CHRIST

AND

CHRISTIANITY

STUDIES ON

CHRISTOLOGY, CREEDS AND CONFESSIONS,
PROTESTANTISM AND ROMANISM, REFORMATION PRINCIPLES,
SUNDAY OBSERVANCE, RELIGIOUS FREEDOM,
AND CHRISTIAN UNION

BY

PHILIP SCHAFF

Wipf & Stock
PUBLISHERS
Eugene, Oregon

Wipf and Stock Publishers
199 W 8th Ave, Suite 3
Eugene, OR 97401

Christ and Christianity
By Schaff, Philip
ISBN: 1-59244-970-0
Publication date 10/28/2004
Previously published by Charles Scribner's Sons, 1885

TABLE OF CONTENTS.

INTRODUCTORY.

THE THEOLOGY OF OUR AGE AND COUNTRY, ... 1–22
Definition of Theology, 1.—Departments of Theology: Exegetical Theology, 2.—Historical Theology, 3.—Systematic Theology, 4.—Practical Theology, 5.—Theology and the Ministry, 6.—The Study of Theology, 6.—Faith and Knowledge, 7.—Theological Character, 9.—Epochs of Theology, 10.—American Theology, 11.—The Voluntary Principle, 13.—Combination of European and American Resources, 14.—Commingling of Denominations, 15.—Christian Union, 16.—Presbyterian Reunion, 19.—The Union Theological Seminary, 20.

I. CHRISTOLOGICAL STUDIES.

CHRIST HIS OWN BEST WITNESS, ... 23–44
The Problem stated, 23.—False Explanations of Christianity, 25.—The Jesus of Imposture, 26.—The Jesus of Fiction, 27.—The Christ of History, 31.—Some traits of Christ's Character, 32.—The external Appearance of Christ, 35.—The Christ of Prophecy, 37.—Christ and Christendom, 40.—Christ and the Human Heart, 42.

CHRIST IN THEOLOGY, ... 45–123
Biblical Christology, 46.—The Ante-Nicene Christology, 50.—The Nicene Christology, 57.—The Chalcedonian Christology, 59.—The Post-Chalcedonian Christology, 62.—Analysis of the Œcumenical Christology, 64.—Critical Estimate of the Œcumenical Christology, 67.—The Orthodox Protestant Christology, 70.—The Scholastic Christology of the Lutheran Church, 72.—The Kenosis Controversy of the Seventeenth Century, 78.—The Reformed Christology, 79.—Comparison of the Lutheran and Reformed Christologies, 86.—Modern Christologies, 94.—The Socinian Christology, 95.—The Unita-

CONTENTS.

rian Christology, 97.—The Swedenborgian Christology, 89.—The Rationalistic Christology, 100.—The Pantheistic Christology, 101.—Schleiermacher's Christology, 104.—Rothe, 105.—Bushnell, 106.—The modern Kenosis Theory, 107.—Criticism of the Kenosis Theory, 115.—Dorner, The Theory of Gradual Incarnation, 119.—Conclusion, 122.

II. POLEMICAL AND IRENICAL STUDIES.

PROTESTANTISM AND ROMANISM, ... 124–127

THE PRINCIPLES OF THE REFORMATION, ... 128–134

CREEDS AND CONFESSIONS OF FAITH, ... 135–152
The Bible and the Creed, 135.—The Confession of Peter, 136.—The Œcumenical Creed, 137.—The Greek Creed, 139.—The Roman Creed, 140.—The Evangelical Creed, 142.—Lutheranism and Reform, 144.—Later Evangelical Creeds, 144.—The Problem of Reunion, 146.—Different kinds of Union, 146.—The Doctrinal Basis already existing, 148.

'THE CONSENSUS OF THE REFORMED CONFESSIONS, ... 153–183
Cranmer's Proposal of a Reformed Consensus, 153.—The Reformed Confessions, 155.—The Harmony of the Reformed Confessions, 158.—Bibliology, 158.—Theology and Christology, 159.—Anthropology and Soteriology, 159.—Predestination, 161.—Ecclesiology, 163.—Sacramentology, 164.—Eschatology, 166.—The Theological Revolution, 166.—The Revival of Evangelical Theology, 167.—The Relation of Modern Evangelical Theology to the Reformed Confessions, 168.—Bibliology, 170.—The Theological Standpoint, 172.—Catholicity, 173.—Moderation of High Calvinism, 174.—The Problem of Predestination, 176.—Infant Salvation, 176.—Religious Liberty, 177.—The Reformed Consensus and the Presbyterian Council, 178.—Conclusion, 183.

III. MORAL AND SOCIAL STUDIES.

SLAVERY AND THE BIBLE, ... 184–212
The Origin of Slavery, 184.—The Curse of Noah, 185.—Patriarchal Slavery, 189.—Slavery under the Mosaic Law, 192.—Greek and Roman Slavery, 197.—The New Testament and Slavery, 200.—Paul and Philemon, 211.—Conclusion, 212.

DIE CHRISTLICHE SONNTAGSFEIER, ... 213–239

CONTENTS. v

THE CHRISTIAN SABBATH, ... 240–275
Origin and authority of the Christian Sabbath, 240.—The Anglo-American and the Continental Theory, 243.—Objections answered, 244.—Advantages of the Anglo-American Theory, 249.—History of Sunday Observance before the Reformation, 252; since the Reformation, 253; in England and Scotland, 255; in New England, 260.—The American Sabbath, 265.—Conclusion, 273.

THE DEVELOPMENT OF RELIGIOUS FREEDOM, ... 276–291
Persecution inconsistent with Christianity, 276.—Persecution in the Middle Ages, 277; after the Reformation, 279.—Causes of Persecution, 283.—Separation of Church and State, 284.—The American Theory of Religious Freedom, 285.—Gradual Growth of Toleration and Freedom, 285.

THE DISCORD AND CONCORD OF CHRISTENDOM, ... 292–310
The Churches of Christendom, 292.—The Greek Church, 293.—The Latin Church, 294.—The Protestant Churches, 294.—Defects and sins of Churches, 295.—Persecution opposed to the spirit of Christianity, 296.—An act of humiliation, 297.—Denominationalism not Sectarianism, 298.—Diversity in Unity, 298.—Denominations necessary and useful, 299.—Liberty favorable to Christianity, 301.—Organic Union never realized nor promised, 301.—Good and evil in Denominationalism, 302.—Christian Union not to be created, 303.—Unity in Doctrine, 303.—Unity in Morals, 305.—Church Polity, 305.—Worship, 306.—Promotion of Christian Union, 307.—Hindrances of Christian Union, 307.—Christian Catholicity, 308.

THE THEOLOGY OF OUR AGE AND COUNTRY.

[Inaugural Address, delivered Oct. 18, 1871, by the author as Professor of Apologetics, Symbolics, and Theol. Encyclopædia in the Union Theol. Seminary, New York. He had entered the actual service of the Seminary two years before, as Professor of Hebrew.]

Christian Theology is the science of the Christian religion, or the knowledge of God, of man, and of their mutual relation under its threefold aspect of original union, subsequent separation by sin, and reunion or reconciliation by Jesus Christ the God-Man and Saviour of mankind. It is the noblest of sciences. It surpasses other sciences in proportion as the Bible which is its text-book, excels other books, and as religion which is its object, towers above the secular concerns of man. It treats of the deepest problems which can challenge the attention of an immortal mind. The boundless wealth of God's revelation, of God's word, of God's plan of salvation, the spiritual experience of God's people in all ages, creation, sin and redemption, life, death and eternity, things past, things present and things to come, all that can purify, ennoble, adorn and perfect human character in this world, the mysteries of the world to come with its endless issues of bliss or woe, the origin, progress and triumph of Christ's kingdom till the final consummation, when "God shall be all in all":—these are the sublime themes of theology, ever fresh and ever new, and carrying in themselves their own best reward.

DEPARTMENTS OF THEOLOGY.

Theology, like the kingdom of Christ itself, has grown up from small beginnings to such magnitude that its thorough study, exclusive of the necessary preparation by a general literary and classical *training, demands now the best years in a man's life. And the more we explore its sacred domain, the more we find out how little we know, and how imperfectly we comprehend. Superficial knowledge alone begets conceit, thorough knowledge makes humble. But even one drop from the ocean of divine wisdom is better than rivers of worldly pleasure. "Now we see in a mirror, darkly, but then face to face; now I know in part, but then shall I know fully even as also I have been fully known."

The whole course of divinity is best divided into four departments: Exegetical Theology, Historical Theology, Systematic Theology, and Practical Theology.

EXEGETICAL THEOLOGY.

Exegetical Theology, or Biblical Science, has for its object the study and exposition of the Book of books, the Book of God for all ages and for all mankind. It embraces, besides Exegesis proper: Sacred Philology; Biblical Archæology; Textual Criticism; Hermeneutics; Critical Introduction to the Old and New Testaments; and Biblical Theology, in the modern technical sense, that is, a systematic, organic view of the Bible religion in its historical, doctrinal and ethical aspects. It covers all the branches of Biblical literature.

Here is a vast field inviting new laborers from year to year, and extending with every new discovery of Bible Mss., and old monuments in Bible lands. Every progress in comparative philology, Egyptology, Assyriology and other branches of ancient lore stimulates new zeal in biblical research. The Bible is now studied more extensively and more critically than ever before. Instead of losing its charm, like other books, it is growing richer and more interesting with every attempt to explore its mines of wisdom and comfort. Edition of the original text follows edition; exegetical helps are multiplying from year to year; one commentary seems only to create a demand for another and better one; and thus the Church will continue preaching and expounding the same Word of life to ever-enlarging congregations to the end of time.

HISTORICAL THEOLOGY.

Historical Theology, or Church History, traces the origin and progress of Christ's kingdom, which is not of this world, but above the world, yet in the world, delivering it from the power of sin and error, and transforming it from within, slowly and surely, by the force of truth and holiness.

Church History is a continuous illustration of the twin parables of the mustard seed which grows to a mighty tree, and the leaven which is to pervade the whole lump of humanity. It is the most important and most interesting part of general history. For the world at large is governed in the interest of Christianity. Secular history is but a John the Baptist pointing to Him who was before him, and decreasing, that Christ may increase. The noble language and literature of Greece, the philosophy of Plato and Aristotle, the conquest of Alexander, the arms and laws of Rome, were tributary to the first coming of Christ, as much as the theocracy of the Jews. And so will all the movements, commotions and revolutions of modern history prepare the way for the final triumph of Christ's kingdom over the whole earth. History is the epos of God, Church History the epos of Christ. All human factors and even the Satanic agencies are ruled and overruled by the Divine factor to the glory of God and the highest happiness of the race.

Historical Theology is, next to the Bible, the richest book of life. It is inexhaustible in its lessons of wisdom. The Bible itself presents its doctrines and precepts mostly in actual facts, and in living examples, clothed in flesh and blood. Church history in the widest sense begins with the race in paradise and accompanies it through the fall and the preparatory stages of redemption down to the advent of Christ. Then it becomes a history of Christianity. This embraces the whole

4 THE THEOLOGY OF OUR AGE AND COUNTRY.

outward and inward life and experience of Christ's Church from the beginning to the present time, the history of missions and persecutions, of doctrines and heresies, of government and discipline, of worship and ceremonies, of charity and philanthropy, in short, all that is of abiding interest and that has contributed to produce the present state of Christian civilization. So vast and various is the field of ecclesiastical history, that one single branch alone—as the life of Christ, or the Apostolic Age, or the reformation of the sixteenth century—is sufficient to occupy years of earnest research.

SYSTEMATIC THEOLOGY.

Systematic or Speculative Theology reflects, in organic unity and completeness, the present consciousness, life and condition of Christendom, as the result of its past history. It comprehends Apologetics, Dogmatics, Symbolics, Polemics, Ethics, and Statistics.

Apologetics defends and vindicates Christianity, as the perfect religion of God for all mankind, against the attacks of infidelity whether Jewish or heathen or nominally Christian, whether they come from philosophy, or criticism, or natural science. It proceeds not from a sense of weakness, but of strength, and from the conviction that the Christian religion is truly what it claims to be, the absolute and final religion. But as this religion is attacked in every age, Apologetics must meet the foe and adapt its method and form to the demands and wants of the time. Its greatest use, however, is its effect upon the church itself rather than upon the assailants. For infidelity proceeds from the heart and will rather than from the brain, and is conquered by moral forces which are stronger than argument.

Dogmatics is a scientific unfolding of the doctrinal system of Christianity from the Bible and Christian consciousness, and in harmony with true reason as enlightened by revelation. Biblical Dogmatics is confined to the teaching of the Scriptures; Church

Dogmatics, to the teaching of the symbolical books; speculative Dogmatics, to the rational vindication of the doctrines of revelation; but a full system of Dogmatics must embrace all these elements as a living whole.

Polemics or Controversial Theology deals with the inner doctrinal differences of Christendom. It has of late assumed a more dignified, less sectarian and more catholic character, under the new name of Symbolics, which includes Irenics as well as Polemics. Symbolics is the science of symbols or creeds. It is comparative dogmatics. It discusses the doctrinal peculiarities of the different denominations as laid down in their authoritative symbols or confessions; calmly weighing the arguments, refuting the errors, and pointing out the way to harmony in the future.

Christian Ethics is a scientific exhibition of Christian life as emanating from, and aiming to imitate, the sinless perfection of the life of Christ. It is related to Moral Philosophy as revelation is to reason, or as the written law to the conscience.

Statistics is a description of the present social status of Christendom, in its various branches, Greek, Latin, and Protestant, with an account of their numerical strength, their polity, government and administration, forms of worship, living institutions and Christian activity.

To Systematic Theology belongs also formal Encyclopædia or an exhibition of theology as an organic whole, showing the relationship of the different parts, and their proper function and aim.

PRACTICAL THEOLOGY.

Practical Theology, with its various branches of Homiletics, Catechetics, Poimenics (commonly called Pastoral Theology), Liturgics, Hymnology, Church Music, Evangelistics, (Mission Work), and Ecclesiology or Theory of Church Polity and Discipline, looks to the future from the experience of the past. It connects the science of religion with its practice, the Professor's chair with the Pastor's pulpit, the Seminary with the congregation.

In this department, the mature results of Exegetical, Historical, and Systematic Divinity, are made available for the edification of the Christian people, through the duties and cares of the gospel ministry. And this process will go on till the whole world is filled with the knowledge and love of Christ.

THEOLOGY AND THE MINISTRY.

From the nature and extent of theology we may form an estimate of the importance of the ministry for which it prepares. I pity the young man who thinks and talks of sacrifices he is making, and of honor he is conferring on the Church, by devoting himself to the clerical profession. God has no need of our poor, feeble services. God rather bestows the highest honor upon us by accepting us as candidates for the stewardship of the mysteries of the kingdom of heaven. What can be more honorable, more glorious, than the calling for which the eternal Son of God himself came in the flesh, and to which the purest and noblest of men, the teachers and benefactors of mankind, have devoted their lives? There is, indeed, as the great Augustin says, "nothing more wretched, mournful and damnable in the eyes of God than the ministry, if it be sought from impure motives, and administered in an impure spirit;" but there is also, he adds, "nothing more blessed in the eyes of God, if the battle be fought in the manner enjoined by our Captain."

The demands upon the ministry are now higher than ever. Ministers ought to be the purest, the noblest, the most useful and charitable of men. They ought to be in the front rank of the civilization of the age, take the lead in all true progress, and maintain the supremacy of religion in the highest walks of learning and literature.

THE STUDY OF THEOLOGY.

The character of Theology suggests the proper spirit and best method of its study.

As a science, Theology must be studied like every other science, with the application of all our cognitive faculties, and with all the enthusiasm for the pursuit of truth. Its vast treasures of knowledge from the Bible and the history of Christianity, in all its forms and phases, can only be appropriated by memory, and arranged by judgment; its deep and intricate problems demand close and earnest thinking. It opens a field for the service of every mental power, and touches at all points on other branches of human learning and literature, as ancient and modern philology, geography, history, philosophy, geology, astronomy, music, poetry, and all the fine arts in their relation to worship.

But as a *sacred* and *spiritual* science, based on a divine revelation and concerned with the eternal interests of man, theology should be studied spiritually as well as intellectually, devoutly as well as thoughtfully, on the knees as well as behind the desk. On its portals we read the inscriptions: *Procul abeste profani. Sancta sancte tractanda. Oratio, meditatio, tentatio faciunt theologum.* Only those who are pure in heart have the promise to see God. The impure will always walk in darkness, or worship idols.

To make God simply an object of philosophical speculation, and logical analysis, is irreverent and profane, and leads to serious error. God is first and last an object of adoration and love. He is sought and found by meditation and prayer rather than by ratiocination. Hence the old adage: *Bene orasse est bene studuisse.* It has been said by Pascal, that while human things must be known before they can be admired and loved, divine things must be loved in order to be known.

FAITH AND KNOWLEDGE.

With equal propriety we must require faith as a condition of knowledge. The greatest theological genius of the nineteenth century (Schleiermacher) has adopted the motto of Anselm and Augustin: *Fides præcedit intellectum.* How can we know God unless we believe Him to exist? And how can we enter into the depths of His character without boundless confidence and trust in his perfections? We must, then, first spiritually apprehend and appropriate the divine objects before we can intellectually comprehend and understand them. Faith is the pioneer in all great undertakings. Faith in ideas guided Plato in his lofty speculations; faith in the existence of a new world led Columbus to the discovery of it; faith produced the Reformation and sustained its leaders in their trials; without faith the art of printing and other modern inventions would be unknown.

But as *pistis* precedes *gnosis*, so on the other hand *pistis* necessarily leads to *gnosis*. The same great divines who gave precedence to faith over knowledge, laid down the correspondent principle: *Credo ut intelligam*, I believe in order that I may understand. Faith is the most fruitful mother of knowledge. The philosophical principle of Cartesius, *De omnibus dubitandum est*, may apply to the functions of rigid historical criticism or legal investigation, but it is false of constructive science. Theology certainly is not born of the barren womb of scepticism or indifferentism to truth, but out of the fruitful soil of faith in God, and love to God and man. In the plerophoria or full assurance of faith, the theologian may boldly climb the giddy heights and descend to the hidden depths of speculation and research, without a misgiving as to the result. Bible truth is fire-proof against the attacks of an infidel science and a philosophy falsely so-called. Our understanding of the Bible may be wrong and need rectification, from time to time, by the progress of knowledge or new discoveries; but the Bible is no more responsible for the mistakes of translators and commentators than the book of nature is for the false and contradictory hypotheses of scientists.

Faith and knowledge, revelation and reason, emanate from the same source, and must return to the same source; they agree in principle and aim, as God agrees with himself, who gave them both, and claims them for his service. It is only a superficial taste of philosophy and science, according to Bacon, that may lead away from God, fully exhausted they lead back to Him. The more thoroughly we know any object, the more nearly we approach the truth; and the nearer we come to the truth, the closer we come to God, who is the source and centre of all truth.

THEOLOGICAL CHARACTER.

The aim of the theological student should be to cultivate the heart as well as the head, to grow in grace as he grows in knowledge, and to make his attainments profitable to his fellow-men. The blending of intellectual and moral strength, of profound learning and devoted piety, constitute a theological character.

Such a theologian is a power and a blessing to his generation. Such were the best among the fathers, the chief schoolmen and mystics, the reformers, and the leading divines of the Protestant churches, who, though dead, still speak words of life, and stimulate to noble thoughts and deeds. It is well for the student to keep constantly before his eyes those truly great and good men who shine as burning lights on the pages of the Greek, Latin and Evangelical Churches from primitive times down to our own day.

It is still better to aspire after the apostolic masters, from whom an Athanasius and Augustin, a Chrysostom and Jerome, an Anselm and Bernard, a Luther and Calvin, have derived their inspiration. Look at St. Paul, who was at once the deepest thinker, the noblest character and the most successful missionary. Remember St. John, the evangelist and seer, who was first and emphatically called the "theologian," who studied at the bosom of the *Theos-Logos*, and saw deeper and with purer heart than mortal ever did before or since; as the mediæval hymnist so inimitably expresses it:

> "*Volat avis sine meta,*
> *Quo nec vates nec propheta*
> *Evolavit altius.*

> *Tam implenda quam impleta,*
> *Numquam vidit tot secreta*
> *Purus homo purius."*

But best and most of all, let us ever look to Christ, the great Captain of our salvation, the Revealer of God, the Wisest of the wise, the Purest of the pure, the Holiest of the holy. Conformity to His spotless image, imitation of His perfect example in His mission of love and good will towards mankind, should be the highest aim and ambition of the theological student. A *Christ-like* theology and ministry is the first and last necessity to the Church and to the world.

EPOCHS OF THEOLOGY.

Every age and nation must produce its own theology, for its peculiar wants and use. We have no right to live on the inheritance of the past; we must make it our own, and enrich it by the fruits of our exertions.

The ancient Greek Church is the mother of œcumenical orthodoxy; she elaborated the fundamental dogmas of the Trinity and the Person of Christ, as laid down in the Apostles' and the Nicene creeds.

The Latin Church devoted her strength to the problems of anthropology, and her noblest offspring is the Augustinian theology, with its profound views and experiences of sin and grace.

The Schoolmen of the middle ages formularized, analyzed and systematized the doctrines of the Fathers, and showed the harmony of revelation and reason; while the Mystics of the same period insisted on a theology of the heart and inward spiritual experience.

With the Reformation was born evangelical theology, from the fresh fountain of the Scriptures, and in heroic conflict with the errors of Romanism. Since that time soteriology and the subjective side of Christianity in its bearing upon the character and comfort of the individual believer have received more attention than ever before. Kliefoth thinks that ecclesiology and

THE THEOLOGY OF OUR AGE AND COUNTRY. 11

eschatology will come next and last; but the burning questions just now are, Christology in its historical aspects, and Bibliology in its relation to modern criticism and science. In our age, Germany is the most fertile field for the cultivation of scientific and critical theology, and is making invaluable additions to the stores of Biblical literature and Church history. In conflict with modern Rationalism there has grown up a new type of evangelical theology, more critical, liberal and comprehensive than the older forms of orthodoxy which preceded the era of scepticism. There is no doubt that even Rationalism, bad and destructive as it was in its immediate effects, did and still does good service in investigating the natural and human aspects of the Bible; but instead of overthrowing, as was the intention, the belief in its supernatural and divine character, it has only supplemented this belief and furnished a broader foundation for it. For the written word of God, like Christ, the personal Word, is theanthropic in origin, nature and aim, and can only be fully understood and appreciated under this two-fold character. The mystery of revelation is God manifest in flesh, and the mystery of Christian life is a heavenly treasure in an earthen vessel.

AMERICAN THEOLOGY.

The time has now fully come for America to produce her own distinctive theology, not indeed in selfish and conceited isolation, but in organic union with the Catholic theology of evangelical Christendom throughout the world. Firmly rooted and grounded in the Scriptures, and in the wisdom and experience of eighteen Christian centuries, American theology should mark a new era in the progressive development of the Church—a development, not of the divine truth itself, which is perfect and unchangeable, but of the human apprehension and application of the truth as it is in Christ and his gospel. For all legitimate and normal progress in theology and religion is simply a *growth in Christ*, "in whom are hid all the treasures of wisdom and knowledge," in whom the whole fulness of the Godhead, and the

12   THE THEOLOGY OF OUR AGE AND COUNTRY.

whole fulness of manhood, without sin, dwell in perfect harmony forever.

American theology, in its first phase, belongs to the Reformed type and is connected with Calvinism through the medium of English Puritanism. It was born in a powerful revival of religion toward the middle of the last century. It may be dated from the profound and devout speculations of the pure and venerable Jonathan Edwards and his successors, who manfully grappled with problems of Christian metaphysics, but moved within the narrow limits of a severe and provincial Calvinism. Since then, the immense growth of our country, and the recent importation of the vast treasures of European learning, have greatly expanded our horizon, opened new avenues of thought and research, and stimulated the native zeal to original contributions in Biblical and historical literature. We may say that all the intellectual and moral forces necessary for a new chapter in the history of sacred letters, are already at work or fast maturing among us.

Our age is not, strictly speaking, a theological age. Theology is no more the all-absorbing and all-controlling science, as it was from the fourth down to the seventeenth century. Mathematics, and the natural sciences, the mechanical and useful arts, trade and politics, have grown to vast dimensions, and invite genius and talent into new channels. The morbid passion for sudden wealth and power, for extravagance and vain show, is a fertile breeder of dishonesty and corruption, and a serious check upon those ideal tendencies and pursuits which, after all, constitute the true nobility and abiding glory of man.

But, on the other hand, our age and country are remarkable for energy, enterprise, liberality and zeal in the cause of general education, and afford unusual facilities for the exchange and spread of ideas and literary productions.

We have, indeed, no such venerable and well-appointed institutions as the great universities of Europe with their scores of distinguished scholars, complete libraries, antiquarian and artistic collections—the growth of many centuries. Most of our teachers, moreover, are too much distracted by extraneous cares and practical duties incident upon the youth of our institutions, while the university professors of Europe can devote that single and undivided attention to their scholastic calling which is necessary to the highest efficiency in any department.

Yet we enjoy, on the other hand, certain advantages even over good old Europe for the cultivation of sacred learning in harmony with the highest religious and moral interests of the race.

THE VOLUNTARY PRINCIPLE.

In the first place, our peaceful separation of Church and State, by throwing Christianity upon the voluntary principle of self-support and self-government, tends to develop a degree of individual interest and liberality for the promotion of religious and theological objects, far greater than exists in those countries where the people are accustomed to look to government for support. Considering the youth of our country, it is astonishing how much has been done already without aid from government and princes. Theological seminaries have been multiplied all over the land, and many a plain layman has immortalized himself by more than princely donations, which will perpetuate his influence for good to the end of time. A noble rivalry exists among different denominations to excel each other in zeal for the training of an able and efficient ministry, which shall make this magnificent country—the richest inheritance ever given to a nation—Immanuel's land for all time to come.

Our voluntary system, moreover, discourages the study for the ministry from any other than the proper motives of love to Christ and to immortal souls, and keeps from its ranks the large number of those who, in state-churches, pursue theology, like an ordinary profession, for a mere living, and thus degrade and paralyze the sacred ministry. Professors and ministers, who disbelieve the very truths which they are appointed to teach and to preach, and who labor to destroy the Church which they ought to build up, could fortunately not maintain themselves in our country. Such men find here more congenial occupation in the fields of secular science, politics, and commerce.

This state of things ought to secure to us a theology more pure, more scriptural, more free from error and more in sympathy with the religious life of the people, than in countries where professors and ministers are officers of the State as well as of the Church, and are elected for theoretical qualifications, with little or no reference to the soundness of their views, and the motives of their hearts.

COMBINATION OF EUROPEAN AND AMERICAN RESOURCES.

Another great advantage is our ready access to the literary treasures of all nations, with a willingness to learn from all. Continental divines rarely know and notice English or American works; they are better acquainted with the remotest past in the east, than with that living Christianity which lies west of their horizon. English divines, with honorable exceptions, are insular, self-sufficient, and much controlled by the spirit of caste which separates "Churchmen" from "Dissenters" and "Dissenters" from "Churchmen."

Our cosmopolitan composition as a nation, to which also in this sense may be applied the motto *E pluribus unum*, tends to beget a more catholic and liberal spirit and disposition. Every book of note which appears in Great Britain, whether it proceed from the Church of England, or the Church of Scotland, or any of the Dissenting bodies, is imported or reproduced in this country. The great German divines of the century are becoming almost as familiar to us as they are to their countrymen; their most valuable works are translated and have even a larger circulation in the United States than in the land of their birth. Scores of American students are annually flocking to German universities, and return well-stored with the latest advances of Continental learning.

The blending of strong English common sense and reverence for holy writ with German learning and perseverance, infused with the freshness and vigor of American life, ought to produce a higher order of theology than either England or Germany alone can give us. Ours is the fault if, with such advantages, we do not improve upon the past and the present. We must retain all that is good in the theology and religion of the Anglo-Saxon race, which, I verily believe, is more deeply imbued with the spirit and power of Christianity than any other people; but on this solid foundation we may build a majestic temple unto the Lord, with precious stones from all the nations of Europe, and every age of Christian civilization.

COMMINGLING OF DENOMINATIONS.

Finally, we have among us nearly all the historic types of Christianity in living representation, on a basis of equality before the law, and with unrestrained liberty of action. The national churches, which in Europe are separated by geographical and political boundaries, and the difference of language, are here brought into direct contact and social intercommunion. In the same town we find the various churches of the Continental and British Reformation, with all the life, vigor and progressive spirit which characterize the genius of Protestantism, as well as the Roman Catholic with her ancient traditions, compact organization, mysterious worship and extravagant claims. Only the Eastern or Greek Church, the oldest of all, has as yet scarcely a name in this young western country, but the noble achievements of her palmy days continue to live among us.

This coëxistence and social commingling of the different phases of Christianity, each representing a peculiar set of ideas and a corresponding mission, must facilitate a thorough acquaintance, remove many prejudices, and foster a spirit of large-hearted Christian liberality and charity. It is said that distance lends enchantment to the view, while familiarity breeds contempt. But the best persons and things improve upon acquaintance. In our land, if anywhere on God's earth, is a field for actualizing the idea of Christian union, which shall gather into

CHRISTIAN UNION.

one the best elements from all ages and branches of Christ's kingdom.

Union among Christians is becoming more and more an imperative necessity if they are to conquer in the great conflict with infidelity and anti-Christ.

"United we stand, divided we fall," is an old and well-tried maxim. "Divide and conquer," has always been the policy of a successful enemy. "When bad men combine," said one of the wisest of British statesmen, "the good must associate, else they will fall one by one an unpitied sacrifice in a contemptible struggle." This is as true of religion as of politics.

But union is not to be sought merely as a means to an end and for the temporary purpose of gaining a victory over a foe. It is to be sought for its own sake, and as a lasting good; it is an essential attribute and will be the crowning glory and joy of the church.

Christian union cannot be enforced, or artificially manufactured. It must grow spontaneously from the soil of Christian freedom. It must proceed from the mighty Spirit of God, which is a spirit of communion. It must rest on the vital union of individual believers with Christ. The closer Christians are united to Christ, their living head, the closer they will be united to each other.

Union is no monotonous uniformity, but implies variety and full development of all the various types of Christian doctrine and discipline as far as they are founded on constitutional differences, made and intended by God himself, and as far as they are supplementary rather than contradictory. True union is essentially inward and spiritual. It does not require an external amalgamation of existing organizations into one, but may exist with their perfect independence in their own spheres of labor. It is as far removed from indifference to denominational distinctions, as from sectarian bigotry and exclusiveness. It is quite consistent with loyalty to that particular branch of Christ's kingdom with which we are severally connected by birth, regeneration, or providential call. Every one must labor in that part of the vineyard where Providence puts him, and where he can do most good. The Church of God on earth is a vast spiritual temple with many stories, and each story has many apartments; to be in this house at all, we must occupy a particular room, which we are bound to keep in order and adorn with the flowers of Christian graces. But nothing should hinder us to live on the best terms of courtesy and friendship with our neighbors and brethren who occupy different apartments in the same temple of God, who love and worship the same Christ, who pray and labor as earnestly as we for the glory of our common Master and the salvation of souls, and with whom we expect to spend an endless eternity in the many mansions of heaven. Why should we not bless those whom God blesses, why not rejoice in the prosperity of their works, though they bear a different name and pursue a different method?

Let Presbyterians, Episcopalians, Congregationalists, Lutherans, Methodists, Baptists, Dutch and German Reformed, and all other Christians, of whatever name, be true to their standards of faith and practice, honestly fulfill their own mission, and do as much good as they can in their own way—there is abundant room of usefulness for them all in this ever-expanding field of labor—only let them disown and abhor the selfish, narrow and uncharitable spirit of sectarian exclusiveness; let them subordinate their denominational peculiarities to the general interests of Christ's kingdom; let them cheerfully and thankfully recognize Christ's image in all its reflections, rejoice in the conversion of every soul, no matter by whose instrumentality it is brought about, and lend a helping hand to every effort to spread the glory of Him who died for all and liveth evermore. Let our motto be:

Christianus sum: Christiani nihil a me alienum puto.

Let us act on the evangelical catholic maxim:

In necessariis unitas, in dubiis libertas, in omnibus caritas.

There are, indeed, differences which can never be reconciled; of two contradictory propositions one must be false and resisted to the end. Between truth and error, between God and Belial, between Christ and Anti-Christ there can be no compromise. Here is room for manly warfare, for Christian polemics—even for martyrdom.

But there are other differences which involve no contradiction and represent only the various aspects of one and the same truth. Such were the differences among the Apostles. Paul and James and Peter and John differed widely in their temper, their mental constitution, and their mode of viewing and stating the truths of the Gospel; and yet they were one in Christ, and their variations help to swell the harmony of inspired teaching. So most of the differences which divide the various creeds of Christendom, point to a higher unity and admit of an ultimate reconciliation in a more comprehensive conception of Christianity in its totality and completeness. We must remember that divine truth is too vast and too comprehensive for one mind or even for one denomination to apprehend and set forth in all its fulness. We must remember that there is an important distinction between theological and religious differences. The deeper we penetrate into the intricate mysteries of theology, the more liberal and charitable we ought to become towards those who view the same truths in a different light. Such liberality is perfectly compatible with strong, positive convictions and an uncompromising attitude towards real error.

It is the noble mission of a truly evangelical catholic theology to study the lineaments of Christ's sinless physiognomy in all his disciples, to acknowledge the merits of his humblest followers, to collect the fragments of truth from every age and denomination, to unite them into a living and beautiful whole, and thus to prepare the reign of peace, when Christians of every name shall see eye to eye, and beat heart to heart, and gather in common adoration around Him who is the divine solution of all human problems, the harmony of all discords, the Alpha and Omega of theology.

PRESBYTERIAN REUNION.

The recent reunion of the Old and New School branches of the Presbyterian Church of the United States is one of the most remarkable and hopeful events in American Church history.[1] It furnishes a practical evidence of the possibility not only of Christian but even of ecclesiastical and organic union, and a refutation of the slander that Protestantism tends only to division and dissolution. This reunion was no compromise between truth and error; it involved no sacrifice of principle or honor; it was not the work of human policy or design; it cannot be traced to any individual agency; it was evidently brought about by the Holy Spirit of God, who seized the minds and hearts of ministers and laymen, made them forget the bitterness of a thirty years' theological war, and melted them together in true Christian harmony. The meeting in Philadelphia which inaugurated the movement, and the one in Pittsburg which brought it to a happy consummation, breathed a truly pentecostal spirit, and commanded the admiration of Christians of all denominations.

Presbyterianism, thus consolidated, far from becoming more sectarian, is all the more catholic and liberal towards sister churches. The success of this reunion justifies the hope of similar movements among kindred branches of the Protestant family. It is time for all unnecessary and useless divisions to pass away. Let the larger bodies which have a historic mission to fulfill, and can work better in separate organizations, remain distinct, but let them at least publicly recognize each other and cultivate a spirit of Christian friendship and love.

We do not even despair of an ultimate union of evangelical Protestantism with evangelical Catholicism, although they are

[[1] The union was completed by a joint meeting of the two General Assemblies in Nov., 1869, at Pittsburg, Pa. The last separate meetings of the Old and New School Assemblies were held in New York in May of the same year. See the Memorial volume on *Presbyterian Reunion*, New York 1870 (568 pages), and Dr. Hatfield's article on *Presbyterian Church U. S.* in the third volume of Schaff-Herzog's *Encycl.*]

now further apart than ever; but this must be preceded by a universal humiliation and repentance, and by a destruction of Popery, which claims to be infallible and therefore irreformable, and holds the Catholic truths in bondage, making void "the word of God by the traditions of men." Then, but not till then, may be realized the dream of a Johannean Church of love that shall exclude all defects of the Petrine Church of authority and the Pauline Church of freedom, and melt the excellences of both into a higher unity. Out of the fiercest struggle comes the greatest victory, and out of the loudest discord the fullest harmony. May God speed the universal pentecost and agape of his one Holy Catholic and Apostolic Church.

THE UNION THEOLOGICAL SEMINARY.

Gentlemen of the Board of Directors:

I have given you an imperfect sketch of the nature and aim of theology, as demanded by the age and country in which we live.

In the spirit of this address I expect, with the help of God, to labor in the professorship to which your confidence has called me. The branches of instruction assigned me are supplementary to other departments, which have grown to such dimensions as to require additional force for thorough cultivation. They embrace *Apologetics, Symbolics* and *Polemics, Introduction to the Holy Scriptures,* and *Theological Encyclopædia,* in connection with *Methodology* and *Bibliography*.[1] Some of these branches are new in our Seminaries, but will no doubt soon become essential in all, as they have been long since in the older institutions of Europe.

My knowledge of the Union Seminary dates from the day of my arrival in America, twenty-seven years ago, when I became personally acquainted with the late Dr. Robinson—then the only

[1] The writer was afterwards transferred to the professorship of "Sacred Literature" (especially the New Testament), but continues to teach Symbolics and Encyclopædia (Propedeutics) in connection with Greek exegesis.]

American scholar of European reputation. Coming from the University of Berlin, in obedience to a call from the German Reformed Church in America, and being furnished with messages of friendship from Ritter and Neander, whom he esteemed as the greatest and best men he had ever seen, I was most cordially welcomed by Dr. Robinson and his cultivated wife to the land of my adoption, and from that time to the day of his death, I enjoyed his friendship.[1]

Dr. Robinson—the first critical explorer of the Holy Land, which is fitly called " the fifth Gospel," shaped the scholastic character and mission of the Union Seminary by his teaching and valuable contributions to Biblical Literature. His colleague, the venerable Dr. Skinner, one of the purest, humblest, and holiest men I ever knew, who has but recently been taken from us in unbroken vigor of body and mind at the rare age of four-score years, impressed upon the Seminary the stamp of his own deep-toned piety and spirituality. Their memories will ever be sacredly cherished in the Churches of America.

Of the living, I will only say that I consider it an honor and a privilege to labor as a colleague with such Christian gentlemen and scholars as the Directors and Professors of the Union Seminary.

I like the name of the institution; it indicates the peaceful spirit and aim of its founders at a time when the *odium theologicum* was raging through the land and rending the Church. It anticipated, as it effectively helped to bring about, the happy reunion of the two branches of Presbyterianism; and it may prove a prophecy of other and larger union movements in the churches of Christ. The past history of the Seminary, its evangelical and catholic spirit, its metropolitan position and advantages, point to a great and noble future. You have it in your power to make it at once, and without dispute, the first school

---

[1] I gave my estimate of Dr. Robinson several years ago, in a biographical article in Herzog's *Theol. Encyclopœdia*, vol. xx. pp. 577–581 [revised German ed., vol. xiii. pp. 13–16, abridged in Schaff-Herzog, vol. iii.]

of sacred learning on this Western Continent, whither "the course of empire takes its way," and to extend its usefulness through all Christian and heathen lands.

"Art is long; time is short."

Let us redeem our time, which is more precious than gold and silver. May we all be found faithful to our trust, and win the crown, to lay it at the feet of Him who alone, by his grace, can " work in us both to will and to work, for his good pleasure."

CHRIST HIS OWN BEST WITNESS.

AN APOLOGETIC ESSAY.

"Thou seemest human and divine,
The highest, holiest manhood Thou."

EIGHTEEN hundred years ago there lived, among a despised nation and in a remote country, a man by the name of Jesus, a carpenter's son, who had no political power, no social position, no secular learning or art, no wealth, no shelter to call his own, and who after a very brief public career was crucified in his youth by his own countrymen as an impostor and a blasphemer. Yet this humble Rabbi, by the force of his doctrine and example, without shedding a drop of blood, save his own, has silently accomplished the greatest moral revolution on record, founded the mightiest spiritual empire, and is now recognized and adored by the civilized nations of the globe as the Son of God and the Saviour of mankind.

This fact is astounding, and stands out alone, unapproached and unapproachable in its glory. It overtowers all other historic events, and throws the achievements of heroes, sages, poets, scholars and statesmen of ancient and modern times far into the shade.

This fact is undisputed, and admitted even by sceptics and infidels. To deny it would be as unreasonable as to deny the sun in heaven, or the existence of man on earth. Let us hear but a few voices of men of acknowledged genius and culture, who widely dissent from the humble faith of Christians, yet testify to the unsurpassed and unsurpassable greatness of Jesus. Goethe, who characterized himself as a decided non-Christian,[1]

---

[1] In a letter to Lavater, 1782: *"Ich bin kein Unchrist, kein Widerchrist, doch ein decidirter Nichtchrist."* He meant that he was an impartial or indifferent outsider.

and as a "child of the world between two prophets,"[1] expressed the conviction, in one of his last utterances that the human mind, no matter how much it may advance in intellectual culture and in the extent and depth of the knowledge of nature, will never transcend the height and moral culture of Christianity, as it shines and glows in the canonical Gospels.[2] Napoleon the Great, after he had subdued and lost again the half of Europe, said, among other striking things: "I search in vain in history to find one equal to Jesus Christ; anything which can approach the gospel. Neither history, nor humanity, nor the ages, nor nature offer me anything with which I am able to compare it or explain it." Strauss, the keenest antagonist of the gospel history, is constrained to admit, that "Jesus represents within the sphere of religion the culmination point, beyond which posterity can never go, yea, which it can not even equal . . . that he remains the highest model of religion within the reach of our thought; and that no perfect piety is possible without his presence in the heart." Renan, the brilliant and eloquent historian of the "Origins of Christianity," concludes his "Life of Jesus" with this tribute to his hero: "'Whatever may be the surprises of the future, Jesus will never be surpassed. His worship will grow young without ceasing; his legend will call forth tears without end; his sufferings will melt the noblest hearts; all ages will proclaim that among the sons of men there is none born greater than Jesus." Mr. Lecky, the able and impartial historian of "Rationalism," and of "European Morals from Augustus to Charlemagne," in speaking in the latter work

[1] "*Prophete rechts, Prophete links,*
   Das Weltkind in der Mitten."

The prophet on the right side was Lavater, and the (pseudo-) prophet on the left, Basedow.

[2] *Gespräche mit Eckermann*, Vol. III, p. 373: "*Mag die geistige Cultur nur immer fortschreiten, mögen die Naturwissenschaften in immer breiterer Ausdehnung und Tiefe wachsen, und der menschliche Geist sich erweitern wie er will: über die Hoheit und sittliche Cultur des Christenthums, wie es in den Evangelien schimmert und leuchtet, wird er nicht hinaus kommen.*"

on the person of the Founder of Christianity, makes this striking and truthful statement: "The simple record of three short years of active life has done more to regenerate and to soften mankind than all the disquisitions of philosophers and all the exhortations of moralists."[1]

This deepest and broadest fact in the history of the race which surrounds us like an ocean from every direction, calls for an explanation. The explanation must be reasonable. The cause assigned must correspond with the effect produced.

Such an explanation we find in the history of Christ and his testimony concerning himself, as recorded by the Evangelists, and believed by Christians of all creeds.

THE FALSE EXPLANATIONS OF CHRISTIANITY.

The gospel history must either be true, or false.

If false, it must be, in its essential, supernatural features, either a wilful *lie,* or an innocent *fiction;* in other words, the product of *imposture,* or of *delusion.*

In both cases the responsibility may be fastened either on Christ Himself, or on the Apostles and Evangelists.

Consequently we may conceive of four infidel constructions of the life of Christ which exhaust the range of logical possibility. They have all been tried from the days of Celsus to those of Renan; and the resources of talent, learning, ingenuity and skill are well nigh exhausted in the attempt to disprove the truth and to prove the falsehood, of the story of Jesus of Nazareth. No new phase of infidelity can be expected which is not of necessity a repetition or modification of one of the four exploded theories. But unbelief, like belief, will go on in the Church militant to the end of time, and every new assault upon the old fortress will be repulsed by the defenders, and, in its defeat, furnish a fresh proof of the truth of Christ's prophecy, that the

---

[1] For these and many similar testimonies, I beg leave to refer to my book on the "*Person of Christ,*" twelfth edition revised and enlarged, publ. by the Am. Tract Society, and Scribner's Sons, in New York, 1882.

gates of Hades shall never prevail against his Church. A brief examination of the infidel theories must suffice for our purpose.

THE JESUS OF IMPOSTURE.

The imposture may be traced either directly to Christ, or to his disciples.

I. The oldest enemies of Christ, the Pharisees and Sadducees of his day, followed by a few obscure infidels of later times, charged Christ himself with being an impostor and a blasphemer, who made his credulous disciples believe that he was the Son of God and the Saviour of mankind, while he knew himself to be a mere man. In this case we must pronounce him a consummate hypocrite, who falls under the condemnation of his own terrible rebuke of hypocrisy. And yet it is now universally acknowledged, even by infidels themselves, that he preached the purest code of morals and lived the purest life, crowned with the noblest death.

How then can one and the same character be at once the very best and the very worst? The contradiction is as monstrous as that white is black and black is white. How could he play the hypocrite in view of poverty, persecution and crucifixion, as his certain and only reward in this life? How could he keep up the play without even for a moment falling out of his role and showing his true colors? How could such a wicked scheme find universal acceptance and produce greater and better results than any which human wisdom and goodness before or since has been able to achieve, or even to conceive?

These questions are unanswerable. The hypothesis is logically so untenable and morally so revolting, that its mere statement is its condemnation. No scholar has seriously endeavored to carry it out.

II. Others fasten the fraud upon the first disciples of Christ, and represent them as the cunning intriguers and successful deceivers, who manufactured the story of the resurrection and persuaded the world into it at the sacrifice of their very lives.

But the first and last impression which the Gospels irresistibly make upon every fair-minded reader is that of the artless simplicity and honesty of the writers. We may contest their learning, critical sagacity, worldly wisdom, and even their common sense, but it is impossible to deny their good faith; it shines forth from every line, it is even strengthened by the many discrepancies in minor details, it was sealed with their whole life, and in the case of Peter and Paul, who testify to all the essential facts, with their own martyrdom. Goethe, as good a judge of literary productions as ever lived, deliberately said: "I consider the Gospels as thoroughly genuine (*durchaus ächt*), for there is reflected in them a majesty and sublimity which emanated from the person of Christ, and which is as truly divine as anything ever seen on earth."

We can conceive of no motive which might have induced these simple-hearted Galilæans to engage in such a dangerous intrigue before all the world. And how could they keep the secret of the conspiracy? And what must we think of the intelligence of the Jews, Greeks, and Romans of that age, that they could be duped by a handful of illiterate fishermen? Was Saul of Tarsus the man to be so easily fooled into a life of martyrdom by a cunning lie of the very men whom he once so bitterly persecuted? Such questions present insuperable difficulties which no learning or ingenuity has been or ever will be able to solve.

The hypothesis of wilful deception in either of its two possible forms is an insult to the dignity of human nature itself, which instinctively shrinks from it. Unable to maintain this ground, infidelity has of late confined itself to the conjecture of innocent fiction.

THE JESUS OF FICTION.

Here again the delusion may be traced either to Christ himself, or to his disciples.

I. The first alternative assumes that JESUS was an ENTHUSIAST who deceived himself, a noble dreamer who imagined that he was the Son of God and the promised Messiah, and died a victim to this delusion.

But the Jesus of the Gospels shows not the faintest trace of fanaticism, or self-delusion. On the contrary, he discouraged and opposed all the prevailing carnal ideas and hopes of the Messiah, as a supposed political reformer and emancipator. He was calm, self-possessed, uniformly consistent, free from all passion and undue excitement, never desponding, ever confident of success even in the darkest hour of trial and persecution. To every perplexing question he quickly returned the wisest answer; he never erred in his judgment of men or things; from the beginning to the close of his public life, before friend and foe, before magistrate and people, in disputing with Pharisees and Sadducees, in addressing his disciples or the multitude, while standing before Pontius Pilate and Caiaphas, or suspended on the cross, he shows an unclouded intellect and complete mastery of appetite and passion,—in short all the qualities the very opposite to those which characterize persons laboring under self-delusion or any mental disease.

II. But may not his DISCIPLES have been SELF-DECEIVED and unduly carried away by the exemplary life and death, the words and deeds of their Master, so as to work up their imagination to the honest belief that he was really the promised Messiah of the Old Testament and a supernatural Being that came down from heaven?

In other words, the gospel history is put on a par with heathen myths (by Strauss), or Christian legends (by Renan), and thus turned into a poem or fiction of an excited imagination, on the basis of a small capital of actual fact.

This is the least discreditable of all false theories, because it leaves room for a high estimate of the moral character of Christ and his apostles. Christ must have been a very extraordinary person to account at all for the extraordinary impression he made, and the Apostles may escape with the complimentary censure of an excess of pious imagination and admiration.

But the Evangelists are singularly free from imaginative coloring. They are the most objective and sober of all historians; they abstain from every intrusion of their own feelings and reflections, even' when they record the most exciting scenes, the bitterest persecution and the deepest sufferings of their Master. Their individuality is lost in the events which are supposed to speak best for themselves without note or comment. How different in this respect from the Apocryphal Gospels, which abound in the crude inventions of a morbid imagination. We are moreover at a loss to conceive that the Apostles and Evangelists, gifted, as they were, with as clear eyes and as sound common sense as other observers, could make such a radical mistake as is here supposed. How could so many deceive themselves at the same time and in the same way? Is it at all likely that five hundred persons, to whom the risen Christ is said to have appeared at the same time, should dream the same dream? And all this not in a period of childlike simplicity and ignorance, but in a period of high culture and sceptical criticism, in a land and among a people where the story of Jesus was everywhere known, and surrounded by bitter hostility eager to dispel and expose the delusion. How could the keen, sharp and persecuting Paul be so thoroughly converted to an empty fiction? How incredible that some illiterate fishermen should have invented a far higher and more perfect life and character than the poets, philosophers and historians of Greece and Rome. The poet in this case, as Rousseau, himself an unbeliever, well said, must have been greater than the hero. It takes more than a Jesus (*i. e.* a greater than the greatest, which is an impossibility) to invent a Jesus. And how could an *imaginary* resurrection which took place only in the visionary faith of the disciples, or, as Renan says, " in the passion of a hallucinated woman," lay the foundation of such a rock-like institution as the Christian Church?

Just here the mythical and legendary hypothesis breaks down completely, and is driven to the only alternative of truth, or fraud. Innocent fiction will not do in the case of the resurrection of Christ, or even the resurrection of Lazarus, of which Spinoza remarked that, if he could believe it, he would embrace the whole Christian system, because, as the greatest of Christ's miracles, it involves the less.

In this case Renan, unable to find a better solution, departs from his own theory, and is not ashamed to resort to the wretched hypothesis of a fraud, contrived by Lazarus and his two sisters, and weakly connived at by Jesus himself in the vain hope of producing a revolution in his favor among the unbelieving Jews. And such a Jesus who could willingly play the charlatan, and thus outrage the principle of ordinary honesty, Renan would make us believe nevertheless to have been the greatest and purest of men who ever walked on earth, and who will never be surpassed in time to come! *Credat Judæus Appella.*

The false theories then are perfect failures as far as an explanation of the great fact of Christ is concerned. They put a severer tax on our credulity than orthodoxy itself. Instead of solving or diminishing difficulties, they increase them, and substitute a moral monstrosity in the place of a supernatural miracle. They are calculated to shake the faith in man as well as in God. They contradict each other, and one has in turn refuted the other. After completing its course, infidelity in its latest phase, when brought to the test of the resurrection miracle, is forced to resort to its first and most disreputable form, and thus to fall under its own sentence of condemnation, which it pronounced upon the exploded scheme of fraud.

And, indeed, this is the only alternative: the gospel history is either true, or it is a shameless, wicked fraud in which Christ himself was the chief actor. The shrewd, cunning Pharisees and Sadducees who watched his movements with the vigilance of intense jealousy and hatred, felt this; they heard his amazing speeches with their own ears; they witnessed his miracles with their own eyes; how gladly would they have denied them and resorted to the mythical or legendary fiction-theory of modern times; but being unable to contradict the testimony of their senses and the common observation of the people, they derived his miracles from Beelzebub, and crucified Christ as an impostor. But the resurrection and the triumph of Christianity on the ruins of the Jewish theocracy was the triumphant answer to this wicked calumny.

Let us add the testimony of an able and liberal Unitarian who, after a careful critical examination of the records of Christ's history, comes to this irresistible conclusion : " Wonderful is the character of Jesus. And hardly less wonderful is the manner in which it is portrayed in the Gospels, undesignedly, by brief, sketchy narratives of a variety of incidents, strung together with only the slightest regard to their right order and connection, and yet yielding a result of unequalled moral beauty and of a world-saving power,—a result, self-consistent, all-consistent, and spontaneous, because, let me reiterate, the incidents narrated are *true*."[1]

Verily, the history of Jesus, his words and miracles, his crucifixion and resurrection, witnessed by the rulers and the people, friend and foe, Herod and Pilate, Jews and Romans, related by his disciples, with unmistakable simplicity and honesty, proclaimed from Jerusalem to Rome, believed by contemporaries of every grade of culture, sealed by the blood of martyrs, producing the mightiest results, felt and demonstrated in its power from day to day wherever his name is known, is the best authenticated history in the world.

THE CHRIST OF HISTORY.

The more we examine the Christ of the Gospels, the more we find that he carries in himself his own best evidence, like the sun which proves its existence and power by shining on the firmament to all but the blind. "I am one," he says, "that beareth witness of myself."

Much as the Evangelists differ in minor details and in their stand-point and aim, they nevertheless present only the various

[1] *Jesus*, by W. H. Furness, Philadelphia, 1870, p. 223.

aspects of the one and the same Christ. Matthew, writing for Jewish readers, sets him forth as the new Lawgiver and King of Israel in whom all the prophecies are fulfilled; Mark paints him, in fresh, rapid sketches, for the world-conquering Romans, as the mighty Son of God and worker of miracles of power; Luke, the physician and Hellenist, describes him to Greek readers as the Healer of diseases, the Friend of sinners, the Saviour of the lost, the sympathizing and ideal Son of Man; John who wrote last and wrote for Christians of all nations and ages, gives us the Gospel of the incarnate Logos, the only Begotten of the Father, who became flesh and dwelt among us full of grace and truth. But these are not contradictory, but complementary pictures of one and the same person.

The essential identity of the Christ of the Synoptists is universally conceded. As to the identity of the Synoptic and the Johannean Christ, it has indeed been disputed by a small class of modern critics; but the Church at large has never doubted it, and the common reader of the Gospels can perceive no difference affecting in the least degree the character and authority of Christ. Certainly in all the features of his moral character and the object of his mission, as well as in the principal events of his earthly life there is the most perfect agreement among the canonical Gospels. He is in all of them the same original, consistent, unselfish, sinless and perfect being from the beginning to the close of his public life.

SOME TRAITS OF CHRIST'S CHARACTER.

His character is *original* beyond all other men who have a just claim to originality. History furnishes no parallel to Jesus of Nazareth. The fertile imagination of poets has never conceived a character like his. No system of moral philosophy among the ancient Greeks and Romans set up such a standard of purity and perfection as Christ not only taught but practiced. All the other great teachers fell confessedly behind their own standard of virtue; Christ was more than his doctrine; his doctrine is but a reflection of his life. His character cannot be explained from any resources of his age; neither the orthodoxy of the Pharisees, nor the liberalism of the Sadducees, nor the mysticism of the Essænees could produce it; on the contrary he stands in antagonism to all. He came out from God and taught the world as one who owed nothing to the world, its schools, its libraries, its wise and good men. Though living in the world and for the world, he was not of the world, but far above it as the heaven is above the earth.

Christ's character is uniformly *consistent*. There is no man, however wise and good, who is not more or less inconsistent, who does not occasionally fall below his own standard, yield to the pressure of circumstances, allow himself to be carried away by passion or excitement, betray his native weakness, falter in the path of virtue. But Christ is the same in doctrine and conduct from the beginning to the end, before friend and foe, in private and public life, in action and suffering. He had never to retract a word, never to regret a deed, never to ask the pardon of God or man. His calmness and serenity were never disturbed; he never felt unhappy or desponding, and, at the close of his ministry, he could say to his heavenly Father in the presence of his intimate friends and disciples: "I glorified Thee on the earth, having finished the work which Thou hast given me to do."

Christ's character is absolutely *unselfish*. Love to God and man is the virtue of virtues, the fulfillment of the law, the bond of perfection, and the source of all true happiness. Selfishness, its very opposite, is the most radical and most universal of sins and failings. Our natural instincts prompt us to think first and last of ourselves; while our Christian instincts direct our attention to the good of our neighbor. We may despise the maxim of the famous statesman that "every body has his price." There were noble men and women in all ages and lands who sacrificed themselves for the good of others. But it is only too true that outside of Christianity there is little disinterested benevolence in the world. Even the best of men are more or less influenced in their good deeds by love of money or power or honor and glory. With the ancient Greeks and Romans pride and ambition were acknowledged to be the ruling passions and strongest motives of action. But in the life of Christ as told in the gospel story, there is not a trace of selfishness in any form, and his bitterest foes could not charge him with love of gain or any earthly good. He grew up, lived and died in poverty. His public life was one continued series of acts of benevolence and mercy. His miracles had for their aim, to feed the hungry, to heal the sick, to give sight to the blind, to expel evil spirits, to comfort the broken-hearted, to lead to repentance, faith, and a better life. He went about doing good to the bodies and souls of men, and his example has ever acted and acts at this day all over the Christian world as an inspiration of the noblest, purest and most useful deeds of charity. Ask the philanthropists and benefactors of the race in every age, ask the missionaries of the cross from St. Paul down to our time, ask the sisters of mercy, the founders of orphan homes, hospitals, houses of refuge, the emancipators of slaves, the reformers of prisons, the promoters of temperance, of peace and good will among men, ask them the question, who prompted them to their deeds of self-sacrificing devotion to their suffering fellow-men, and they will respond with one voice, It is Jesus of Nazareth who died on the cross to save sinners from temporal and eternal ruin.

To sum up all, Christ's character is *sinless* and *perfect*. This is an amazing fact, and nothing less than a moral miracle in the midst of a sinful world. Every human being is involved in the fall of the race. Those who are the humblest and know themselves best, are most ready to feel and to admit their own imperfections. I need only name Abraham, Moses, David, St. Peter, St. Paul, and St. John, who tower so high above ordinary men by the profound conviction of their sinfulness and guilt before God no less than by their genius, piety and influence in the history of religion. Even the noblest among the heathen, as Sakya-Muni, Socrates, Plato, Seneca, Epictetus, Plutarch, and Marcus Aurelius, prove the same fact.

But Jesus forms one absolute exception to a universal rule. Endowed with the keenest moral sensibilities and tenderest sympathies, moving in a corrupt age of this wicked world, and tempted as we, yea more than we are, by unbelief, ingratitude, malignity, denial and treason, he yet maintained a spotless innocence to the last. He never harmed a human being, never failed in word or deed, never fell out of harmony with his Heavenly Father. He was ever true to his mission of mercy, and lived solely for the glory of God and the good of mankind. He united, in even symmetry, the opposite graces of dignity and humility, strength and gentleness, severity and kindness, energy and resignation, active and passive obedience even to the death on the cross, and furnished an exemplar of perfect humanity for universal imitation.

If this was the character of Jesus—and who will deny it?—we must in the name of consistency and common sense accept his testimony concerning his person and work and admit the truth of his stupendous claims, which from any other mouth would be universally condemned as wicked blasphemy, but which from his lips sound with all the force of self-evident truth. If he was the wisest and holiest of men, he must truly be what he professes to be, the Son of God, the promised Messiah, the Saviour of the world.

THE EXTERNAL APPEARANCE OF CHRIST.

It is a remarkable fact that the Evangelists, while they give us such a full and harmonious exhibition of the character of Jesus in his own words and deeds, make no allusion to his physical appearance. They observe absolute silence about his countenance, his stature, the color of his hair and eye, his dress, his daily habits. Not even the beloved John who leaned on his Master's bosom and beheld "his glory" face to face, has a single hint on this subject. In this respect our instincts of natural affection have been wisely overruled, that all superstitious worship of pictures may be cut up by the root. We should not cling to the Christ in the flesh, but to the Christ in the spirit and in glory.

The prophetic descriptions of the Old Testament which were understood to refer to Christ, gave rise to two opposite theories, since they represent him on the one hand, as "a root out of dry ground, having no form nor comeliness," and, on the other hand, as "fairer than the children of men" and "altogether lovely." They are not irreconcilable if we distinguish between the state of humiliation and the state of exaltation, and again, in the state of humiliation, between sensuous and spiritual beauty of appearance. The ante-Nicene church under persecution, and the post-Nicene church in power differed here as they did in their outward condition. Justin Martyr and Tertullian were certainly wrong when they imagined Jesus to have been homely. But their view was not generally entertained even in their age; for the pictures in the Roman catacombs represent him, allegorically, as a handsome shepherd carrying a lamb on his shoulders or in his arms. Jesus in the days of his flesh had probably nothing extraordinary or imposing in his personal appearance that would strike the superficial observer, and in his dress and mode of daily life he no doubt conformed to the habits of his countrymen, as well as in his language and even in the peculiarities of the dialect of Galilee. Hence the woman of Samaria at once recognized him as a Jew. Yet we can hardly think of him as a Jew. We cannot associate him with the lineaments of any particular nationality. He is the universal man for universal imitation. He had not the physiognomy of a sinner. The spiritual beauty, purity and peace of his sinless soul in unbroken harmony with God must have shone through the thin veil of the flesh and flashed from his eye. This accounts for the overawing impression of his majesty on the profane traffickers in the temple-court, and on the band of soldiers in Gethsemane. On the Mount of transfiguration he anticipated the lustre of his future glory, when his "face did shine as the sun, and his garments became white as the light." With such hints Christian art was left to its own conceptions of ideal beauty in delineating the human face divine of the Saviour of mankind. The greatest painters and sculptors have not succeeded in satisfying their own aspirations. The subject is inexhaustible.

THE CHRIST OF PROPHECY.

Though descended from heaven, Christ stands firmly on earth, as the universal man, "most human, and yet most divine." He is intertwined with all the fortunes of the race, and casts his lustre back through the long ages of the past to the very beginning of the race, and forward to all ages of the future.

It is an undeniable fact that at the time of Christ the Jewish nation was filled with Messianic expectations which, though carnally misunderstood and perverted, had their roots in the Scriptures of the Old Testament and bear testimony to them. A long series of prophecies and types runs in unbroken line from the fall of man to the advent of Christ, and looks steadily towards a final redemption not only of the chosen people but of the whole human family. Though varied in form and admitting of a growing fulfillment, they are yet one and consistent in spirit and aim, and were wonderfully confirmed at last by actual fulfillment. The proto-gospel of the serpent-bruiser, the promises given to Noah, to Abraham, Isaac, and Jacob, to David and his royal house, the symbol of the brazen serpent in the wilderness for the healing of the people, the daily sacrifices, and the pregnant symbolism of the tabernacle and the temple, the prediction of a future great prophet and lawgiver, the meek and lowly King of Zion, his sufferings for the sins of the people, and his exaltation and everlasting reign, apply, in their highest and deepest sense, to *Jesus of Nazareth*, and *to no other person in history*. Isaiah, the prince and evangelist among the prophets, unrolls a picture of the Messiah so complete that none but those blinded by dogmatic prejudice can fail to find here the lineaments of our Saviour with his atoning death and glorious triumph. And finally to make certainty doubly certain, immediately before Christ, appeared his great forerunner (whose historical existence no one denies), as the personal embodiment of the Old Covenant, leading his own pupils to Jesus as the Lamb of God, and then disappearing like the dawn of the morning in the glory of the risen sun.

Christ knew and confessed himself to be the promised Messiah of whom Moses wrote and the prophets; he claimed all the prerogatives and exercised all the functions of the Messiah; he read himself on every page of the book of God. And, truly, he is the light and the life of the Old Testament; without him it is a sealed book to this day, in him it is revealed.

The wonderful harmony between the Christ of prophecy and the Christ of history has at all times justly been regarded as one of the strongest proofs of his divine character and mission, and has led to the conversion of many thinking and inquiring minds from Justin Martyr down to the present day. It is impossible to resolve this harmony into accident or to trace it to human divination and sagacity. It is the exclusive privilege of the divine mind to foreknow the distant future and to read the end from the beginning.

But the Christ of prophecy and type is not confined to the Jewish religion; he may be traced, in a modified form, even in the providential currents of the heathen world before his advent on earth. He is the desire of *all* nations. The civilization and literature of Greece, the military and political power of Rome prepared the way for his coming as well as the theocracy of the Jews. The noblest mission of the Greek language was to become the silver basket for the golden apple of the gospel. The chief aim of Alexander's conquests and the consolidation of nations under the Roman rule was to break down the partition walls between nations, and to prepare them for a universal religion. The Greek fathers justly recognized in the scattered truths of the ancient poets and philosophers sparks of the light from the Logos before his incarnation. Plato almost prophesied Christ when he described " the righteous man as one who, without doing any injustice, yet has the appearance of the greatest injustice, and proves his own justice by perseverance against all calumny unto death;" and when he predicted that, if such a righteous man should ever appear on earth, " he would be scourged, tortured, bound, deprived of his sight, and, after having suffered all possible injury, nailed to a post." Even amidst the blundering symbols, allegories and fictions of heathen mythology, the Avatars and Grand Llamas of Brahminism and Buddhism, the divine incarnations and the human deifications of ancient Greece and Rome, we may see caricatures and carnal anticipations of the great mystery of godliness: "God manifest in the flesh." They express the irrepressible longing of the human mind and heart after union with the divine, the groping in the dark after the unknown God who became known in Christ. The prodigal son of idolatry, after wasting his substance in riotous living, remembered his Father's house and prepared to return to him in penitence and faith, when the Father met him more than half way and received him to his loving heart. Tertullian speaks with reference to the nobler heathen of the *testimonia animæ naturaliter Christianæ*, of the testimonies of the soul which is constituted and predestinated for Christianity, and which, left to its truest and noblest instincts, turns to the one true God, as the flower to the sun, as the needle to the magnet.

Thus Christ sums up the whole meaning of ancient history, fulfilling the unconscious as well as the conscious prophecies and types of the past, the preparatory revelations of God and the aspirations of the human heart. In the widest sense it is true that he came not to destroy but to fulfil.

This is beautifully expressed by the German poet Lenau:

"*Die Sehnsucht die zum Himmel lauschte
Nach dem Erlöser je und je;*

Die aus Prophetenherzen rauschte
In das verlassne Erdenweh ;

Die Sehnsucht, die so lange Tage
Nach Gotte hier auf Erden ging,
Als Thräne, Lied, Gebet und Klage:
Sie ward Maria und empfing."

CHRIST AND CHRISTENDOM.

As Christ stands at the end of the ancient world, so he stands also at the beginning of the new. He is at once the ripest fruit of history before, and the fertile seed of history after, his coming. He is the turning-point in the biography of our race, the glory of the past and the hope of the future. Christ and Christianity are inseparable ; the achievements of Christianity are the achievements of Christ, its founder and ever present head ; and if Christianity cannot perish, it is because Christ lives, the same yesterday, to-day, and forever.

For eighteen centuries the Christian church has stood firm and unshaken, assailed indeed by winds and storms from all directions, yet ever growing stronger and spreading wider : a perpetual testimony to Christ, feeding on his words, living of his life, singing his praise in every zone, commemorating his life-giving death in every communion service, and celebrating his resurrection on every returning Lord's day. Christianity has taken the lead in all the great movements of modern history : it has regenerated the tottering Roman empire, civilized the Northern barbarians, produced the Reformation of the sixteenth century, abolished cruel laws, mitigated the horrors of war, restrained violence and oppression, infused a spirit of justice and humanity into governments and society, advocated the rights of the poor and suffering, stimulated moral reform and progress, founded literary and benevolent institutions without number, and is the chief author and promoter of all that is good and praiseworthy and enduring in our modern society.

Human nature is indeed still as depraved as ever, stained with the same vices, vexed with the same cares, saddened with the same sorrows as in times of old; but, taking even the lowest utilitarian view, we may say with Benjamin Franklin, in his wise letter to Tom Paine, "Man is bad enough with religion, he would be far worse without it; therefore do not unchain the tiger." Whatever is bad and deplorable exists *in spite* of Christianity, whatever is pure and holy and tends to promote virtue, happiness and peace, is due chiefly to the direct or indirect influence of Christ and his gospel. And whatever hopes we may and must entertain for the future progress and amelioration of the race, they depend upon him who alone can bring about by his good and holy Spirit that millennium of peace when

' Earth is changed to Heaven, and Heaven to earth,
One kingdom, joy and union without end."

Yet in the midst of abounding corruptions, Christ continually acts and reacts, and fulfills his mission of peace and good will to mankind. Who can measure the restraining, ennobling, cheering, sanctifying impulses which are from day to day and from hour to hour proceeding from the example of Christ, as preached from the pulpit, taught in the school, read in the Bible, and illustrated in the lives of his followers? Much as Christians are divided on points of doctrine, polity and ceremonies, they are united in devotion and love to their heavenly Master, derive the same holy motives from him, and endeavor, however feebly, to attain the same standard of perfection set up by him.

This unity of Christendom is strikingly illustrated in the vast treasure-house of hymnology whose power for good cannot be easily over-estimated. As I said in another place: "The hymns of Jesus are the Holy of holies in the temple of sacred poetry. From this sanctuary every doubt is banished, here the passions of sense, pride and unholy ambition give way to the tears of penitence, the joys of faith, the emotions of love, the aspirations of hope, the anticipations of heaven; here the dissensions of rival churches and theological schools are hushed into silence; here the hymnists of ancient, mediæval, and modern times, from every section of Christendom,—profound divines, stately bishops, humble monks, faithful pastors, devout laymen, holy women— unite with one voice in the common adoration of a common Saviour. He is the theme of all ages, tongues and creeds, the divine harmony of all human discords, the solution of all dark problems of life. What an argument this for the great mystery of God manifest in flesh, and for the communion of saints. Where is the human being however great and good that could open such a stream of grateful song, ever widening and deepening from generation to generation to the ends of the earth?"[1]

CHRIST AND THE HUMAN HEART.

The experience of the Christian church for these eighteen hundred years is repeated day by day in every human soul which is seriously concerned about the question of personal salvation. We are placed by Divine Providence in a world of sin and death; we are made in God's image, endowed with the noblest faculties, destined to be the prophets, priests, and kings of nature, filled with unsatisfied longings and aspirations after truth, holiness, and peace; yet bound to this earth, ever drawn away from our own ideals by sensual passions, selfish desires, and surrounded by temptations from within and without. We who are born to the freedom of the sons of God, are slaves of sin; we who are destined for immortality and glory, must suffer and die; descended from heaven, we end in the tomb, and return to dust.

Who solves this mysterious problem of life? Who breaks the chains of darkness? Who removes the load of guilt? Who delivers us from the degrading slavery of sin? Who secures peace to our troubled conscience? Who gives us strength against temptation, and enables us to realize our noble vocation? Who inspires our soul with love to God and man? Who, in the midst of abounding corruption and depravity, upholds our faith in man, as the image of God and special object of his care? Who

[1] Preface to. "*Christ in Song*," New York, 1868; London, 1869.

keeps up our hope and courage when earthly prospects vanish, the dearest friends depart, and the future looks dismal and threatening? Who dispels the terrors of the tomb and bids us hail death as a messenger that summons us to a higher and better world where all the problems of earth are solved in the light and bliss of heaven? To all these questions, which may be hushed for a while by the follies of passion, the intoxication of pleasure, the eager pursuit of wealth or knowledge, but which sooner or later irresistibly press themselves upon the attention of every serious mind, there is but one answer: "Lord, where shall we go but to thee? Thou alone hast words of eternal life, and we know and believe that thou art the Christ, the Son of the living God." Apostles and evangelists, martyrs and confessors, fathers and reformers, profound scholars, and ignorant slaves, mighty rulers and humble subjects, experienced men and innocent children—all, all point, in this great and all-absorbing question of salvation, not to Moses, not to Socrates, not to Mohammed, not to philosophy, art, or science, but to Christ, as the Way, the Truth, and the Life. He and he alone has a balm for every wound, a relief for every sorrow, a solution for every doubt, pardon for every sin, strength for every trial, victory for every conflict. He and he alone can satisfy the infinite desires of our immortal soul. Out of Christ life is an impenetrable mystery; in him it is gloriously solved. Out of him there is nothing but scepticism, nihilism, and despair; in him there is certainty and peace in this world, and life everlasting in the world to come. Our hearts are made for Christ, and "they are without rest until they rest in Christ."

This was one of the deepest thoughts of St. Augustin, and the same sentiment has found poetic expression in the finest Christian ode produced in America, in opposition to modern unbelief.[1]

[1] "Our Master," by Whittier.

"In joy of universal peace, or sense
 Of sorrow over sin,
Christ is his own best evidence,
 His witness is within.

No fable old, nor mythic lore,
 Nor dream of bards and seers,
No dead fact stranded on the shore
 Of the oblivious years,—

But warm, sweet, tender, even yet
 A present help is He;
And faith has still its Olivet,
 And love its Galilee.

The healing of his seamless dress
 Is by our beds of pain;
We touch Him in life's throng and press,
 And we are whole again.

Through Him the first fond prayers are said
 Our lips of childhood frame.
The last low whispers of our dead
 Are burdened with His name.

O Lord and Master of us all!
 Whate'er our name or sign,
We own Thy sway, we hear Thy call,
 We test our lives by Thine.

Apart from Thee all gain is loss,
 All labor vainly done;
The solemn shadow of Thy cross
 Is better than the sun.

Alone, O love ineffable!
 Thy saving name is given:
To turn aside from Thee is hell,
 To walk with Thee is heaven.

Our Friend, Our Brother, and our Lord,
 What may Thy service be?
Nor name, nor form, nor ritual word,
 But simply following Thee.

The heart must ring the Christmas bells,
 Thy inward altars raise,
Its faith and hope Thy canticles,
 And its obedience praise."

CHRIST IN THEOLOGY.

CHRIST is the centre of the moral universe, the Holy of holies in history. Christ in the Gospels, Christ in the Church, Christ in the pulpit, Christ in the school, Christ in theology, Christ in poetry, Christ in art, Christ in the soul, Christ in holy lives of men and women devoted to the welfare of the race,—wherever we meet him, he appears as the purest, loveliest, highest object of contemplation, and commands above all human beings our affection and veneration. He is nearest to us, and yet high above us, at once our friend and brother, and our Lord and Saviour.

We propose to give a popular summary of the history of Christ in the thoughts and creeds of Christendom.[1]

We approach the task with the conviction that Christ is far higher and deeper and broader than all Christologies. No single mind, no church or sect has ever exhausted the fulness of his divine-human personality. Every age must grapple anew with "the great mystery of godliness," and make it alive and fruitful for its own intellectual and spiritual benefit.

> "Our little systems have their day;
> They have their day and cease to be:
> They are but broken lights of Thee,
> And Thou, O Lord, art more than they.

---

[1] For further statements, criticisms, proofs, and literature, the author refers to the doctrinal sections in his *Church History* (revised ed. 1882 sqq., vols. I., II. and III.), to his article *Christology* in the "Rel. Encyclopædia," vol. I. 451-467, and especially to the well-known masterly work of his beloved teacher and friend Dr. Dorner, *Entwicklungsgeschichte der Lehre von der Person Christi* (2nd ed. Berlin 1851, 1853, 2 vols.), which was translated into English by W. L. Alexander and D. W. Simon (Edinb. 1864, in 5 vols.).

> "Let knowledge grow from more to more
> But more of reverence in us dwell;
> That mind and soul according well,
> May make one music as before."

BIBLICAL CHRISTOLOGY.

Christology, or the doctrine of Christ's Person, is based upon the life and testimony of Christ, as represented, historically, in the Gospels, and as reflected, doctrinally and experimentally, in the Acts and Epistles. It treats of the mystery of the incarnation and embraces three distinct and yet inseparable points: the humanity of our Lord, his divinity, and their relation to each other in his one person. His divine-human personality forms the basis of his work, which is the redemption, reconciliation, and re-union of men with God. It is the central fact and truth of Christianity. It was the one article of St. Peter's creed, and it forms the chief part of the Apostles' Creed. The leading evangelical divines of Europe and America are coming to agree more and more in this estimate of its importance; and the ever-increasing number of Lives of Christ strengthens the Christocentric character of modern theology. Yet care must be taken not to emphasize the incarnation at the expense of the doctrines of the atonement by Christ's death, and the regeneration by the Holy Spirit.

The biblical Christology begins with the Messianic prophecies of the Old Testament, which is the preparation for the New. Christ is the heart of the Scripture, and the key to its spiritual understanding. All revelations of God look to him as the final revelation. The promise of the Messiah runs like a golden chain through the whole Old Testament. The history of redemption begins immediately after the fall. Before their expulsion from Paradise our first parents received as an anchor of hope the protevangelium of the woman's seed that should crush the serpent's head and destroy the power of sin. The Messianic promise binds together the primitive, the patriarchal, the Mosaic, the prophetic, the exilian, and the post-exilian periods.

The whole history of Israel, its deliverance from the land of bondage, the Mosaic legislation and worship, the daily sacrifices, the festivals and sacred rites, the representative persons and events, typically foreshadow the Redeemer and the redemption. The later prophets, especially Isaiah, draw that mysterious person of the future in such lineaments as apply to Jesus of Nazareth, and to no other. The New Testament, as Augustin said, is concealed in the Old, the Old Testament is revealed in the New. At last the law and the prophecy culminate in John the Baptist and his witness to Jesus as the Lamb of God that taketh away the sin of the world.

The New Testament Christology may be summed up, with Dr. Dorner, in the sentence: "In Christ has appeared the perfect revelation of God, and at the same time the perfection of humanity." He unites in his person the nearest approach which God can make to man, and the nearest approach which man can make to God. All the Evangelists and Apostles agree in representing Jesus of Nazareth as the Messiah, as the Lord and Master, and as the only Saviour of the race from sin and death. They teach unanimously that he combines in one harmonious personality the twofold character of a unique Divine Sonship and a unique sinless Manhood, and that by this very constitution he is qualified to be the only Mediator between God and man. Their faith and doctrine are rooted and grounded in their personal experience which was to them more certain than their own existence. Simon Peter spoke in the name of all when he confessed: "Lord, to whom shall we go? Thou hast the words of eternal life. And we have believed and know that thou art the Holy One of God."

All the essential elements of the apostolic Christology are clearly contained in Christ's own testimony concerning himself, and are confirmed by his life and work.

Jesus exhibits himself constantly under the twofold aspect of the Son of Man and the Son of God, in a sense that applies to no other being. He strongly asserts his humanity, and calls himself (about eighty times in the Gospels) *the Son of Man;* not *a* son of man, among other descendants of Adam, but *the* Son of Man emphatically; as the representative of the whole race; as the second Adam, descended from heaven; as the ideal, the perfect, the absolute man, the head of a new race, the King of Jews and Gentiles, the model man for universal imitation. While putting himself on a *par* with us as *man*, he claims at the same time as *the* Son of Man, superiority over all, and freedom from sin. He thus stands solitary and alone as the one and only spotless human being in the midst of a fallen race, as an oasis of living water and fresh verdure, surrounded by a barren desert of sand and stone. He never fell out of harmony with God and with himself: he alone needed no repentance, no conversion, no regeneration, no pardon. This sinlessness of Christ is the great moral miracle of history which underlies all his miraculous works, and explains them as natural manifestations of his person.

On the other hand Jesus as emphatically asserts his divinity, and calls himself not simply *a* son of God among other children of God by adoption, but *the Son of God* above all others, in a peculiar sense; the Son by nature; the Son from eternity; the Son who alone knows the Father, who reveals the Father to us, who calls him, not "our" Father (as we are directed to pray), but "my" Father. He is, as his favorite disciple calls him, "the only-begotten Son" (or "*God* only-begotten,"[1] according to some of the oldest manuscripts). The Nicene divines express this by the phrase "eternally begotten of the essence[2] of the Father."

He is thus represented to us by himself and his disciples as a divine-human being, truly God and truly man in one person; and his words and acts and sufferings have a corresponding effect. Hence he calmly puts forth astounding claims, which in the mouth of every other man, no matter how wise and how good, would sound like blasphemy or madness, but which

[1] Μονογενὴς Θεός (for ὁ μονογενὴς υἱός).   [2] Οὐσία.

from his lips appear as natural as the rays of light emanating from the sun. He declares again and again that he was sent from God, to teach this world what he did not learn from any school or any book, but directly from the Father. He invites all men to come to him that they may find rest and peace. He calls himself the Light of the world, and the Way, the Truth, and the Life. He claims and exercises the power to forgive sins, and to raise the dead. He says, "I am the Resurrection and the Life," and promises eternal life to every one that believes in him. Even in the moment of his deepest humiliation, he proclaimed himself the King of truth, and the Ruler and Judge of mankind. His kingdom is to be co-extensive with the race, and everlasting as eternity itself. And with this consciousness he sent forth his disciples to preach the gospel of salvation to every creature, forewarning them of persecution and martyrdom, and promising no reward in this life, but pledging them his presence to the end of the world, and a crown of glory in heaven. He co-ordinates himself in the baptismal formula with the eternal Father and the eternal Spirit, and allows himself to be worshipped by the sceptical Thomas as his "Lord" and his "God."

This central truth of Christ's divine-human person and work is set forth in the New Testament writings, not as a logically-formulated dogma, but as a living fact and glorious truth, as an object of faith, a source of comfort, and a stimulus to a holy life, in humble imitation of his perfect example. This is sufficient for all practical purposes. The simple narrative of the Gospels has been, is now, and always will be far more powerful for the general benefit of mankind than all the systems of dogmatic theology and moral philosophy.

But the mind of the Church must meditate, reflect, reason, philosophize and theologize. It must endeavor to grasp, comprehend, and define the truth, and to vindicate and guard it against error. The New Testament itself furnishes ever new impulse and food for knowledge. The fruitful germs of a

Christology we find already in Peter, Paul, and John, and their teaching must ever guide all sound Christological speculation.

THE ANTE-NICENE CHRISTOLOGY.
From A. D. 100 to the Council of Nicæa A. D. 325.

The ecclesiastical development of this fundamental dogma started from Peter's confession of the Messiahship of Jesus, and from John's doctrine of the incarnate Logos.

It was stimulated by two opposite heresies which agitated the church during the second century, but were overruled for the advancement of deeper knowledge of the truth. These are EBIONISM and GNOSTICISM; the one essentially Jewish, the other essentially heathen; the one affirming the humanity of Christ to the exclusion of his divinity, the other running into the opposite error by resolving his humanity into a delusive show or empty phantom; both agreeing in the denial of the incarnation, or the real and abiding union of the divine and human in the person of our Lord.

Besides, there arose in the second and third centuries two forms of *Unitarianism* or *Monarchianism*, that is Antitrinitarianism.

(1) The RATIONALISTIC or DYNAMIC Unitarianism—represented by the ALOGIANS, THEODOTUS, ARTEMON, and PAUL OF SAMOSATA—either denied the divinity of Christ altogether, or resolved it into a mere power,[1] although they generally admitted his supernatural generation by the Holy Spirit.

(2) The PATRIPASSIAN and SABELLIAN Unitarianism maintained the divinity of Christ, but merged it into the essence of the Father, and so denied the independent, pre-existent *personality* of Christ. So PRAXEAS, NOETUS, CALLISTUS (Pope CALIXTUS I.), BERYLLUS OF BOSTRA, and SABELLIUS. The last was the most subtle and profound of these Unitarians, and taught a trinity of mode and of revelation, but not a trinity of persons.

[1] Δύναμις.

In antagonism with these errors the Church maintained the full divinity of Christ (*versus* Ebionism and rationalistic Monarchianism), his full humanity (*versus* Gnosticism and Manichæism), and his independent or distinct personality (*versus* Patripassianism and Sabellianism). The dogma was developed in close connection with the dogma of the Trinity, which resulted, by logical necessity, from the deity of Christ, and the deity of the Holy Spirit on the basis of the fundamental truth of Monotheism. For if there is but one God, and yet a divine Son and a divine Spirit as well as a divine Father, there must be a trinity of divine persons as well as a unity of divine essence.

The ante-Nicene Christology passed through many obstructions, loose statements, uncertain conjectures and speculations; but the instinct and main current of the Church was steadily towards the Nicene and Chalcedonian creed-statements, especially if we look to the worship and devotional life as well as to theological literature. Christ was the object of worship, prayer, and praise (which implies his deity) from the very beginning, as we must infer from several passages of the New Testament, from the heathen testimony of Pliny the Younger concerning the singing of hymns to Christ as *God*, from the "Gloria in Excelsis," which was the daily morning hymn of the Eastern Church as early as the second century, from the "Tersanctus," from the Hymn of Clement of Alexandria to the divine Logos, from Eusebius and many other testimonies. Christ was *believed* to be divine, and *adored* as divine, before he was clearly *taught* to be divine. Faith preceded theology. Many a martyr in those days of persecution died for his faith in the divinity of our Lord, with very imperfect knowledge of this doctrine. It is unfair to make the Church responsible for the speculative crudities, the experimental and tentative statements, of some ante-Nicene fathers, who believed more than they could clearly express in words. In the first efforts of the human mind to grapple with so great a mystery, we must expect many mistakes and inaccuracies. The ante-Nicene rules of faith as we find them in the writings of Irenæus, Origen, Tertullian, Cyprian, etc., are essentially agreed among themselves and with the Apostles' Creed, so called, as it appears, first in the fourth century, especially at Rome and Aquileia. They all confess the divine-human character of Christ as the chief object of the Christian faith, but in the form of facts, and in simple, popular style, not in the form of doctrinal or logical statement. The Nicene Creed is much more explicit and dogmatic in consequence of the preceding contest with heresy; but the substance of the faith is the same in the Nicene and Apostles' Creeds.

The Apostolic Fathers so called who lived at the close of the first and the beginning of the second century, give us only plain, practical assertions, and reminiscences of apostolic preaching for the purposes of edification. Clement of Rome (in the newly discovered portion of his Epistle to the Corinthians) says that "God, the Lord Jesus Christ, and the Holy Spirit are the faith and the hope of the elect." This is the first clear post-apostolic statement of the Trinity which implies, like the baptismal formula and the Apostolic benediction, the recognition of the divinity of Christ. Ignatius of Antioch does not hesitate to call Christ "*God*," without qualification. Polycarp of Smyrna calls him "the *eternal* Son of God," and associates him in his last prayer with the Father, and the Holy Spirit.

The theological speculation on the person of Christ began with Justin Martyr, and was carried on by Clement of Alexandria and Origen, in the East; by Irenæus, Hippolytus, and Tertullian, in the West.

JUSTIN MARTYR (d. 166) takes up the Johannean Logos idea, which proved a very fruitful germ of theological speculation. It was prepared by the Old Testament personification of the word and wisdom of God, assumed an idealistic shape in Philo of Alexandria, and reached a realistic completion in St. John. Following the suggestion of the double meaning of the Greek *Logos* (*ratio* and *oratio*, *reason* and *word*), Justin distinguishes in the Logos two elements, the immanent and the transitive; the revelation of God *ad intra*, and the revelation *ad extra*. He teaches the procession of the Logos from the free will (not the essence) of God by generation, without division or diminution of the divine substance. This begotten Logos he conceives as a hypostatical being, a person distinct from the Father, and subordinate to him. He represents God, the Son, and the prophetic Spirit, as joint objects of Christian worship.[1] Peculiar is his doctrine of the seminal Logos,[2] or the Word disseminated among men, *i. e.*, Christ before the incarnation, who scattered elements of truth and virtue among the heathen philosophers and poets, although they did not know it. He held the liberal view that all who lived according to the light of the Logos were unconscious Christians. A similar view was taught by Zwingli in the time of the Reformation.

CLEMENT OF ALEXANDRIA (d. 220) sees in the Logos the ultimate principle of all existence (without beginning, and timeless), the revealer of the Father, the sum of all intelligence and wisdom, the personal truth, the author of the world, the source of light and life, the educator of the race, who at last became man to make us partakers of his divine nature. Like some other ante-Nicene fathers (Justin Martyr, Tertullian, and Origen), he conceived the outward appearance of Christ's humanity in the state of humiliation to have been without form or comeliness (Isa. 53: 2, 3); but he made a distinction between two kinds of beauty,—the outward beauty of the flesh, which soon fades away; and the moral beauty of the soul, which is permanent, and shone even through the servant-form of our Lord.

ORIGEN (d. 254) felt the whole weight of the Christological problem, but obscured it by foreign speculations, and prepared the way both for the Arian heresy and the Athanasian orthodoxy, though more fully for the latter. On the one hand he closely approaches the Nicene Homoousian by bringing the Son into union with the essence of the Father, and ascribing to him

[1] Σεβόμεθα καὶ προσκυνοῦμεν, *Apol.* I. 6.   [2] Λόγος σπερματικός.

the attribute of eternity. He is, properly, the author of the Nicene doctrine of *eternal* generation of the Son from the *essence* of the Father (though he usually represents the generation as an act of the *will* of the Father). But on the other hand he teaches subordinationism by calling the Son simply God,[1] and a second God,[2] but not *the* God.[3] In his views on the humanity of Christ, he approached the semi-Gnostic docetism, and ascribed to the glorified body of Christ ubiquity (in which he was followed by Gregory of Nyssa). His enemies charged him with teaching a double Christ (answering to the lower Jesus, and the higher Soter of the Gnostics), and a merely temporary validity of the body of the Redeemer. As to the relation of the two natures in Christ, he was the first to use the term "God-man,"[4] and to apply the favorite illustration of fire heating and penetrating the iron, without altering its character.

The Western Church was not so fruitful in speculation, but, upon the whole, sounder and more self-consistent. The keynote was struck by IRENÆUS (d. 202), who, though of Eastern origin, spent his active life in the south of France. He carries special weight as a pupil of Polycarp of Smyrna, and through him a grand-pupil of St. John, the inspired master. He likewise uses the terms "Logos" and "Son of God" interchangeably, and concedes the distinction, made also by the Valentinians, between the *inward* and the *uttered* word, in reference to man, but contests the application of it to God, who is above all antitheses, absolutely simple and unchangeable, and in whom before and after, thinking and speaking, coincide. He repudiates also speculative or *a priori* attempts to explain the derivation of the Son from the Father. This he holds to be an incomprehensible mystery. He is content to define the actual distinction between Father and Son by saying that the former is God revealing himself; the latter, God revealed. The one is the ground of revelation; the other is the actual, appearing

---

[1] Θεός.   [2] Δεύτερος Θεός.   [3] Ὁ Θεός, or αὐτό-Θεος.
[4] Θεάνθρωπος.

revelation itself. Hence he calls the Father "the invisible of the Son;" and the Son "the visible of the Father." He discriminates most rigidly the conceptions of generation and of creation. The Son, though begotten of the Father, is still, like him, distinguished from the created world as increate,—without beginning, and eternal; all plainly showing that Irenæus is much nearer the Nicene dogma of the essential identity of the Son with the Father than Justin Martyr and the Alexandrians. If, as he does in several passages, he still subordinates the Son to the Father, he is certainly inconsistent, and that for want of an accurate distinction between the eternal Logos and the incarnate Christ. Expressions like "My Father is greater than I," which apply only to the Christ of history, in the state of humiliation, he refers also, like Justin and Origen, to the eternal Logos. On the other hand he is charged with leaning in the opposite direction,—towards the Sabellian and Patripassian views,—but unjustly. Apart from his frequent want of precision in expression, he steers in general, with sure biblical and churchly tact, equally clear of both extremes, and asserts alike the essential unity and the eternal personal distinction of the Father and the Son. The incarnation of the Logos he ably discusses, viewing it both as a restoration and redemption from sin and death, and as the completion of the revelation of God and the creation of man. In the latter view, as finisher, Christ is the perfect Son of Man, in whom the *likeness* of man to God (the *similitudo Dei*), regarded as moral duty, in distinction from the *image* of God (*imago Dei*), as an essential property, becomes for the first time fully real. According to this, the incarnation would be grounded in the original plan of God for the education of mankind, and independent of the fall. It would have taken place even without the fall, though in some other form. Yet Irenæus does not expressly teach this. Speculation on abstract possibilities was foreign to his realistic cast of mind. He vindicates at length the true and full humanity of Christ against the docetism of the Gnostic schools. Christ must be man, like us, in body, soul, and spirit, though without sin, if he would redeem us from sin, and make us perfect. He is the second Adam, the absolute, universal man, the prototype and summing up[1] of the whole race. Connected with this is the beautiful idea of Irenæus (repeated by Hippolytus), that Christ made the circuit of all the stages of human life to redeem them all. To carry this out he extended the life of Jesus to fifty years, and supported it by a mistaken inference from the loose conjecture of the Jews (John 8 : 57), and by an appeal to tradition. He also teaches a close union of the divinity and humanity in Christ, in which the former is the active principle, and the seat of personality, the latter the passive and receptive principle.

TERTULLIAN of North Africa (about 220) taught a trinity of subordination. He bluntly calls the Father the whole divine substance, and the Son a part of it, illustrating their relation by the figures of the fountain and the stream, the sun and the beam. He would not have two suns, he says; but he might call Christ "God," as Paul does in Rom. 9 : 5. The sunbeam, too, in itself considered, may be called sun, but not the sun a beam. Sun and beam are two distinct things (*species*) in one essence (*substantia*), as God and the Word, as the Father and the Son. But we should not take figurative language too strictly, and must remember that Tertullian was especially interested to distinguish the Son from the Father, in opposition to the Patripassian Praxeas. In other respects he did the Church Christology material service. He propounds a threefold hypostatical existence of the Son (*filiatio*): (1) The pre-existent, eternal immanence of the Son in the Father, they being as inseparable as reason and word in man, who was created in the image of God, and hence in a measure reflects his being; (2) The coming-forth of the Son with the Father for the purpose of the creation; (3) The manifestation of the Son in the world by the incarnation. He advocates the entire, yet sinless humanity of Christ, against both the docetistic Gnostics and the Patripas-

---

[1] 'Ανακεφαλαίωσις, *recapitulatio.*

sians. He accuses the former of making Christ, who is all truth, a half lie, and by the denial of his flesh, resolving all his work in the flesh into an empty show. He urges against the latter that God the Father is incapable of suffering and change.

HIPPOLYTUS of Rome (d. 236) was likewise a subordinationist in his doctrine of the trinity.

CYPRIAN (d. 258) of Carthage, a pupil of Tertullian, marks no progress in this or any other doctrine, except that of the Catholic unity and the episcopate. He was not so much a theologian as an ecclesiastic, and typical high-churchman.

DIONYSIUS, Bishop of Rome (d. 269), a Greek by birth, came nearest the Nicene view. He maintained distinctly, in his controversy with Dionysius of Alexandria, the unity of essence, and the threefold personal distinction of Father, Son, and Spirit, in opposition to Sabellianism, tritheism, and subordinationism. He showed that instinct of orthodoxy and that art of anathematizing heresy which were already familiar to the popes. His view is embodied in a fragment preserved by Athanasius.

THE NICENE CHRISTOLOGY.

From A. D. 325 to A. D. 381.

The Nicene Christology is the result of the struggle with ARIANISM and SEMI-ARIANISM, which agitated the Eastern Church for more than half a century from A. D. 318 to 381.

The Arian heresy denied the strict deity of Christ (his co-equality with the Father), and taught that he is a subordinate divinity, *different in essence* from God,[1] pre-existing before the world, yet not eternal,[2] that he is himself a creature of the will of God out of nothing;[3] that he created this present world and became incarnate for our salvation.

Arianism disappoints the expectations of reason and faith alike: by teaching the incarnation of a pre-existent Logos, it encounters the chief objection to the orthodox Christology; and by lowering this pre-existent Christ to the rank of a crea-

[1] Ἑτεροούσιος.   [2] Ἦν ποτε ὅτε οὐκ ἦν.   [3] Κτίσμα ἐξ οὐκ ὄντων.

ture, it robs him of that divinity which alone can be a proper object of faith and worship. It starts with a zeal for the unity and the unchangeableness of God; and yet ends in dyotheism, the doctrine of an uncreated God, and a created God. It is (as Neander calls it) "a prosy intellectualism." It runs rampant at last into deism and sheer humanitarianism. Its doctrine of freedom contains the germ of Pelagianism.

Semi-Arianism occupied an untenable middle ground between the Arian *hetero-ousia*, or *difference* of essence, and the orthodox *homo-ousia*, or *equality* of essence; and substitutes for both the elastic term *homoi-ousia*, or *similarity* of essence, which might be contracted into an Arian, or stretched into an orthodox sense, according to the spirit and tendency of the men who held it.

In opposition to these heresies, the orthodox church firmly maintained and defended, with superior ability, rigor, and perseverance, the doctrine of the eternal deity of Christ or the essential oneness of the Son with the Father. It was briefly expressed by the word *homo-ousia*, or equality of essence. This doctrine was regarded in the Nicene age as the very corner-stone of the Christian religion, the *articulus stantis vel cadentis ecclesiæ*. Its chief champion was the heroic ATHANASIUS, bishop of Alexandria (d. 373), who devoted his whole life to this doctrine, never 'wavering, though standing at one time, "*unus versus mundum*," and suffering twenty years of exile. Hence he is justly called "the Great," and "the father of orthodoxy." Next to him, his friends, the three Cappadocian bishops,—Basil, Gregory of Nazianzus, and Gregory of Nyssa,—were the ablest defenders of the Nicene faith, during the ascendancy of Arianism.

The orthodox doctrine triumphed in the first œcumenical council, convened by Constantine the Great, at Nicæa, A. D. 325, and, after a new and longer struggle, it was re-asserted in the second œcumenical council, convened by Theodosius the Great, at Constantinople, A. D. 381. It is briefly and tersely

CHRIST IN THEOLOGY. 59

laid down in the chief article of the Nicæno-Constantinopolitan Creed, which has stood ever since like an immovable rock :—

("We believe) ... in one Lord Jesus Christ, the only-begotten Son of God, begotten of the Father before all worlds [God of God], Light of Light, very God of very God, begotten, not made, being of one substance with the Father; by whom all things were made; who for us men and for our salvation came down from heaven, and was incarnate by the Holy Ghost of the Virgin Mary, and was made man."

Nicæa has long since lost its glory and is now a miserable Turkish village. But the Nicene Creed still rings throughout orthodox Christendom and is incorporated in the most solemn acts of worship.

"The faith of the Trinity lies,
Shrined forever and ever in those grand old words and wise;
A gem in a beautiful setting; still at matin-time,
The service of Holy Communion rings the ancient chime;
Wherever in marvellous minster, or village churches small,
Men to the Man that is God, out of their misery call;
Swelled by the rapture of choirs, or borne on the poor man's word,
Still the glorious Nicene confession unaltered is heard;
Most like the song that the angels are singing around the throne,
With their Holy! holy! holy! to the great Three in One."

THE CHALCEDONIAN CHRISTOLOGY.

This finds its normal expression in the Chalcedonian statement of 451. It was the answer of the orthodox Church to the heresies which related to the proper constitution of Christ's theanthropic person, or the relation between the divine and human nature.

These heresies are chiefly three: viz.,

1. APOLLINARIANISM, a partial denial of the humanity, as Arianism is of the deity, of Christ. Apollinaris the Younger, bishop of Laodicea in Syria (d. 390), on the basis of the Platonic trichotomy, ascribed to Christ a human body[1] and animal soul,[2] but not a human spirit or reason.[3] He put the divine Logos in the place of the rational soul, and thus substituted a flesh-bearing God[4] for a real Godman,[5]—a mixed middle being

[1] Σῶμα. [2] Ψυχὴ ἄλογος. [3] Ψυχὴ λογική, νοῦς, πνεῦμα.
[4] Θεὸς σαρκοφόρος. [5] Θεάνθρωπος.

for a divine-human person. From this error it follows, either that the rational soul of man was not redeemed, or that it needed no redemption. When John says that the Logos became "flesh," and when Paul says that Christ appeared "in the likeness of the flesh of sin," we are to understand by "flesh"[1] not simply the body,[2] but the whole nature of man, body, soul, and spirit. Christ became like us in all things, sin only excepted.

2. NESTORIANISM (from Nestorius, Patriarch of Constantinople, d. in exile 440) admitted the full deity and the full humanity of Christ, but put them into loose mechanical conjunction, or affinity [3] rather than a vital and personal union;[4] and hence it objected to the popular orthodox term "mother of God,"[5] as applied to the Virgin Mary, while willing to call her "mother of *Christ*"[6] or "mother of our Lord" (Luke 1: 43).

3. EUTYCHIANISM (from Eutyches, presbyter at Constantinople, d. after 451) is the very opposite of Nestorianism, and sacrificed the distinction of the two natures in Christ to the unity of the person, to such an extent as to make the incarnation an absorption of the human nature by the divine, or a deification of human nature, even of the body: hence the Eutychians thought it proper to use the phrases "God is born," "God suffered," "God was crucified," "God died."

The third and fourth œcumenical councils (at Ephesus and Chalcedon) settled the question of the precise relation of the two natures in Christ's person, as the first and second (325 and 381) had decided the doctrine of his divinity. The decree of the Council of Ephesus, A. D. 431, under the lead of the violent Cyril of Alexandria, was merely negative, a condemnation of the error of Nestorius, and leaned a little towards the opposite error of Eutyches. This error triumphed temporarily in the justly so-called "Robber Synod," likewise held at Ephesus, in 449, under the dictatorship of Dioscurus of Alexandria, who inherited all the bad, and none of the good, qualities of his

[1] Σάρξ. [2] Σῶμα. [3] Συνάφεια. [4] Ἔνωσις. [5] Θεοτόκος, *Dei-para*. [6] Χριστοτόκος.

predecessor, Cyril. But Dyophysitism re-acted; and Dioscurus and Eutyches were condemned a few years afterwards by the Council of Chalcedon, A. D. 451, at which bishop Leo I. of Rome by correspondence exerted a commanding influence. This council gave a clear and full statement of the orthodox Christology as follows:

"Following the holy Fathers, we all with one consent teach men to confess one and the same Son, our Lord Jesus Christ, the same perfect in Godhead and also perfect in manhood; truly God and truly man, of a rational soul and body; consubstantial (co-equal) with the Father according to the Godhead, and consubstantial with us according to the Manhood; in all things like unto us, without sin; begotten before all ages of the Father according to the Godhead, and in these latter days, for us and for our salvation, born of the Virgin Mary, the Mother of God, according to the Manhood; one and the same Christ, Son, Lord, Only-Begotten, to be acknowledged in two natures, *inconfusedly, unchangeably, indivisibly, inseparably;* the distinction of natures being by no means taken away by the union, but rather the property of each nature being preserved, and concurring in one Person and one Subsistence, not parted or divided into two persons, but one and the same Son, and only begotten, God the Word, the Lord Jesus Christ; as the prophets from the beginning [have declared] concerning him, and the Lord Jesus Christ himself has taught us, and the Creed of the holy Fathers has handed down to us."

The same doctrine is set forth in a more condensed form in the second part of the *Symbolum Quicunque,* or the (falsely so-called) Athanasian Creed, which probably originated in Gaul during the seventh or eighth century.

"Furthermore it is necessary to everlasting salvation: that he also believe rightly [faithfully] the Incarnation of our Lord Jesus Christ. For the right Faith is, that he believe and confess: that our Lord Jesus Christ, the Son of God, is God and Man; God, of the Substance [Essence] of the Father; begotten before the worlds: and Man, of the Substance [Essence] of his Mother, born in the world. Perfect God and perfect Man; of a rational soul and human flesh subsisting; equal to the Father, as touching his Godhead; and inferior to the Father as touching his Manhood. Who although he is God and Man; yet he is not two, but one Christ. One; not by conversion of the Godhead into flesh, but by assumption of the Manhood into God. One altogether; not by confusion of Substance [Essence], but by unity of Person. For as the rational soul and flesh is one Man; so God and Man is one Christ. Who suffered for our salvation; desended into Hades, rose again the third day from the dead. He ascended into heaven; He sitteth on the right hand of God the Father Almighty. From thence He shall come to judge the living and the dead. At whose coming all men shall rise again with their bodies, and shall give account for their own works."

THE POST-CHALCEDONIAN CHRISTOLOGY.

The Chalcedonian decision did not stop the controversy, but called for a supplementary statement concerning the *two wills* of Christ, corresponding to the *two natures*.

Eutychianism revived in the form of MONOPHYSITISM,[1] or the doctrine that Christ had but one composite nature.[2] It makes the humanity of Christ a mere accident of the immutable divine substance. The liturgical shibboleth of the Monophysites was "God crucified," which they introduced into the Trisagion[3]: hence they are also called *Theopaschites*.[4] The tedious Monophysite controversies convulsed the Eastern Church for more than a hundred years, weakened its power, and facilitated the conquest of Mohammedanism.

The fifth œcumenical council, held at Constantinople, 553, made a partial concession to the Monophysites, but did not reconcile them. They separated, like their antipodes, the Nestorians, from the orthodox Greek Church, and continue to this day under various names and organizations,—the Jacobites in Syria, the Copts in Egypt, the Abyssinians, and, the most important of them, the Armenians.

Closely connected with Monophysitism was MONOTHELETISM,[5] or the doctrine that Christ has but *one will*, as he has but one person. The orthodox maintained that will is an attribute

---

[1] From μόνη φύσις, one nature.
[2] Μία φύσις σύνθετος, or μία φύσις διττή.
[3] Ἅγιος ὁ Θεός, ἅγιος ἰσχυρός, ἅγιος ἀθάνατος, ὁ σταυρωθεὶς δι' ἡμᾶς, ἐλέησον ἡμᾶς.
[4] Θεοπασχῖται.
[5] From μόνον and θέλημα.

CHRIST IN THEOLOGY. 63

of nature, rather than of person, and consequently that Christ had *two* wills corresponding to the two natures,—a human will and a divine will,—both working in harmony. The Monotheletic controversy lasted from 633 to 680. The Emperor Heraclius proposed a compromise formula,—one divine human energy;[1] but it was opposed in the West.

The sixth œcumenical council, held in Constantinople, 689 (also called the Third Constantinopolitan Council, or the Conc. Trullanum I.), condemned the Monotheletic heresy, and repeated the Chalcedonian Creed of one Christ in two natures, with the following supplement concerning the two wills:—

"And we likewise preach *two natural wills*[2] in him [Jesus Christ], and *two natural operations*[3] undivided, inconvertible, inseparable, unmixed,[4] according to the doctrine of the holy fathers; and the two natural wills are far from being contrary (as the impious heretics assert), but his human will follows the divine will, and is not resisting or reluctant, but rather subject to his divine and omnipotent will. For it was proper that the will of the flesh should be moved, but be subjected to the divine will, according to the wise Athanasius."

The same council condemned Pope Honorius as a Monotheletic heretic, and his successors confirmed it. This undeniable fact figured conspicuously in the Vatican Council (1870) as an unanswerable argument against papal infallibility, and was pressed by bishop Hefele and other learned members of the council, although they afterwards submitted to an infallible modern pope and council *versus* infallible old popes and councils. Monotheletism continued among the Maronites on Mount Lebanon (who, however, afterwards submitted to the Roman Church), as well as among the Monophysites, who are all Monothelites.

With the sixth œcumenical council closes the development of the ancient Catholic Christology. The Adoption controversy, which arose in Spain and France toward the close of the eighth century, turned upon the question whether Christ as man was the Son of God by nature (*naturaliter*), or simply by adoption

[1] Μία θεανδρικὴ ἐνέργεια. [2] Δύο φυσικὰς θελήσεις ἤτοι θελήματα.
[3] Δύο φυσικὰς ἐνεργείας. [4] Ἀδιαιρέτως, ἀτρέπτως, ἀμερίστως, ἀσυγχύτως.

64 CHRIST IN THEOLOGY.

(*nuncupative*). The Adoptionists maintained the latter, and shifted the whole idea of sonship from the person (to whom it belongs) to the nature. Their theory was a modification of the Nestorian error, and was condemned in a synod at Frankfort-on-the-Main 794; but it did not result in a positive addition to the creed statements.

The scholastic theology of the middle ages made no real progress in Christology, and confined itself to a dialectical analysis and defence of the Chalcedonian dogma, with a one-sided reference to the divine nature of Christ. John of Damascus in the East, and Thomas Aquinas in the West, were the ablest exponents of the Chalcedonian dogma. The mediæval Church while exalting over the glorious divinity of our Lord, almost forgot his real humanity (except his passion), and substituted for it virtually the worship of the Virgin Mary, who seemed to appeal more tenderly and effectively to all the human sensibilities and sympathies of the heart than the exalted Saviour.

ANALYSIS OF THE ŒCUMENICAL CHRISTOLOGY.

The following are the leading ideas of the Chalcedonian or œcumenical Christology, as taught in common by the doctrinal standards of the Greek, Latin, and Evangelical Protestant Churches:—

1. A true *incarnation* of the Logos, *i. e.*, the second person in the Godhead.[1] This is an actual assumption of the whole human nature—body, soul, and spirit—into an abiding union with the divine personality of the eternal Logos, so that they constitute, from the moment of the supernatural conception, one undivided life forever. The incarnation is neither a conversion or transmutation of God into man, nor a conversion of man into God, and consequent absorption of the one, nor a confusion[2] of the two. On the other hand, it is not a mere indwelling[3]

---

[1] Ἐνανθρώπησις Θεοῦ, ἐνσάρκωσις τοῦ Λόγου, *incarnatio Verbi*.
[2] Κρᾶσις, σύγχυσις. [3] Ἐνοίκησις, *inhabitatio*.

CHRIST IN THEOLOGY. 65

of the one in the other, nor an outward, transitory connection[1] of the two factors.

2. The distinction between *nature* and *person*. Nature or substance[2] denotes the totality of powers and qualities which constitute a being; while person[3] is the Ego, the self-conscious, self-asserting, and acting subject. The Logos assumed, not a human person (else we should have two persons,—a divine and a human), but human nature, which is common to us all; and hence he redeemed, not a particular man, but all men, as partakers of the same nature. Yet no council has expressly denied the human personality of Christ.

3. The *God-man*,[4] as the result of the incarnation. Christ is not a (Nestorian) *double* being, with *two* persons, nor a compound (Apollinarian, or Monophysite) *middle* being, a *tertium quid*, partly divine, and partly human; but he is *one* person, both wholly divine, and wholly human.

4. The *duality of natures*. The orthodox doctrine maintains, against Eutychianism, on the one hand, the distinction of natures even after the act of incarnation, without confusion or conversion,[5] and against Nestorianism on the other hand, the union of natures without division or separation;[6] so that the divine will ever remain divine, and the human ever human; and yet the two have continually one common life, and interpenetrate each other, like the persons of the Trinity.[7] According to a familiar figure, the divine nature pervades the human as the fire pervades the iron: the fire is not iron, and the iron is not fire, yet both are inseparable. Another illustration is taken from the relation of soul and body, which are distinct, and yet constitute but one human personality. The two natures are complete, and embrace everything which pertains to them separately, even will (according to the anti-Monothelite decision). Christ has

---

[1] Συνάφεια, *conjunctio*.   [2] Essence, οὐσία.   [3] Ὑπόστασις, πρόσωπον.
[4] Θεάνθρωπος.   [5] Ἀσυγχύτως, *inconfuse*, and ἀτρέπτως, *immutabiliter*.
[6] Ἀδιαιρέτως, *indivise*, and ἀχωρίστως, *inseparabiliter*.
[7] Περιχώρησις, *inhabitatio*, *intercommunio*, *permeatio*.

all the properties which the Father has, except the property of being unbegotten;[1] and he has all the properties which the first Adam had before the fall. He has, therefore (according to John of Damascus), two consciousnesses, and two physical wills, or faculties of self-determination.[2] This is the extreme border to which the doctrine of two natures can be carried, without an assertion of two full personalities; and it is almost impossible to draw the line.

5. The *unity of person*.[3] The union of the divine and human natures in Christ is a permanent state, resulting from the incarnation, and is a real, supernatural, personal, and inseparable union, in distinction from an essential absorption or confusion, or from a mere moral union, or from a mystical union, such as holds between the believer and Christ. The two natures constitute but one personal life, and yet remain distinct. "The same who is true God," says Pope Leo I. in his famous Epistle, which anticipated the decision of Chalcedon, "is also true man; and in this unity there is no deceit; for in it the lowliness of man and the majesty of God perfectly pervade one another. . . . Because the two natures make only one person, we read, on the one hand, 'The Son of *man* came down from heaven' (John 3: 13), while yet the Son of God took flesh from the Virgin; and, on the other hand, 'The Son of *God* was crucified and buried' (1 Cor. 2: 8), while yet he suffered, not in his Godhead as co-eternal and consubstantial with the Father, but in the weakness of human nature." The Athanasian Creed: "As the rational soul and flesh is one man, so God and man is one Christ."

6. The whole *work* of Christ is to be attributed to his person, and not to the one or the other nature exclusively. The person is the acting subject; the nature is the organ or medium. It is the one divine-human person of Christ that wrought miracles by virtue of his divine nature, and that suffered through the

[1] The ἀγεννησία.   [2] Αὐτεξουσία.
[3] Ἕνωσις καθ' ὑπόστασιν, ἕνωσις ὑποστατική, unio hypostatica, or unio personalis.

sensorium of his human nature. The superhuman effect and infinite merit of the Redeemer's work must be ascribed to his person, because of his divinity; while it is his humanity alone that made him capable of, and liable to temptation, suffering, and death, and renders him an example for our imitation.

7. The *Anhypostasia* (*Unpersonality*), or, more accurately, the *Enhypostasia* (*Impersonality*) of the human nature of Christ.[1] The meaning is, that Christ's human nature had no *independent* personality of its own, and that the divine nature is the root and basis of his personality. His humanity was enhypostatized through union with the Logos, or incorporated into his personality. The synod of Chalcedon says nothing of this feature; it was an after-thought developed by John of Damascus. It seems inconsistent with the dyotheletic theory; for a being with consciousness and will has the two essential elements of personality, while an impersonal will seems to be a mere animal instinct. But the orthodox dyotheletism regards the two wills as the attributes of the two natures.

CRITICAL ESTIMATE OF THE ŒCUMENICAL CHRISTOLOGY.

The Chalcedonian Christology is regarded by the Greek and Roman, and the majority of the orthodox English and American divines, as the *ne plus ultra* and *ultimatum* of Christological knowledge attainable in this world. One of the ablest American divines says that "the human mind is unable to go beyond it in the endeavor to unfold the mystery of Christ's complex person;" and he therefore serenely ignores all subsequent Christological controversies and speculations. Another eminent divine notices and criticises several of the more recent "erroneous and heretical doctrines," as he calls them, but abides in the Chalcedonian statement as adopted by the scholastic Calvinists of the seventeenth century.

On the other hand, the Chalcedonian Christology has been

---

[1] Ἀνυποστασία is the negative term, ἐνυποστασία and συνυποστασία (*compersonalitas*) are positive terms for the same idea.

subjected to a rigorous criticism in Germany by Schleiermacher, Baur, Dorner, Rothe, and the modern Kenoticists. It is charged with a defective psychology, and now with dualism, now with docetism, according as its distinction of two natures, or the personal unity, is made its most prominent feature. It oscillates between two extremes, without truly reconciling them; as the orthodox doctrine of the Trinity stands between tritheism and modalism, now leaning to the one, now to the other, when either the tripersonality or the unity is emphasized. It assumes two natures in one person; while the dogma of the Trinity assumes three persons in one nature. It teaches a complete human nature with reason and will, and yet denies its personality. It does not do justice to the genuine humanity of Christ in the Gospels, and to all those passages which assert its real growth. It overshadows the human by the divine. By transferring the personality wholly to the divine nature, it reduces and impoverishes the human nature, although, theoretically, it ascribes to it a human consciousness, and a human will. It puts the final result at the beginning, and ignores the intervening process. If we read the gospel history, we find that Christ was a helpless infant on his mother's breast,—and therefore not omnipotent till after the resurrection, when "all authority in heaven and on earth" was *given* unto him (Matthew 28: 18); he *grew* in wisdom, and *learned* obedience (Luke 2: 40; Heb. 5: 8), and was ignorant of the day of judgment (Mark 13: 32), therefore not omniscient; he moved from place to place, and was therefore not omnipresent before his ascension to heaven; he was destitute of his divine glory, which he was to *regain* after his death (John 17: 5). To confine these limitations and imperfections to his human nature, while in his divine nature he was, *at one and the same time*, omnipotent, omniscient, and omnipresent, even in the manger and on the cross, is to destroy the personal unity of life, and to make two Christs, or a doubleheaded Christ. How can ignorance and omniscience simultaneously co-exist in one and the same mind? How can one and the same individual pervade and rule the universe in the same moment in which he exclaims, "My God, my God, why hast thou forsaken me?" Christ speaks and acts throughout as one undivided Ego.

These are serious difficulties and defects in the Chalcedonian Christology, and call for such a reconstruction or improvement as will conform it to the historical realness of Christ's humanity, to the full meaning of his own sayings concerning himself, and to all the facts of his life. This is now generally felt among the evangelical divines in Germany, where Christological speculation has been most active since the Reformation, and by not a few in other countries. If anything has resulted from the multitude of Lives of Christ, written by learned and able men in this nineteenth century, it is the fact of the perfect and unique divine-human personality of Jesus of Nazareth.

At the same time the Chalcedonian dogma is the ripest fruit of the Christological speculations and controversies of the ancient Church, and can never lose its value. It gave the clearest expression to the faith in the incarnation for ages to come. It saves the full idea of the God-man as to the essential elements, however imperfect the philosophical form in which it is cast. It defines with sound religious judgment the boundary-line which separates Christological truth from Christological error. It guards us against two opposite dangers,—the Scylla of Nestorian dualism, and the Charybdis of Eutychian Monophysitism, or against an abstract separation of the divine and human, and an absorption of the human by the divine. It excludes also every kind of mixture of the two natures, which would result in a being that is neither divine nor human.

With these safeguards, theological speculation may boldly and hopefully move on, and penetrate deeper and deeper into the central truth of Christianity. Protestantism cannot consistently adopt any doctrinal or disciplinary decisions of popes or councils as an infallible finale, but must reserve the right of further research and progress in the apprehension and appropriation of Christ

THE ORTHODOX PROTESTANT CHRISTOLOGY.

and his infallible teaching according to the Scriptures as the only rule of faith.

The churches of the Reformation (Lutheran, Anglican, and Calvinistic) adopted in their confessions of faith, either in form or in substance, the three œcumenical creeds, and with them the ancient Catholic doctrines of the Trinity, and the Incarnation. They condemned the errors of the old and new Antitrinitarians, including the Socinians, who taught that Jesus was raised by his own merit to a participation in the divine honor and dignity. The Socinians, like the Anabaptists, were everywhere (except in Poland and Transylvania), imprisoned, exiled, or executed, and the unfortunate Servetus, who denied the Trinity, was burnt as a heretic and blasphemer, under the eyes of Calvin, and with the full approval of the mild Bullinger and Melanchthon. These were cruel measures contrary to the spirit of the New Testament as well as to our modern ideas of religious liberty, but they show how fully the Reformers agreed in Christology with the traditional creed of the Catholic church.

We quote the statements of the principal Protestant Confessions.

The Augsburg Confession, the chief doctrinal standard of the Lutheran Church (1530), Art. III. (*De Filio Dei*), says:—

"Also they teach that the Word, that is, the Son of God, took unto him man's nature in the womb of the blessed Virgin Mary, so that there are two natures, the divine and the human, inseparably joined together in unity of person; one Christ, true God and true man: who was born of the Virgin Mary, truly suffered, was crucified, dead, and buried, that he might reconcile the Father unto us, and might be a sacrifice, not only for original guilt, but also for all actual sins of men."

The Belgic Confession, composed in French by the martyr Guy de Brès, for the churches of Flanders and the Netherlands (1561), and revised by the National Synod of Dort (1619), gives a full statement of the doctrine of the Incarnation in Art. XVIII. and XIX., from which we extract the following :—

"We confess that God did fulfill the promise which he made to the fathers through the mouth of the prophets when he sent into the world at the time appointed by him, his only-begotten and eternal Son, who took upon him the form of a servant and became like unto men, really assuming the true human nature, with all its infirmities, sin excepted, being conceived in the womb of the blessed Virgin Mary, by the power of the Holy Ghost, without the means of man; and did not only assume human nature as to the body, but also a true human soul, that he might be a real man. For since the soul was lost as well as the body, it was necessary that he should take both upon him to save both. . . . In truth he is our IMMANUEL, that is to say, *God with us*. We believe that by this conception the person of the Son is inseparably united and connected with the human nature; so that there are not two Sons of God, nor two persons, but two natures united in one single person; yet each nature retains its own distinctive properties. . . . Wherefore we confess that he is *very God* and *very Man:* very God by his power to conquer death, and very man that he might die for us according to the infirmity of his flesh."

The Heidelberg Catechism (1563), which is the doctrinal standard of the German and Dutch Reformed Churches, in answer to Question XV., "What manner of Mediator and Redeemer must we seek," says :—

"One who is a *true* and *sinless man*, and yet more powerful than all creatures; that is one who is at the same time *true God*."

The Second Helvetic Confession, by Bullinger of Zurich (1566), which was extensively adopted by the Reformed churches in Europe, chap. 11 :—

"We acknowledge, therefore, that there are in one and the same Jesus Christ our Lord two natures, the divine and the human nature; and we say that these two are so conjoined or united, that they are not swallowed up, confounded or mingled together, but rather united or joined together in one person, the properties of each nature being safe and remaining still: so that we do worship one Christ our Lord, and not two; I say, one, true, God and man; as touching his divine nature, of the same substance with the Father, and as touching his human nature, of the same substance with us, and 'like unto us in all things, sin only excepted.'"

The Thirty-nine Articles of the Church of England (1562 and 1571), Art. II.:—

"The Son, which is the Word of the Father, begotten from everlasting of the Father, the very and eternal God, and of one substance with the Father, took man's nature in the womb of the blessed Virgin, of her substance; so that two whole and perfect natures, that is to say, the Godhead and Manhood, were joined together in one Person, never to be divided, whereof is one Christ, very God and very man; who truly suffered, was crucified, dead, and buried, to reconcile his Father to us, and to be a sacrifice not only for original guilt, but also for [all] actual sins of men."

The Westminster Confession (1647), which gives the clearest and strongest expression to the faith of the strictly Reformed or Calvinistic Churches, thus states the doctrine of Christ's person in chap. viii. § 2:—

"The Son of God, the second person in the Trinity, being very and eternal God, of one substance and equal with the Father, did when the fulness of time was come, take upon him man's nature, with all the essential properties and common infirmities thereof, yet without sin, being conceived by the Holy Ghost in the womb of the Virgin Mary, of her substance; so that two whole, perfect, and distinct natures, the Godhead and the Manhood, were inseparably joined together in one person, without conversion, composition, or confusion. Which person is very God, and very man, yet one Christ, the only Mediator between God and men."

The Westminster Shorter Catechism, (1647), which is famous for clear and terse definitions, says (Qu. 21):—

"The only Redeemer of God's elect is the Lord Jesus Christ, who, being the eternal Son of God, became man, and so was, and continueth to be, God and man, in two distinct natures, and one person, forever."

THE SCHOLASTIC CHRISTOLOGY OF THE LUTHERAN CHURCH.

On the general basis of the Chalcedonian Christology, and following the indications of the Scriptures, as the only rule of

CHRIST IN THEOLOGY. 73

faith, the Lutheran scholastics, at the close of the sixteenth, and during the seventeenth century, built some additional features, and developed new aspects of Christ's person.[1] The propelling cause was the Lutheran doctrine of the real presence or omnipresence of Christ's body in the Lord's Supper, which gave rise to controversies with the Zwinglians and Calvinists, and among the Lutherans themselves.

The Lutheran Christology goes beyond the Chalcedonian statement in two points, the doctrine of the relationship of the two natures, and the doctrine of the two states, of Christ. Both points were developed with great metaphysical depth and acumen, but carried to the very verge of pantheism, which obliterates the distinction between the divine and the human, and to the verge of docetism, which destroys the realness of Christ's humanity. The whole system is artificial, and goes far beyond the popular comprehension, but was a necessary logical and theological development.[2]

I. The doctrine of the *Communication of Attributes* (*Communicatio Idiomatum*) is derived from the personal union (*unio personalis*) and the communion of the two natures (*communio naturarum*). It is maintained that the attributes or properties[3] of one nature are communicated to the other nature, or to the whole person of Christ. There are four possible kinds or *genera*

---

[1] The chief dogmatic divines of the Lutheran Church, after Luther and Melancthon, are Martin Chemnitz, Jacob Andreæ, John Brenz (or Brentius), John Gerhard, Calov, Quenstädt, Hutter, Baier, König, Hollaz. Modern Lutheran divines, as Thomasius, von Hofmann, Liebner, Gess, Kahnis, Luthardt and others, depart from the Formula of Concord and adopt the *Kenosis* theory. See below. Philippi adheres closely to the Lutheran orthodoxy.

[2] Luther himself, when not influenced by his eucharistic views, favored a more natural theory, and laid great stress on the full humanity of Christ. See Dorner, *System der christl. Glaubenslehre* II. 328 sqq. Dorner thinks that the eucharistic controversy was rather a disturbing element in the development of the Lutheran Christology. But Luther himself very strongly taught the ubiquity. See my work on *Creeds*, I. 286 sqq.,; Köstlin, *Luther's Theologie*, II. 118, 154, etc.; Weisse, *Die Christologie Luthers*, second ed. 1855; and Steitz on Ubiquity in Herzog, first ed. vol. XVI. 557 sq. and XXI. 382.

[3] Ἰδιώματα, *proprietates* (from ἰδίωμα, peculiarity, property).

of such communication, but the Lutheran orthodoxy admits only three.

(1) The *genus idiomaticum*,[1] whereby the properties of one nature are transferred and applied to the whole person. For this are quoted such passages as Rom. 1: 3; 1 Pet. 3: 18; 4: 1. Some divines distinguish again three species in this genus.[2]

(2) The *genus apotelesmaticum*,[3] whereby the redemptory functions and actions[4] which belong to the whole person are predicated only of one or the other nature. Comp. 1 Tim. 2: 5 sq.; Heb. 1: 2 sq.

(3) The *genus majestaticum* or *auchematicum*,[5] whereby the human nature is clothed with and magnified by the attributes of the divine nature, as omnipotence, omniscience, and omnipresence. For this are quoted John 3: 13; 5: 27; Matt. 11: 27; 28: 18, 20; Eph. 1: 23; Rom. 9: 5; Phil. 2: 10; Col. 2: 9.

Under this third head the Lutheran Church claims a certain ubiquity or omnipresence for the body of Christ,[6] on the ground of the personal union of the two natures; but as to the extent of this ubiquity there were two distinct schools, which are both

---

[1] Ἰδιωματικόν, *peculiar, characteristic*. The act is called ἰδιοποίησις, *appropriatio*.

[2] The first species is called ἰδιοποίησις, *appropriatio*, when human attributes are predicated *de concreto divinæ naturæ*. Acts 3: 15; 20: 28; 1 Cor. 2: 8; Gal. 2: 20. The second species is called κοινωνία τῶν θείων, when divine attributes are predicated *de persona Verbi incarnati*. John 6: 62; 8: 58; 1 Cor. 15: 47. The third species is called ἀντίδοσις, *alternatio* or *reciprocatio*, when both divine and human attributes are predicated *de concreto personæ sive de Christo*. Heb. 13: 8; Rom. 9: 5; 2 Cor. 13: 4; 1 Pet. 3: 18.

[3] From ἀποτέλεσμα, completion (ἀποτελέω, to bring to an end). It is also called *genus κοινοποιητικόν*, from κοινωνία ἀποτελεσμάτων, *communio operum officii*.

[4] The ἀποτελέσματα, used in a wider sense of the offices of Christ.

[5] Αὐχηματικόν, from αὔχημα, *gloria*.

[6] *Ubiquity* is the term by which the Zwinglians described the Lutheran doctrine of the illocal omnipresence of the *humanity*, and more particularly of the *body* of Christ. It is therefore not quite identical with *omnipresence*, which is used of the *divine* nature.

represented in the Formula of Concord (1577). The Swabian Lutherans, under the lead of John Brentius and Jacob Andreæ, maintained an *absolute* ubiquity of Christ's humanity from his very infancy, thus making the incarnation not only an assumption of the human nature, but also a deification of it, although the divine attributes were admitted to have been *concealed* during the state of humiliation. The Saxon divines, whose chief was Martin Chemnitz, called this view a monstrosity, and taught only a *relative* ubiquity, depending on Christ's will (hence called *volipræsentia*, or *multivolipræsentia*). Christ *may* be present with his *whole* person wherever he pleases to be, and he *is* present where he promised to be, namely in the eucharist, and on such special manifestations as when he appeared to dying Stephen and to Saul at Damascus. The Formula of Concord (which was the joint work of Andreæ and Chemnitz and several other Lutheran divines) teaches, in the first part (the *Epitome*), the absolute ubiquitarianism of the Swabian school, and, in the second part (the *Solida Declaratio*), the relative or hypothetical ubiquitarianism of the Saxon school. Either view furnished a dogmatic basis for the Lutheran doctrine of the real presence of Christ in the eucharist. It is by an inherent quality that the very body and blood of the Lord are supposed to be present "in, with, and under" the bread and wine, which otherwise remain unchanged. But the absolute ubiquity would deprive the eucharistic presence of its specific character, and put it on a par with the divine omnipresence.

The Roman Catholic church secures the real presence in a different way, namely by the *miracle* of transubstantiation, which is supposed to be repeated wherever and whenever the mass is celebrated by the priest in the moment he pronounces the words of institution. The mediæval schoolmen and modern Roman divines ascribe *omnipresence* only to the divine nature and person of Christ, *unipresence* to his human body in heaven, and a miraculous *multipresence* to his body and blood in the sacrament of the altar. The Reformed divines who deny the real presence in the *corporeal* sense, and give the words of institution a figurative interpretation, reject the doctrine of ubiquity in any shape as inconsistent with the nature of a body, and substitute for a corporeal real presence a spiritual real or dynamic presence.

(4) A fourth conceivable kind of communication is the transfer of the properties of the human nature to the divine nature. This might be called the *genus kenoticum*, or *tapeinoticum*,[1] since it implies a self-humiliation and self-limitation of the divine nature to the limits of the human nature. But the old Lutheran orthodoxy decidedly rejected this form as being inconsistent with the unchangeableness of God.[2] A modern school of Lutherans, however, called *Kenoticists*, assert it, and thus complete the doctrine of the communication of attributes, or, rather they substitute the fourth kind for the third. (See below).

II. The doctrine of the TWOFOLD STATE of Christ,—the state of *humiliation*[3] and the state of *exaltation*.[4] This is based upon Phil. 2: 5–11. The state of humiliation embraces the supernatural conception, birth, circumcision, education, earthly

---

[1] From κένωσις, and ταπείνωσις, the nouns of the corresponding verbs used by Paul, Phil. 2: 7, 8: ἑαυτὸν ἐκένωσε (he emptied himself) and ἐταπείνωσεν ἑαυτόν (he humbled himself).

[2] The Formula of Concord (Pt. I. ch. VIII. p. 612) rejects as a blasphemous perversion such an interpretation of Matt. 28: 18 ("All power is given unto me," etc.) as would imply that " in his state of humility Christ had, according to his divine nature, divested himself and abandoned that power." (*Rejicimus damnamusque quod dictum Christi*, Matth. 28: 19: ' *Mihi data est omnis potestas in coelo et in terra,*' *horribili et blasphema interpretatione a quibusdam depravatur in hanc sententiam: quod Christo secundum divinam suam naturam in resurrectione et ascensione ad coelos iterum restituta fuerit omnis potestas in coelo et in terra perinde quasi, dum in statu humiliationis erat, eam potestatem etiam secundum Divinitatem deposuisset et exuisset.*)

[3] *Status humiliationis* or *exinanitionis*. Some divines, as Hollaz, analyse it so as to distinguish and to include in this state four elements: 1) the κένωσις, 2) the λῆψις μορφῆς δούλου, 3) the ὁμοίωσις ἀνθρώπων, and 4) the ταπείνωσις ὑποστατική.

[4] *Status exaltationis*, the state of the ὑπερύψωσις (Phil. 2: 9), δόξασις (John 17: 5), στεφάνωσις (Heb. 2: 9), ἐνθρωνισμός (Heb. 8: 1).

CHRIST IN THEOLOGY. 77

life, passion, death, and burial of Christ. The state of exaltation includes the descent into hell (which the Lutherans regard as a triumph over hell, herein differing from the Reformed divines), the resurrection, the ascension, and the sitting at the right hand of God.

The Lutheran creed, however, refers the two states only to the human nature of Christ, and regards the divine nature as unchangeable, and hence incapable of any humiliation or exaltation. This is consistent with the rejection of the *genus kenoticum*. The humiliation therefore consists not in the act of incarnation or the assumption of human nature, still less in a renunciation of the divine essence or attributes, but simply in the temporary renunciation of the outward and public manifestation of his divinity, except when he performed miracles. In other words, his human nature, though in full possession of the divine glory by virtue of its union with the divine nature, yet voluntarily renounced the plenary use and exercise of the divine majesty and power, and instead led a life of poverty and lowliness, and assumed the limitations and infirmities (but not the sin) of humanity. The humiliation began with the first moment of conception and continued to the last moment of rest in the grave. The exaltation consists in the assumption, by this human nature, of the full exercise and manifestation of the divine glory after the completion of the work of redemption. It began with the return of Christ into life, exhibited itself to the world of the dead by the descent into hell, and to the world of the living by the resurrection and ascension, and it continues forever.

This doctrine of the two states is not clearly set forth in the Formula Concordiæ, because the theologians at that time were not yet agreed. It asserts that Christ, even according to his human nature, was in *possession* of the divine glory during his earthly life, but leaves open the question of the *extent* of the renunciation of the glory or the *use* of the divine attributes. The Lutherans of the Saxon School inclined to a total renunciation, those of the Swabian School, admitted only a partial renunciation, or rather they resolved the renunciation into a mere concealment. This question was more fully discussed forty years later between Giessen and Tübingen.

THE KENOSIS CONTROVERSY OF THE SEVENTEENTH CENTURY.

This is the last chapter in the history of the orthodox Lutheran Christology (for the *modern* kenotic theory is not so much a further development in the same direction as a new departure). In the early part of the seventeenth century there arose a subtle controversy about the *Kenosis* and *Krypsis* between the Lutheran divines of the University of Giessen [1] and those of the University of Tübingen.[2] It was, as already intimated, a continuation or revival of the controversy between the Saxon and the Swabian divines concerning relative or absolute ubiquity, but it carried the question further. The exegetical basis is the Pauline passage on the self-emptying and self-humiliation of Christ, Phil. 2 : 7, 8.

Both parties stood on orthodox Lutheran ground, that is, they held with the Formula of Concord to the doctrine that Christ, even in the state of humiliation, and according to his human nature, was in full *possession*[3] of the divine attributes; but they differed as to the *use*[4] he made of these attributes.

The divines of Giessen taught the *Kenosis* or entire *renunciation* of the use,[5] but they made an exception in the case of the miracles in which Christ manifested his divine power.

The Tübingen divines advocated the *Krypsis*, or concealment, that is the *secret use* of all divine attributes.[6] They assumed that the possession necessarily implies the use. Consequently Christ, in his human nature, by virtue of its union with the divine, was actually, though secretly, omnipotent, omniscient,

[1] Balthasar Mentzer, Feuerborn (his son-in-law), and Winkelmann.
[2] Thumm, Hafenreffer, Osiander, Nicolai.
[3] Κτῆσις, *Besitz*.   [4] Χρῆσις, *Gebrauch*.
[5] Κένωσις χρήσεως, *abstinentia ab usu*, *Entäusserung des Gebrauchs*.
[6] Κρύψις χρήσεως.

CHRIST IN THEOLOGY. 79

and omnipresent during the state of humiliation from the cradle to the grave; he ruled the world and filled all things even at the time when he was a helpless infant and when he was expiring on the cross. The only difference, then, between the two states is that between a hidden and a manifest exercise of one and the same Almighty power.

The Kenotic theory of Giessen agrees better with the grammatical meaning of *Kenosis* and with the facts of Christ's life, but by conceding the exceptional use of omnipotent power, in the performance of miracles, it yields the principle of the other theory.

The Kryptic theory of Tübingen is more logical from Lutheran premises, and substitutes an active for a purely passive possession of divine attributes, but it obliterates the difference between the two states; it makes the exaltation already begin with the assumption of the human nature by the divine Logos; it reduces the exaltation to a mere manifestation of a state already existing; it goes to the very verge of Gnostic docetism, which resolves the earthly life of Christ into a magical illusion.

The controversy was waged with violence, and threatened to weaken the Protestant cause at a very critical period. The Lutheran princes interfered. In their name, Hoe von Hoenegg, court-preacher at Dresden issued, in 1624, a *Solida Decisio*, essentially favoring the cause of the Giessen Kenoticists; but the Tübingen divines defended their position till the controversy was lost in the disastrous events of the Thirty-years' War, without leading to any positive result.

More than two hundred years afterwards the Kenotic controversy was renewed, but in a modified form, and on a new basis (see below).

THE REFORMED CHRISTOLOGY.[1]

The scholastic Christology of the Reformed or Calvinistic

[1] The Reformed church embraces the German, Swiss, French, Dutch, and English branches. The most prominent Reformed divines who have carefully

churches in the seventeenth century adhered upon the whole more closely to the Chalcedonian formula than the Lutheran, but prepared the way for a fuller appreciation of the genuine humanity of Christ. It embraces three aspects, the communion of natures, the threefold office, and the two states of the God-man.

I. THE PERSONAL or HYPOSTATIC UNION OF THE TWO NATURES IN CHRIST. This is of such a character that the full integrity of natures and of their properties continues, and that none is absorbed by the other. A distinction is made between the *immediate* union of the human nature with the Logos-personality, and the *mediate* union of the two natures without mixture and confusion, and yet without division and separation, according to the Chalcedonian formula.

The effect of this union is a threefold *communion* or *communication*.

(1) A communication of *graces* or *charismata*, whereby the person of the Logos gives to the human nature a preëminence over all creatures and the consequent honor of adoration, together with all other charismata, as knowledge, wisdom, power, and especially impeccability (the *non posse peccare*); yet without disturbing the natural development of the humanity of Christ during his state of humiliation. The *honor adorationis* belongs to his humanity not as such, but by virtue of its assumption into unity with the divine Logos, who is in himself an object of adoration.

(2) A communication of the *properties* (*idiomata*) of each

studied the Christological problem are Calvin, Bullinger, Beza, Olevianus, Ursinus, Zanchi, Peter Martyr, Sadeel, Danæus, Bucan, Wolleb, Keckermann, Heidegger, Piscator, Pictet, Franc. Turretin, Marck, Wyttenbach, Lampe. See a list of their dogmatic works in Heppe's *Dogmatik der evang.-reformirten Kirche*, Elberfeld 1861. To them should be added the Westminster divines of the seventeenth century, and the great Anglican Episcopal divines, Hooker, Bull, Waterland, Pierson. Christological speculation, however, was carried on so far almost exclusively on the continent of Europe. Most of the Anglican and Presbyterian divines in England and America adhere to the Chalcedonian statement as a finale, and confine themselves to an analysis and illustration of it.

nature to the person, so that the divine human *person* of Christ may be said to be almighty, omnipresent, omniscient, and that Mary may be called the mother of *God*[1] inasmuch as she gave birth to him who is also God; though a distinction must be made between the *concretum* (*Deus, homo*) and the *abstractum* (*Deitas, humanitas*) of the two natures. This corresponds to the *genus idiomaticum* of the Lutherans.

(3) A communication of the *operations*,[2] that is the concurrence of the two natures in the accomplishment of the mediatorial work,[3] so that this proceeds from the person of the God-man through the distinct efficacy of each nature, but is the one work of the theanthropic person. This corresponds to the *genus apotelesmaticum* of the Lutherans.

So far the two Confessions are agreed, and differ only in the mode of statement. But the Reformed theologians deny the communication of the *properties of one nature to the other nature*, either in the form of the *genus majestaticum* (asserted by the Lutheran divines) or in the form of the *genus tapeinoticum* (which is denied also by the orthodox Lutherans, but held by the modern Kenoticists).[4] The attributes of the divine nature, according to the Reformed theologians, cannot be transferred to the human, because the human nature is limited and incapable of the infinite; nor can the attributes of the human nature be transferred to the divine, because the divine nature is unchange-

[1] Θεοτόκος, *Deipara*. The safer scriptural term is "Mother of our Lord."
[2] *Communicatio* ἀποτελεσμάτων.
[3] *Concursus ad operationes mediatorias.*
[4] The Reformed objections to the Lutheran doctrine of the *communicatio idiomatum*, especially the *genus majestaticum* and the doctrine of the two states, is clearly stated in the *Admonitio Christiana de libro Concordiæ*, which appeared in Latin and German at Neustadt (hence also called *Admonitio Neostadiensis*), in 1581. It was prepared by Zach. Ursinus, one of the two authors of the Heidelberg Catechism. Among modern Reformed divines, Dr. Hodge (*Syst. Theol.* II. 416) objects to the Lutheran doctrine, that it " destroys the integrity of the human nature of Christ. A body which fills immensity is not a human body: a soul which is omniscient, omnipresent, and almighty, is not a human soul. The Christ of the Bible and of the human heart is lost, if the doctrine be true." He does not seem to appreciate the difficulties on the other side.

able and incapable of limitation and imperfection. The Reformed divines reject especially the eucharistic ubiquity of the body of Christ. They reason that omnipresence, whether absolute or relative, is inconsistent with the necessary limitation of a human body, as well as with the Scripture facts of Christ's ascension to heaven, and promised return. The *genus majestaticum* can never be fully carried out, unless the humanity of Christ is also eternalized. The attributes, moreover, are not an outside appendix, but inherent qualities of the substance to which they belong, and inseparable from it. Hence a communication of attributes would imply a communication or mixture of natures. The divine and human natures can indeed hold free and intimate intercourse with each other; but the divine nature can never be transformed into the human, nor the human nature into the divine. Christ possessed all the attributes of both natures; but the natures, nevertheless, remain separate and distinct. The familiar illustrations of the iron and the fire, of the body and the soul, favor the Reformed rather than the Lutheran theory; for the fire, while it pervades the iron, does not communicate its properties to the iron, nor the iron its properties to the fire. The soul resides in and interpenetrates the body; but its spiritual qualities, as cognition and volition, are not communicated to the body; nor are the physical qualities of the body, as weight and extension, communicated to the soul.

According to the Reformed Christology, therefore, the two natures in Christ's person cannot and do not entirely cover each other. The Divine Logos is not confined or shut up in the humanity of Christ, but is omnipresent; the Logos is *totus in carne Christi*, but he is also *totus extra carnem Christi*. In other words, he is whole, but not wholly or exclusively in the humanity of Christ.

II. THE MEDIATORIAL OFFICE OF CHRIST. This is threefold, prophetic, priestly, and kingly. It is included in the official name Christ, *i. e.* the Messiah, the Anointed. He was

CHRIST IN THEOLOGY. 83

anointed at his baptism by the Holy Spirit above measure (John 3 : 34), and thus fully furnished for all the three offices, which were typically foreshadowed in the theocracy of the Old Testament, and united and completed in him. Both natures coöperate in the execution of the mediatorial office.

(1) The *prophetic* office (*prophetia, munus propheticum*) is the full revelation of the divine will concerning our salvation. It includes (*a*) the external promulgation of the saving truth; (*b*) the internal illumination by the Holy Spirit; and in a wider sense (*c*) also his miraculous works and martyr-death, by which he confirmed and sealed his doctrine. Christ executes the prophetic office, in the Old Covenant through Moses and the prophets, in the New Covenant by direct teaching, and indirectly through the apostles and teachers of the church.

(2) The *priestly* or *sacerdotal* office (*sacerdotium, munus sacerdotale*) embraces (*a*) the *satisfaction, i. e.* the voluntary self-sacrifice of Christ to God for the propitiation (*expiatio*) and reconciliation (*reconciliatio*) of sinners (Heb. 2 : 17 ; 9 : 14, 15); and (*b*) the continual *intercession* for the elect (Heb. 7 : 25). The former includes his perfect active obedience or fulfillment of the law, and his perfect passive obedience in bearing the punishment of sin on the cross.

(3) The *kingly* or *royal* office (*munus regium*), is the government of the church by the word and the Holy Spirit, and its protection against all enemies. A distinction is made between the kingdom of nature (*regnum naturale, essentiale*, or *universale*), which is ruled by Christ as the eternal Son of the Father, together with the Father and the Holy Spirit, and the kingdom of grace (*regnum personale*, or *œconomicum*), which embraces all true Christians, and belongs to Christ as the God-man, because he purchased it with his blood. The latter will pass from a state of humiliation (*regnum gratiæ*) or militant state to a state of glory (*regnum gloriæ*) or triumphant state, and last forever, but subject to the Father that "God may be all in all" (1 Cor. 15 : 24, 28).

The doctrine of the threefold office of Christ was suggested by Eusebius and other Greek fathers, but properly introduced into theology by Calvin,[1] and the Heidelberg Catechism,[2] and taught by all the Reformed divines down to Heppe and Ebrard. In the Lutheran church it seems to have been first adopted by John Gerhard and prevailed till the middle of the eighteenth century (although some Lutheran scholastics distinguished only two offices, and included the prophetic in the sacerdotal). Ernesti (a Lutheran) set it aside,[3] but Schleiermacher (Reformed) revived it, and gave it new popularity in both confessions.

III. THE STATES OF CHRIST. Based on Phil. 2: 5–11.

(1) *The State of Humiliation (Status Humiliationis* or *Exinanitionis*). It is the state in which Christ, according to his divine nature, emptied or deprived himself of the use and manifestation of his divine glory, and in which he, according to his human nature, submitted himself with extreme humility to the law of God in all things necessary for the redemption of the sinner. The humiliation does not consist in the act of the incarnation as such, for the Logos might have assumed human nature and manifested his divine glory in it, but it consists in the assumption of "the form of a servant,"[4] or the fallen human nature (*i. e.* human nature with the consequences of the

---

[1] *Institutio Christ. Religionis* II. 15, 1 : " *Statuendum hoc principium est, tribus partibus constare quod ei* [*Christo*] *injunctum a Patre munus fuit. Nam et Propheta datus est, et Rex, et Sacerdos.*"

[2] *Quest.* 31: "Why is He called Christ that is, Anointed? Because He is ordained of God the Father, and anointed with the Holy Ghost, to be our chief Prophet and Teacher, who fully reveals to us the secret counsel and will of God concerning our redemption; and our only High Priest, who by the one sacrifice of His body has redeemed us, and ever liveth to make intercession for us with the Father; and our eternal King, who governs us by His word and Spirit, and defends and preserves us in the redemption obtained for us." The next question applies this threefold office to every Christian who " by faith is a member of Christ, and thus a partaker of his anointing."

[3] In two programmes *De officio Christi triplici*, Lips. 1768 and 1769.

[4] Μορφὴ δούλου, literally "of a slave." Phil. 2: 7.

fall, but without sin).[1] Some theologians make a proper distinction between *exinanition*[2] and *humiliation*,[3] and confine the former to the life, the latter to the death of Christ.

The whole state of humiliation embraces four grades: birth, life of poverty, death, and descent into Hades. While Christ's body was buried and lay in the tomb, his soul descended into Hades; yet the person of the Logos remained united with the assumed humanity. The descent is, however, not to be understood in the sense of a locomotion. Some Calvinists, following Calvin and the Heidelberg Catechism, understand it figuratively of the taste of eternal punishment on the cross;[4] others identify it with the burial or make the article in the Creed to mean simply: He continued in the state of death.[5] Both these interpretations plainly depart from the original meaning of the article in the Creed, and destroy its distinctive importance.[6]

(2) *The State of Exaltation* (*Status Exaltationis*). This belongs likewise to the whole person of Christ; the divine nature laying aside the assumed form of a servant and manifesting its

---

[1] As the Westminster Confession, Ch. VIII. sect. 2, has it: "The Son of God .... did take upon him man's nature, with all the essential properties and *common infirmities* thereof, yet without sin." Heb. 2: 17; 4: 15. Westminster Larger Cat., Qu. 46: "The estate of Christ's humiliation was that *low condition*, wherein he, for our sakes, emptying himself of his glory, took upon him the form of a servant," etc.

[2] Κένωσις. Phil. 2: 7, ἑαυτὸν ἐκένωσεν. *Selbstentäusserung.*

[3] Ταπείνωσις. Phil. 2: 8, ἐταπείνωσεν ἑαυτόν. *Selbsterniedrigung.*

[4] The Heidelberg Catechism in answer to Qu. 44: "Why is it added: He descended into Hades (German *Todtenreich*)?" says: 'That in my greatest temptations I may be assured that Christ, my Lord, by His inexpressible anguish, pains, and terrors which He suffered in His soul on the cross and before, has redeemed me from the anguish and torment of hell.'" A true idea, but not an explanation of the descensus which took place *after* the death on the cross.

[5] So the Westminster Larger Catechism, Qu. 50: "Christ's humiliation after his death consisted in his being buried, and continuing in the state of the dead, and under the power of death till the third day, which hath been otherwise expressed in these words, He descended into hell."

[6] The different views of the Reformed divines on the descensus are given in the theological *Synopsis* of the Leiden Professors (Lugd. Bat. 1652), as quoted by Heppe, *Dogmatik der evang. reform. Kirche*, p. 358 sq.

full majesty; the human nature being freed from all infirmities and exalted and glorified. The state of exaltation comprehends also four grades, namely the resurrection, the ascension, the sitting at the right hand of the Father, and Christ's coming again to judge the world. The sitting at the right hand of God signifies the elevation of the incarnate Logos to such participation in the majesty of God that he now rules, as eternal high priest and King, over all things in heaven and on earth.[1]

COMPARISON OF THE LUTHERAN AND REFORMED CHRISTOLOGIES.

With all the essential agreement of the two Confessions in Christology on the common basis of the Chalcedonian creed statement, there is an interesting difference between them which deserves special notice.[2]

The Lutheran Christology emphasizes the union of the two natures of Christ on the metaphysical principle that the finite is capable of the infinite,[3] or that the human nature may become partaker of the divine nature and it carries this union to the extent of clothing the humanity of Christ with divine attributes. The Reformed Christology emphasizes the distinction of

[1] The Larger Westminster Catechism, Qu. 54, thus explains this article: "Christ is exalted in his sitting at the right hand of God, in that as Godman he is advanced to the highest favor with God the Father, with all fullness of joy, glory, and power over all things in heaven and earth; and doth gather and defend his church, and subdue their enemies; furnisheth his ministers and people with gifts and graces, and maketh intercession for them." It is worth noticing that the Westminster Confession is silent about the two states, but the Westminster Larger Catechism, which was finished October 1647, gives a full statement of it in Quest. 46 to 56. The Shorter Catechism, which was completed a year later (see Schaff's *Creeds*, I. 784), presents a concise summary in Quest. 27 and 28.

[2] It has been discussed with great subtlety by Schneckenburger (a Lutheran divine from Würtemberg, but Professor of theology in the Reformed University of Bern, Switzerland, where he died (1848), in his two works: *Zur kirchlichen Christologie. Die orthodoxe Lehre vom doppelten Stande Christi nach lutherischer und reformirter Fassung*, Pforzheim, 1848, 2d (title) ed. 1861; and *Vergleichende Darstellung des lutherischen u. reformirten Lehrbegriffs, herausgegeben durch Edw. Güder*, Stuttgart, 1855, 2 parts.

[3] *Finitum capax est infiniti.* This must be taken in a passive sense; otherwise it is manifestly absurd, as the finite can never fill or hold the infinite.

the divine and human on the opposite metaphysical principle that the finite cannot adequately hold or fully include the infinite;[1] and it carries this to the border of an abstract separation. Hence the former is often charged with a leaning to Eutychianism and Monophysitism, the latter with a leaning to Nestorianism; but both proceed alike from the dyophysitic basis. Lutheranism desires to exalt human nature and to bring it into the closest possible contact with the divine; Calvinism shrinks from lowering the divine majesty and bows reverently before the infinite superiority of God over man.

Neither one nor the other philosophical premise can be carried out absolutely. Man is made in God's image and may by faith in Christ become a partaker of the divine nature,[2] but the closest intimacy between God and his children, between Christ and the believer will not obliterate the distinction between the infinite and eternal Creator and the finite creature of time, between the absolute perfection of the Redeemer and the relative perfection of the redeemed. Theology will in due time find a higher and better solution of the problem than either the Formula of Concord, or the Westminster standards contain; in the meantime it may be well to admit that they here, as well as elsewhere, represent different and complementary elements of truth.

The two salient points on which the Lutheran and the Calvinistic Christologies come in conflict, are the ubiquity of Christ's humanity, and his state of humiliation. They are intimately connected, and have their root in the adoption or rejection of the third kind of communication of attributes, the *genus majestaticum*, which the one asserts, and the other rejects. They have also an important bearing upon the doctrine of the real presence in the eucharist.

I. THE UBIQUITY OF CHRIST'S HUMANITY. The Reformed divines assert with one accord the realness and consequent essential limitations of Christ's body, even in its glorified state, and deny the doctrine of ubiquity both in the shape of a pantheistic

---

[1] *Finitum non est capax infiniti.*   [2] Comp. 2 Pet. 1: 4 θείας κοινωνοὶ φύσεως.

omnipresence and of a eucharistic multipresence. They prove their position not only philosophically by the nature of material substance, but also and chiefly on exegetical grounds by the facts of the gospel history, the birth of Christ, his locomotion from place to place, and his ascension to heaven, from which he will visibly return to judge the world.

The great dogmatic argument of the Lutherans for ubiquity was the impossibility of separating the divine and human in Christ, so that wherever his person is, his human nature must be likewise. To this the Reformed replied that the argument would prove too much, namely an absolute omnipresence of the God-man; that the human nature is not locally in the Logos-person (as if the Logos were a place), and that the Logos is not confined or included in the human nature, but is also actively present outside of it and everywhere.[1]

The chief exegetical argument for the eucharistic ubiquity is derived from the literal meaning of "this *is*," in the words of institution. But while Luther here adopted the literal method of interpretation, he resorted to a figurative interpretation of the throne and right hand of God in heaven, and called the literal view childish. God, he maintained, is not really seated in heaven, like an earthly monarch, nor is Christ seated alongside of him with a golden crown on his head, but God's throne is his majesty and his right hand is his almighty and omnipresent power.[2]

We may fully admit this, and admit also that Christ's glori-

[1] Dr. Martensen, one of the ablest divines of the Lutheran church, charges the Lutheran theory with confounding the limited omnipresence of *Christ* with the unlimited omnipresence of the *Logos*, and endeavors to mediate between the two confessions by the idea of a growing or ever expanding ubiquity of Christ (*ein lebendiger organisch wachsender Christustempel*). *Die Christliche Dogmatik*, German ed. § 174–179 (p. 369 sqq.)

[2] I am not aware that any Reformed divine ever denied this. On the contrary it is clearly asserted that the *sessio ad dextram* must be understood "figuratively and metaphorically of the supreme dignity and rule of Christ." See the proof passages in Heppe, *Dogm. der evang. reform. Kirche* (Elberf. 1861), p. 364 sq.

fied humanity is above the limitations of space, and not subject to the ordinary laws of matter. It may move with more than lightning speed, and fill the heavens above and the church below with its power. Otherwise he could not have visibly appeared to the dying Stephen in Jerusalem, and the persecuting Saul near Damascus. Nevertheless the ascension of Christ and his sitting at the right hand of power are facts and no empty figures of speech, or mere visions of the disciples. Heaven is a reality as much as earth or hades. The Bible gives our soaring thoughts and prayers a helpful resting-place by directing us to the throne of grace and glory. No Christian can give up the precious hope of the personal re-appearance of Christ, and of seeing him face to face in his heavenly majesty. We must in humility confess that we know little or nothing about the *locality* of heaven, and the nature of *spiritual* bodies. We do not know whether heaven is inside or outside the visible Universe, whether it is very far or very near and round about us. Astronomy gives no light on the subject, but it sets aside our popular terms "above" and "below the earth," as well as the literal rising and setting of the sun. What is above us during the day time is beneath us during the night, and what is above to the inhabitants of one continent is below to their antipodes. Yet we *do* know from an authority higher and more certain than science, that there are many mansions in our Father's house, and that Christ has there prepared a place for his disciples.

There is a mystery here which we cannot expect to solve in our present limited state of knowledge. But for all practical purposes there is a possibility of harmonizing the Lutheran and Reformed views. We find it in the idea of a *dynamic* and *operative* presence of the *theanthropic* Christ not only in the eucharist, but in the whole Christian life and in the church "which is his body, the fulness of him that filleth all in all."[1]

[1] Eph. 1: 23 and 4: 10. These passages are often quoted for the doctrine of ubiquity. See the commentaries. Bishop Ellicott on 1: 23 calls the doctrine of the omnipresence of Christ "an eternal truth of vital importance," but on 4: 10 he says: "The doctrine of the ubiquity of Christ's *Body* derives

As the sun in heaven shines upon every object on earth and is wholly present without division or diminution in every ray of light and heat, so Christ is wholly present with his saving power in all his ordinances and in the heart of every true believer who by faith is made a member of his body, yea "flesh of his flesh and bone of his bone." This idea gives us the benefit of a real and effective presence without the objections which hold against the dogma of the ubiquity of the body on the one hand, and the localization and isolation of it on the other. It allows full force to the fact of Christ's ascension to the Father in heaven and to his unbroken personal presence in the church on earth. For it is the Godman in his one and undivided personality who promised to be with his disciples "all the days unto the end of the world" (Matt. 28 : 20.)[1]

II. THE STATES OF CHRIST. Here there are two points of difference, the *Subject* of humiliation, and the meaning of the *Descent into Hades*.

(1.) The Reformed Christology regards the *God-man* as the subject of the two states: his divine nature was in a state of humiliation as regards its external manifestation or the conceal-

no support from this passage (*Form. Conc.* p. 767), as there is no reference here to a diffused and ubiquitous corporeity, but to a pervading and energizing omnipresence; comp. Ebrard, *Dogmatik*, § 390, vol. II. 139, and notes on ch. 1 : 20. The true doctrine may perhaps be thus briefly stated :—Christ is perfect God, and perfect and glorified Man; as the former he is present *everywhere*, as the latter he can be present *anywhere*." Bishop Andrews, as quoted by Ellicott, says: "Christ is both in heaven and earth : as He is called the Head of his Church, He is in heaven, but in respect of his body which is called Christ He is on earth."

[1] The ablest modern discussions of this difficult problem are by Steitz, Martensen, and Dorner. To them must be added a brief paper of Dr. Roswell D. Hitchcock: *The Theanthropic Ubiquity*, in the "Journal of Christian Philosophy" ed. by John A. Payne, New York, (30 Bible House), vol. II. No. 4, pp. 381–389, July, 1883. Dr. H. thus expresses his view: "In this sense is the Godman ubiquitous, that He may anywhere, at any moment, reveal himself in his God-manhood to the willing soul. Such ubiquity, which may be called *potential*, best explains the vision of martyred Stephen, the vision of Paul near Damascus, the beatific vision of the dying, so well accredited in instances without number."

ment of its glory *(ratione occultationis)*; his human nature was in a state of humiliation as compared with its subsequent exaltation. The incarnation itself, or the assumption of "the form of a servant," is the beginning of humiliation.

The Lutheran Christology ascribes the two states only to the *human nature* of Christ, and excludes the incarnation from the humiliation. The divine nature, being unchangeable, admits of no humiliation; it resided with all its fulness in the human nature of Christ from the moment of its conception, and was only concealed or veiled for a time; while the human nature began in the same moment to be exalted by its assumption into union with the divine nature. Consequently the two states were *simultaneous* from the cradle to the cross. The self-exinanition or *kenosis* of the Logos consisted simply in the renunciation by the *human* nature of the *full* and *open use* of divine attributes which that human nature actually *possessed* from the first moment of its existence in the womb of the Holy Virgin. The Lutheran theory thus resolves the whole difference between the two states into a difference of outward manifestation, and a difference of duration; for the humiliation ceased with death, while the exaltation continues forever and ever.

The settlement of this difference depends on the exegesis of the classical Christological passage in the second chapter of Philippians (vers. 5-11). Paul presents here a concise summary of the entire history of Christ, in its three states, the pre-existent state in "the form of God" (ver. 6); the incarnate earthly state in "the form of a servant" (the *kenosis* and *tapeinosis*) to the death on the cross (vers. 7 and 8), and the exalted post-resurrection state of the God-man in heaven (vers. 9-11). The general subject in all these states is the same, namely, the Person of our Lord; yet the particular subject of the *kenosis* must be the *preëxistent* divine Person of our Lord, and cannot be the *incarnate* Christ or his *humanity;* for this never was in "the form of God," and could not lay it aside, unless we assume an *eternal* humanity of Christ. The verb "being originally,"[1] ver. 6, points to a time prior to the incarnation. Consequently the *kenosis* or the act of self-emptying must be identical with the incarnation or the assumption of "the form of a servant." And, surely, nothing else can be meant by the additional phrase "being made in the likeness of men." It is the same idea which John expresses by the phrase, "the Word became flesh."[2]

This is the exegesis of the Greek fathers, the Reformed theologians, and the majority of the modern commentators of all confessions.[3] It is confirmed by the parallel passage 2 Cor. 8:

---

[1] This is the proper meaning of ὑπάρχων, from ἀρχή, *beginning*; hence *to begin to do*, then *to begin to be*, or *to be in the beginning*. Thomasius and Ellicott explain it "from all eternity." The participle in connection with ἡγήσατο indicates the past: "although he was," or "when he was."

[2] John 1: 14: ὁ λόγος σὰρξ ἐγένετο.

[3] Chrysostom (and his successors), Augustin, Beza, Calvin (in ver. 6), Tholuck, Wiesinger, Weiss, Ewald, Lechler, Grimm, C. F. Schmid, R. Schmidt, Braune (in Lange), Meyer, Alford, Ellicott, Lightfoot, Lumby, and the Lutheran Kenoticists (Thomasius, Hofmann, Liebner, Gess, Kahnis, etc.). Weiss says (Com. on *Philippians*, 1859, p. 146): "*Die Ansicht der Griechen ist entschieden festzuhalten und nicht gegen die altlutherische preiszugeben.*" So also in his *Bibl. Theol. des N. T.* fourth ed. (1884), p. 429 sq. Meyer and Lightfoot are equally emphatic. The other interpretation, however, which makes Christ *secundum humanum naturam* the subject of the *Kenosis*, is advocated by very distinguished divines, Ambrose, Luther (in part by Calvin on ver. 7), Calov, Bengel, De Wette, Philippi, Schneckenburger, Beyschlag, and also quite recently by Dorner (*Gesammelte Schriften*, 1883, p. 221 note), for two reasons: 1) The relative "who," in ver. 6, refers back to "Christ Jesus," ver. 5. True, but to his *person*, not to his human nature. He is the subject of the whole passage, and the more immediate reference is defined by the context; so also in 2 Cor. 8: 9 and Col. 1: 13, 15. See Meyer and Ellicott *in loc.* 2) Only the *incarnate* or *historical* Christ can be held up as our example for imitation, not the preëxistent divine Christ. But the incarnation has its ethical root and motive in the self-denying, condescending love of Christ, and this is the strongest possible stimulus to a corresponding disposition and action on our part. Comp. Matt. 5: 48; Eph. 5: 1. Bishop Lightfoot thus paraphrases the difficult passage in Philippians: "Reflect in your own minds the mind of Christ Jesus. Be humble, as He also was humble. Though existing before the worlds in the Eternal Godhead, yet he did not cling with avidity to the prerogatives of his divine majesty, did not ambitiously display his equality with God; but divested himself of the glories of heaven, and took upon him the nature of a servant, assuming the likeness of men. Nor was this all. Having thus appeared among men in the fashion of a man, he humbled him-

9 : " Ye know the grace of our Lord Jesus Christ, that, though he was rich, yet for your sakes he became poor,[1] that ye through his poverty might become rich." The phrase, "he was rich," corresponds to the phrase, " being in the form of God ; " and the phrase, " he became poor," corresponds to the phrase, " he emptied himself." The self-emptying is only a stronger term for self-impoverishment, and both are the acts of infinite grace that we might be filled with divine riches.

(2.) The Reformed Christology regards the *Descent of Christ into Hades* as the last grade in the state of humiliation, the Lutheran Christology makes it the first grade in the state of exaltation. The former regards it as a part of the suffering, the latter, as a part of the triumph, of Christ.

Neither view is strictly correct, or in harmony with the original meaning of the article in the Creed. The descensus was an actual fact between the death and the resurrection of Christ, and hence forms the tradition from the state of humiliation to the state of exaltation. (This is ignored by the Calvinists). But it was an ascent to Paradise as well as a descent into Gehenna. (This is ignored by the Lutherans who make it a triumph over hell). It is certain from Christ's own lips (Luke 23 : 43) that immediately after the crucifixion he went to Paradise, which is a state of bliss, and hence is promised as a *reward* to the penitent robber. It is certain moreover from Peter's pentecostal sermon (Acts 2 : 27, 31), that between death and resurrection while Christ's body lay in the sepulchre, his spirit was in Hades, that is, in the realm of the dead ; and from Peter's Epistle it appears that in that mysterious triduum he preached to the souls of the departed (1 Pet. 3 : 19 ; 4 : 6). Consequently the descensus was a self-manifestation of Christ and his work to the *whole* spirit-

self yet more, and carried out his obedience even to dying. Nor did he die by a common death : he was crucified, as the lowest malefactor is crucified. But as was his humility, so also was his exaltation," etc. Comp. also the doctrinal discussion of this whole subject in my *Creeds of Christendom*, vol. I. 328.

[1] 'Επτώχευσε.

world, and affected the condition of both the pious in Paradise and the ungodly in Gehenna, as a savor of life unto life to the believing who waited in hope for his coming, and as a savor of death unto death to the impenitent who rejected the offer of salvation. It was a part of his universal mission; for he lived and died for the ages before as well as those after his coming.[1]

MODERN CHRISTOLOGIES.

We now proceed to the modern Christologies which depart from the Chalcedonian dogma, both in the Lutheran and Reformed type of its development. They agree in the attempt to substitute a Christ-personality with one consciousness and one will for a dyophysitic Christ with a double consciousness and a double will. But we must distinguish two different classes, which may be compared to the two classes of Monarchians in the ante-Nicene age.

One class of modern Christologies is humanitarian and rationalistic, and lowers the personality of Christ to the level of human personalities, though with the admission of his elevation above all other men in the degree of perfection. Here belong the Socinian, Unitarian, and Pantheistic Christologies. The other class

[1] The original idea of Hades or Sheol in Jewish theology comprehends Paradise (or Abraham's Bosom) and Gehenna (or Place of Punishment). In the Parable of Dives, Luke 16: 22, 23, Hades is the general term, and includes the two opposite states of Lazarus and Dives, who are represented as being separated by an impassable gulf (ver. 26), yet in communication with each other, consequently in an intermediate condition. Paradise must not be identified with the final heaven of the saints, nor Gehenna with the final Hell of the lost. Paradise and Gehenna belong to the αἰὼν οὗτος, Heaven and Hell to the αἰὼν μέλλων or the state after the parousia and resurrection. Christ's descent into Hades, however, must have produced a marked change in both regions of Hades. The Protestant eschatology, in its righteous indignation against the injurious superstitions of the Romish doctrine of purgatory, obliterated the distinction between Hades and Hell (Gehenna), even in the translations of the Bible both German and English, and overlooked the intermediate state altogether. The Revised English version has wisely restored the distinction in all the passages where Hades occurs (Matt. 11: 23; 16: 18; Luke 10: 15; 16: 23; Acts 2: 27, 31; Rev. 1: 18; 6: 8; 20: 13, 14). The popular eschatology needs a thorough reconstruction.

CHRIST IN THEOLOGY. 95

is trinitarian and mystic, and saves the eternal deity and the incarnation of Christ. Here belong the Swedenborgian, the modern Kenotic, and the gradual incarnation theories.

THE SOCINIAN CHRISTOLOGY.

The Socinian system was matured by two Italians, Lelius Socinus (or Lelio Sozzini, of Siena, b. 1525, d. at Zürich 1562), and his nephew Faustus Socinus (b. 1539, at Siena, d. in Poland 1604), and authoritatively stated in the Rakow Catechism (1605, etc.)[1]

The Socinian Christology falls below Arianism (which admitted the preëxistence and the incarnation of the Logos), and resembles the Christology of the dynamic Unitarians in the third century (Theodotus, Artemon, Paul of Samosata), who saw in Christ a mere man, though supernaturally conceived, and filled with divine power operating in him from the beginning. It denies the preëxistence, and consequently the incarnation of the Logos, and explains away such passages as John 1 : 1, 3, 10; 8 : 58; Col. 1 : 15; Phil. 2 : 6; Heb. 1 : 3, by referring them merely to the beginning of the gospel, the spiritual creation, a preëxistence in the design of God, etc. "The Logos was God," means simply, he was divine in wisdom and power, but not in nature or essence. The divine nature is unchangeable, the infinite cannot become finite; immensity cannot dwell in space, nor omniscience in an ignorant child; in one word, the incarnation of God is an impossibility. The idea of a suffering and dying

---

The Rakow Catechism appeared in several languages, in an English translation by Th. Rees, London 1818. The Socinian Christology was anticipated by some Antitrinitarian Baptists (Denk, Hetzer. etc.) who are condemned in the Augsburg Confession (1530) as "new Samosatenes" (Art. I: "*Damnant Samosatenos, veteres et neotericos*"). The Second Helvetic Confession (1566) rejects in ch. iv. the errors of the "*Monarchici*." In the Lutheran Formula of Concord (*Epit.* art. xii) the Socinians are probably included under the name "New Arians," who are condemned for teaching "that Christ is not true, substantial natural God of the same essence with the Father and the Holy Ghost; but that he has been merely in such wise adorned with divine majesty with the Father as that he is nevertheless inferior to the Father."

God is not only absurd, but horrible. The New Testament clearly asserts the full and pure humanity of Christ, by calling him a man (John 8: 40; Rom. 5: 15; 1 Cor. 15: 21, 22), or the son of man (in the Gospels). He derived his doctrines from the Father, he prayed to the Father, wrought miracles by the help of the Father, subordinated himself to the Father, and asserted expressly his partial ignorance (Matt. 26: 18; John 5: 19; 14: 28; Matt. 13: 23, etc.). Moreover, Christ could not be our example for imitation, if he were God.

By nature, then, Christ is only a man and his existence began with his conception and birth. Nevertheless he is distinct from all other men by several peculiarities, and has become by grace and by his own merits the Son of God in a preëminent sense. Socinianism admits his supernatural conception by an immediate act of divine omnipotence, without the agency of man; his sinless life and character; his miracles; his resurrection and ascension. It asserts the peculiar doctrine that Jesus before he entered upon his public ministry, was once or twice miraculously carried up to heaven (like Paul) and directly instructed by the Father concerning the way of salvation.[1] In reward for his perfect obedience he was raised to the right hand of God, made a partaker of his majesty and the sovereign ruler of the church, but at the final judgment he will surrender the government to the Father that "God may be all in all." He has therefore been deified after his resurrection, and hence is justly called "the true God" (1 John 5: 20), and deserves divine honor and worship no less than the Father (John 5: 22, 23; Acts 1: 24; Phil. 2: 9–11). The Socinians refused to recognize those as Christians who refused divine honors to Christ. In this respect they differ from the rationalistic Unitarians. But the idea of an acquired and communicated divinity is untenable; for divinity in any

---

[1] This idea of a *raptus in cœlum* was based upon John 3: 13, 31; 6: 38, 62; 16: 28, and illustrated by Paul's translation in spirit to the third heaven (2 Cor. 12: 2, 3), and by the conversation of Moses with Jehovah on Mount Sinai, which is an antitype of heaven.

CHRIST IN THEOLOGY. 97

proper sense must be essential, without beginning and without end. Hence the irresistible logical tendency of Socinianism is towards full-grown rationalism and humanitarianism.

THE UNITARIAN CHRISTOLOGY.

Socinianism exerted considerable influence on the theological thinking in the Lutheran and Reformed churches of Europe and aided in bringing on the reign of rationalism. As a system of thought and as an ecclesiastical organization it was revived or rather newly introduced in England by Priestley towards the end of the last, and in New England in the beginning of the present century, under the technical name of UNITARIANISM.[1] The modern Unitarians agree with the Socinians in the objections to the orthodox creed, and reject the Trinity, the divinity of Christ and the Holy Spirit, the doctrine of hereditary sin and total depravity, and the doctrine of the atonement, but they have no confessional standard, and allow great latitude of thought and teaching both in the orthodox and heretical direction. They allow on the one hand a purely humanitarian or rationalistic Christology, and on the other a very near approach to the divinity and worship of Christ.

The most conservative as well as the most distinguished American Unitarian is WILLIAM ELLERY CHANNING, a very spiritual and devout man and noble Christian philanthropist. He opposed on the one hand the bony Puritan orthodoxy of his day which almost ignored the human nature of Christ, but on the other

[1] The leaders of English Unitarianism are Joseph Priestley (b. near Leeds, 1733, d. in Pennsylvania, 1804, more distinguished as a natural philosopher, than as a theologian), and Theophilus Lindsey (b. in Cheshire, 1723, died in London 1808). Priestley wrote a *History of Corruptions of Christianity* (1782), and *Early Opinions concerning Jesus Christ* (1786). He derived the orthodox doctrines of the Trinity of God and the Divinity of Christ from Platonic speculations. American Unitarianism is traced to Dr. James Freeman, minister of King's Chapel, Boston, who removed from the Book of Common Prayer all reference to the Trinity, and the Deity and worship of Christ (1783), to Dr. Henry Ware, who was elected Hollis Professor of Divinity in Harvard College. (b. 1805, d. 1845), and especially to Dr. Channing, of Boston, (b. in Rhode Island, 1780, d. at Burlington, Vermont, 1842).

7

hand also the radical Unitarianism which made him a mere man. He wrote one of the most eloquent essays on the moral perfection of Christ's character, and humbly followed his example. He saw in him the highest revelation of God and the ideal of humanity. He acknowledged his divine origin, his sinlessness, his authority, his miracles, especially his resurrection. He firmly believed in the historical credibility of the Gospels, and among his last utterances are strong protests against the mythical theory of Strauss and Theodore Parker. In earlier years he seems to have been a high Arian, at least he professed in 1832 to be "inclined to the doctrine of the *preëxistence* of Christ;" but he was no metaphysician and preferred to dwell on the historical Christ and his perfect humanity; yet he always remained a supernaturalist.

The Unitarian Christology is logically inconsistent in admitting the human perfection of Christ, and yet denying his divinity which rests on *his own* testimony; for he claims to be the Son of God, to have existed before Abraham, to have power to forgive sins and to raise the dead, to be one with the Father, to be the Saviour of the human race. If he was a perfect man, his testimony must be true; if his testimony is false, he must have been self-deceived or a deceiver, and cannot be our example. The very perfection of Christ's humanity is a proof of his divinity.

THE SWEDENBORGIAN CHRISTOLOGY.

The very opposite of the rationalistic and humanitarian theories is that remarkable mystic system which claims to rest on divine revelation and the spiritual visions of the Seer of the North, Emmanuel Swedenborg (1688–1772). But as his views are not very clear and lie outside the historical current of thought, they had no effect upon the development of Christology.[1]

---

[1] See especially his "*The True Christian Religion;*" "*The Doctrine of the New Jerusalem concerning the Lord;*" and the "*Arcana Cœlestia.*" A brief summary of his system is contained in his *Summaria Expositio Doctrinæ Novæ Ecclesiæ,* Amsterd. 1769; English translation (*A Brief Summary of the Doctr. of the New Church*), Lond. and N. York 1878 (115 pages). Swedenborg wrote volumes

Swedenborg likewise denies the orthodox doctrine of the Trinity, *i. e.* three distinct persons in the Divine essence, and charges it with tritheism, but he maintains in the strictest sense the deity of Christ and of the Holy Spirit. He substitutes for a trinity of persons a trinity of one and the same person. So far he seems to agree with Sabellianism; but his theory is quite peculiar and asserts the eternal humanity of God. The Father is the essential Divinity, the Son the Divine Humanity, the Holy Spirit the Divine Proceeding or Divine Operation. This trinity centres in Christ. He is the only true God, the Lord or Jehovah from eternity, the Creator and Redeemer. He is called the Son of God, not with reference to an eternal generation which has no meaning, but on account of his Divine humanity; and he is called the Son of Man with reference to his passion, to redemption, salvation, regeneration, and judgment. A distinction is made between the Divine humanity "in first principles," and the Divine humanity "in ultimates." God was a man from the beginning, and thus are explained the theophanies and anthropomorphic expressions of the Old Testament. God can only be conceived and worshipped under human form. Heaven itself has the shape of a man. The eternal Lord assumed material humanity from the mother in order to save mankind and to become visible, but he exchanged it after the crucifixion for a spiritual (or as Swedenborg calls it, a "substantial") humanity of the state of glorification. This is the Divine humanity "in ultimates." He was the Son of Mary, but is so no more; "for by acts of redemption he put off the humanity which he derived from his mother, and put on a humanity from his Father; in consequence of which the humanity of the Lord is divine, and in him God is man, and man God. That he put off the humanity from the mother, and put on a humanity from his Father, which is a divine humanity, is evident from the circumstance that he

of folio pages in Latin *currente calamo*, with scarcely a correction. A copy of the photolithographed edition of Tafel (in 12 vols. fol., 1870) is in the Swedenborg Publication Society Library, Cooper Institute, New York.

never called Mary his *mother* but *woman* (John 2 : 3, 4; 19 : 26, 27; Matt. 12: 46–49)."[1]

THE RATIONALISTIC CHRISTOLOGY.

We return to the further progress of Christological speculation in Germany.

The orthodox Christology of the seventeenth century had emphasized the divinity of Christ, and left his humanity more or less out of sight (although it was always recognized in theory). Rationalism arose, towards the close of the eighteenth century, as a reaction against symbolical and scholastic orthodoxy, and ran into the opposite extreme: it ignored the divine nature, and fell back upon a purely human or Ebionitic Christ. Its force, as well as its weakness, consists in the examination and assertion of the human element in Christ and in the Bible.

The philosophy of Kant favored a higher form of rationalism which emphasized the moral ideal. The great thinker of Königsberg asserted the superiority of the practical reason over the theoretical, and believed as a practical philosopher what he denied or could not prove as a theoretical philosopher. He bowed before the majesty of the moral law within him and the starry heavens above him, as the two phenomena which filled his mind with ever-growing reverence and awe. He regarded Christ as the representative of the moral ideal, but he made a distinction (renewed by Strauss) between the ideal Christ and the historical Christ, and did not consider it his province as a philosopher to enter into a discussion of the relation of the two.[2]

[1] *The True Christian Religion*, section 102. In the same place Swedenborg claims to have had a conversation with Mary in the spiritual world, where she appeared to him clothed in white raiment, and said " that she had been the mother of the Lord, but that He put off all humanity He had from her, so that therefore she now worships Him as her God, and is unwilling that any should acknowledge Him as her Son, because in Him all is divine."

[2] *Religion innerhalb der Grenzen der blossen Vernunft*, 1792. *Works*, ed. by Rosenkranz, X. 69 sqq. Dorner discusses Kant's Christology very fully, in his *Entwicklungsgesch.*, etc., II., p. 974 sqq. See also Lipsius, *Dogmatik* (2nd ed. 1879), p. 488 sq.

THE PANTHEISTIC CHRISTOLOGY.

With the revival of evangelical faith in Germany, the divine element in Christ was again duly appreciated by theologians. Hegel and Schleiermacher mark a new epoch in Christological speculation, with two tendencies,—the one, pantheistic; the other, humanistic; and these, again, were followed by original reconstructions and modifications of the Catholic doctrine of the God-man. The pantheistic tendency of Hegel is congenial to the maxim of the Lutheran Confession, that the finite is capable of the infinite; the humanistic tendency of Schleiermacher, to the genius of the Reformed Confession, which guards the genuine humanity of Christ against confusion with the divine. The former starts from the divine, the latter from the human element; but both may unite, and do often unite when they proceed from naturalistic premises. Both Hegel and Schleiermacher gave impulse to orthodox as well as negative and destructive tendencies.

Schelling and Hegel favored the Christian doctrines of the trinity and the incarnation, but gave them a pantheistic meaning. Hegel, especially, taught the *essential unity* of God and man, and a *continuous* incarnation of God in the human race as a whole. From his philosophy proceeded two antagonistic schools, one called the right or conservative wing, represented by Daub, Marheineke, and Göschel, the other the left or radical wing, represented by Baur, Strauss, and Biedermann. The former endeavored to harmonize the Hegelian ideas with the orthodoxy of the church and to reconstruct the doctrine of a God-man. The other broke with the historical creeds and asserted an irreconcilable conflict between the ideal Christ and the historical Christ.

STRAUSS resolved the gospel history into a series of poetical myths or legends, and the Christian dogmas into empty dreams.[1] He denies the possibility of a miracle, because it interrupts the

[1] The former in his *Life of Jesus*, 1835; the latter in his *Christian Dogmatics*, 1840.

uniform and unchangeable laws of nature; and he denies that the infinite can "pour out its fulness into a single individual." It is only humanity as a *whole* or as a race, which is one in essence with God. Humanity is the incarnate God, the child of nature and spirit, of a visible mother and of an invisible father; humanity is the worker of miracles in subjugating nature; humanity dies, rises, and ascends to heaven; it is by faith in humanity that we are justified and saved. Nevertheless Strauss assigns to Christ the highest position in this respect that he *first* awoke to a consciousness of the union of God and man, and that he represents this union in its purest and strongest form. At one time he went so far as to say that " Christ remains the highest model within the reach of our thought; and no perfect piety is possible without his presence in the heart."[1]

BIEDERMANN, proceeding from the same pantheistic principles, places Christ highest in the scale of humanity, not only in the past, but for all time to come.[2]

[1] See his essay *Vergängliches und Bleibendes im Christenthum* (in *Friedliche Blätter*, Altona 1839). In his second or popularized *Life of Jesus* (1864), p. 208, he admits that Christ presents such a harmony of soul from beginning to end as had no need of returning and beginning another life. See the passages in Schaff's *Person of Christ*, p. 269 sq. Strauss ended at last in the philosophical bankruptcy of atheistic materialism, as openly confessed in his *Old and New Faith*, and was buried without any religious ceremony in his native city of Ludwigsburg (1874). But I learn from good authority that in his last hours of intense pain (caused by cancer of the stomach) which he bore with stoic resignation, he repeatedly exclaimed within the hearing of the deaconess who attended him, "Lord, have mercy upon me!" Dr. Baur, his teacher, was a very honest and earnest scholar, and made the remarkable concession that he could find no psychological or critical solution of the conversion of St. Paul except in a miracle of divine grace, which presupposes the still greater miracle of Christ's resurrection. Baur published no Christological theory of his own, but a very learned and able History of the doctrine of the Trinity and Incarnation, in 3 vols. (Tübingen 1841-'43).

[2] *Christl. Dogmatik* (Zürich, 1869), p. 691 : "*Jesus ist als die historische Offenbarung des Erlösungsprincips der historische Erlöser. Desswegen ist die Person Jesu zugleich für alle Zeiten das welthistorisch gewährleistende Vorbild für die Wirksamkeit des Erlösungsprincips.*" He then goes on to evolve the philosophical truth from the orthodox Christology, including even the *enhypostasia* of the human nature. He says, p. 693: "*Die chalcedonensische Bestimmung wie*

KEIM, likewise an independent pupil of Baur, made it his life-work to elaborate a Life of Jesus of Nazareth from purely historical and critical principles, but he arrived at far more positive conclusions than Strauss, and virtually refuted the mythical theory. He substitutes for the subjective vision-hypothesis of the resurrection (as held by Strauss and Renan) an actual, though spiritual, resurrection and ascension of Christ, and his objective reappearance to his disciples from heaven. He strongly asserts the sinlessness of Christ as being implied in his word and work, though it may not be capable of absolute historical proof as an experimental fact. He says that the person of Jesus in his gigantic elevation above his and all succeeding ages "makes the impression of mysterious loneliness, superhuman miracle, divine creation."[1]

Thus the most advanced school of critical research by legitimate progress forsakes its former negations and makes considerable approach to the Christological faith of the church.

untrennbarer so unvermischter Einheit der beiden Naturen im Gottmenschen war in der Kirchenlehre nothwendiger Ausdruck der Wahrheit, dass im absoluten religiösen Selbstbewusstsein die Absolutheit des Geistes und die creatürliche Endlichkeit des Ich die beiden logisch wohl zu unterscheidenden, aber thatsächlich ungetrennten Momente des Einen persönlichen Lebensprocesses dieses Selbstbewusstseins bilden; wobei die lutherische Fassung der communicatio idiomatum das Verhältniss beider Momente an sich, die reformirte ihr Verhältniss in der Wirklichkeit zum Ausdruck bringt."
A similar view is held by R. A. Lipsius, *Dogmatik*, p. 476, 480 (Braunschweig, 2nd ed. 1879).

[1] *Geschichte Jesu von Nazara* (Zürich 1867-72, 3 vols.), III. 662. Comp. his *Der geschichtliche Christus*, Zürich 1866. It is remarkable that Lange and Keim, both authors of a Life of Christ, the one from the standpoint of evangelical faith, the other from the standpoint of sceptical criticism, filled successively the theological chair in Zürich, to which Strauss had been called in 1839, but of which he was deprived by the vigorous protest of the people of the canton. Lange was afterwards (1854) called to Bonn, Keim to Giessen (where he died, 1879). Ebrard, who wrote a vigorous work in defense of the Gospel History against Strauss, was also several years Professor at Zürich. Alexander Schweizer, a pupil of Schleiermacher, and Biedermann, a Hegelian, are still connected (in 1884) with that Swiss University. Both of these are Swiss by birth, all the others named are Germans.

SCHLEIERMACHER'S CHRISTOLOGY.

SCHLEIERMACHER (1768–1834) marks an epoch in German theology and a progress from Rationalism to a new phase of evangelical faith. His Christology starts from the human personality of Christ and ascends to the highest form of humanitarianism, but fully recognizes also the *supernatural* or *divine* element in that mysterious person whom he adored and loved as his Lord and Redeemer, from his Moravian childhood to the solemn communion scene on his deathbed.

He regards Christ as a perfect man, in whom, and in whom alone, the ideal of humanity (the *Urbild*) has been fully realized.[1] He emphatically asserts Christ's essential sinlessness and absolute perfection,[2] and a peculiar real and abiding indwelling or being of the Godhead in him,[3] by which he differed from all men. He admits him to be "a moral miracle." This means a great deal for a divine of the boldest and keenest criticism in matters of history. He was willing to surrender almost every miracle of action in order to save the miracle of the person of Christ. From this historic Christ issues an incessant flow of a new spiritual life with all its pure and holy emotions and aspirations after sinlessness.

Schleiermacher adopts the Sabellian view of the Trinity as a threefold manifestation of God in creation (in the world), redemption (in Christ), and sanctification (in the church). He therefore has no room for an eternal *personal* pre-existence and *personal* incarnation of the Logos. His conception of the abstract unity and simplicity of the Godhead excludes the immanent Trinity of persons. He also rejects the dyophysitic basis of the Chalcedonian dogma, and substitutes for it a full human personality filled with the divinity.[4]

---

[1] *Urbild* or *archetype* is much more than *Vorbild* or *example*. The *Urbild* fully coincides with the historical Christ in Schleiermacher's system.

[2] "*wesentliche Unsündlichkeit*," and "*schlechthinige Vollkommenheit*."

[3] *ein eigentliches Sein Gottes in ihm.*

[4] See Schleiermacher's *Der Christl. Glaube* §§ 92–99 (vol. II. 26–93), and the sharp criticism of Strauss, *Die Christl. Glaubenslehre im Kampf mit der modernen*

CHRIST IN THEOLOGY. 105

To most of his pupils Schleiermacher was a John the Baptist who led them to the higher school of Christ.

One of the best Christological works which proceeded from his school, is Ullmann's "*Sinlessness of Jesus.*"[1] It has an abiding doctrinal and apologetic value independently of all speculative theories. Bushnell's "*Moral Character of Christ*" may be mentioned in this connection as an American parallel.

ROTHE.

RICHARD ROTHE (d. at Heidelberg, 1866), the greatest speculative divine of the nineteenth century, next to Schleiermacher, and influenced by him as well as Hegel, yet independent of both, especially in the department of Ethics, likewise dissents from the orthodox doctrine of the Trinity and the Incarnation. He objects to the Chalcedonian creed that it goes far beyond the simplicity of biblical teaching and makes the union of the divine and human physical rather than moral. Yet he fully admits the divine-human character of the one personality of Christ. He lays great stress on the ethical feature in the development of Christ, by which alone he can become our Redeemer and Example. God, by a creative act, called the second Adam into existence in the bosom of the old natural humanity. Christ was *born* of a woman, yet not *begotten* by man, but *created* by God (as to his humanity), hence free from all sinful bias, as well as actual sin. His development was a real, but normal and harmonious, religious moral growth, and a correspondingly increasing indwelling of God in him.[2] There

Wissenschaft, II. 175 sqq. Schleiermacher's posthumous lectures on the Life of Christ are perhaps his least satisfactory production, and in a purely critical point of view prepared the way for the *Leben Jesu* of Strauss, but his doctrinal and religious relation to Christ was radically different.

[1] *Die Sündlosigkeit Jesu*, Gotha, seventh ed. 1863. A new English translation by Sophia Taylor, Edinburgh 1870.

[2] See his *Dogmatik* (published after his death, from MSS., by Schenkel, 1870), vol. II. 168 (note [2]): "*Der Process der sittlichen Lebensentwicklung des zweiten Adams ist gleich wesentlich beides, eine stätige Menschwerdung Gottes und eine stätige Gottwerdung des Menschen (des zweiten Adams).*"

was not a single moment in his conscious life in which he stood not in personal union with God; but the absolute union took place with the completion of the personal development of the second Adam. This completion coincided with his perfect self-sacrifice in death. Henceforth he was wholly and absolutely God (*ganz und schlechthin Gott*), since his being is extensively and intensively filled with the true God; but we cannot say, *vice versa*, that God is wholly the second Adam; for God is not limited by an individual person. The death of Christ on earth was at the same time his ascension to heaven and his elevation above all the limitations of material existence into the divine mode of existence,[1] which, however, implies also his perpetual presence with his church on earth (Matt. 28 : 20).

I add the following noble confession of Rothe's humble belief: "The ground of all my thinking, I can truly say, is the simple faith of Christians, which (independently of dogma or any system of theology), for these eighteen hundred years, has overcome the world. It is my last certitude to which I am ready without any hesitation cheerfully to sacrifice every other pretended knowledge which asserts itself against this faith. I know no other firm ground on which I could anchor my whole being, and particularly my speculations, except that historical phenomenon which is marked by the holy name Jesus Christ. He is to me the unimpeachable Holy of Holies of humanity, the highest Being known to man, and a sun-rising in history which alone spreads light on all other objects."[2]

BUSHNELL.

The Christology of HORACE BUSHNELL, a very vigorous and independent American divine (d. at Hartford, Conn., 1876), resembles the views of Schleiermacher and Rothe. It was first delivered in his *Concio ad Clerum*, at the annual commencement of Yale College, New Haven (Aug. 15, 1848), and was published, together with two other discourses (delivered at Cambridge and

---

[1] A return to the μορφὴ θεοῦ.
[2] *Theol. Ethik*, vol. I. Preface p. XVI. (sec. ed. 1867.)

Andover), and a preliminary dissertation on the *Nature of Language as related to Thought and Spirit*, under the title, *God in Christ* (new ed., New York, 1877). It gave rise to his trial for heresy. Bushnell was not a German scholar; but he read Schleiermacher's essay on Sabellius as translated by Professor Moses Stuart in the *Biblical Repository*, and says that " the general view of the Trinity given in that article coincides " with his own view, and confirmed him in the results of his own private struggles. He maintains the full divinity of Christ, but on the Sabellian basis. He rejects the theory of " three metaphysical or essential persons in the being of God," with three distinct consciousnesses, wills, and understandings; and he substitutes for it simply a trinity of revelation, or what he calls an "instrumental trinity," that is, three impersonations, in which the one divine being presents himself to our human capacities and wants, and which are necessary to produce mutuality, or terms of conversableness between us and him, and to pour his love most effectually into our feeling. " God may act," he says, "a human personality, without being measured by it." The real divinity came into the finite, and was subject to human conditions. There are not two distinct subsistences in the person of Christ,—one infinite, and the other finite; but it is the one infinite God who expresses himself in Christ, and brings himself down to the level of our humanity, without any loss of his greatness, or reduction of his majesty. At the same time, Bushnell holds to the full yet sinless humanity of Christ; and the tenth chapter of his work on *Nature and the Supernatural* is one of the ablest and most eloquent tributes to the sinless perfection of the moral character of Christ.

THE KENOSIS THEORY.[1]

The modern KENOSIS theory, that is, the theory of SELF-EXINANITION or SELF-EVACUATION, differs from the theories

[1] The Literature on the Kenosis theory is little known among English readers; hence we give it in full. JOH. L. KÖNIG: *Die Menschwerdung Gottes*, Mainz, 1844. GOTTFRIED THOMASIUS (Erlangen, d. 1875): *Beiträge zur kirchl. Chris-*

just noticed, by its orthodox premises and conclusions as far as

tologie, 1845; and *Christi Person und Werk,* Erlangen, 2d ed. 1856–64, 3 vols. (vol. II. 63 sqq., 128 sqq., 185 sqq.). J. CHR. CONR. VON HOFMANN (Erlangen, d. 1877): *Schriftbeweis,* Nördlingen, 2d ed. 1857 sqq. LIEBNER (of Leipzig, d. 1871): *Die christl. Dogmatik aus dem christolog. Princip.,* Göttingen, 1849, (I. 286 sqq.). EBRARD (Erlangen): *Christl. Dogmatik,* Königsberg, 1851 and 1852, 2 vols. (II. 34 sqq. 143 sqq.) J. P. LANGE (Bonn): *Positive Dogmatik,* Heidelb 1851 (pp. 595-782). GESS (Prof. in the Mission Institute at Basel, afterwards in the University of Breslau): *Lehre von der Person Christi,* Basel, 1856; rewritten under the title *Christi Person und Werk,* Basel, Part I., 1870, Part II., 1878. MARTENSEN (Copenhagen, d. 1884): *Christl. Dogmatik,* Berlin, 1853 (Engl. transl. by Urwick, Edinb. 1866). DELITZSCH (Leipzig): *Syst. der bibl. Psychologie,* 1855, 2d ed. 1861, (pp. 325 sqq.) J. BODEMEYER: *Die Lehre von der Kenosis,* Göttingen, 1860. KAHNIS (Leipzig): *Die Luther. Dogmatik,* Leipz., 1861-68, 3 vols. (III. 343 sqq.), sec. ed. abridged in 2 vols. SCHÖBERLEIN (d. at Göttingen, 1880): *Die Geheimnisse des Glaubens,* Heidelb. 1872. ROBERT KÜBEL (Tübingen): *Das Christliche Lehrsystem nach der heil. Schrift,* Stuttgart, 1873 · and his art. *Christologie* in Herzog² vol. III. 211–216. LUTHARDT (Leipzig): *Kompendium der Dogmatik,* Leipz. 6th ed. 1882 (p. 208 sq., very brief). VAN OOSTERZEE (Utrecht, d. 1882): *Christian Dogmatics,* Eng. trans. 1874 (vol. II. 514 and 543 (very moderately and cautiously Kenotic). FR. GODET (Neuchatel): Essay on *Jesus Christ,* in his *Studies on the New Testament,* transl. by Lyttleton, Lond. 1876; and his *Com. on the Gospel of John,* 3d ed. 1881. E. DE PRESSENSÉ (Paris): *Life of Christ* (first French ed., 1866, also transl. into English and German), and *La divinité de Jésus-Christ,* in the "*Revue Chretienne,*" III. 641 sqq. HENRY M. GOODWIN: *Christ and Humanity,* New York (Harpers) 1875. HOWARD CROSBY: *The True Humanity of Christ,* New York (Randolph) 1881.

For an adverse criticism of the Kenosis theory see DORNER: *Entwicklungsgesch.,* II. 126 sqq. (Engl. transl. Divis. II. vol. III. 100 sqq.); and especially the first of his three Essays on the "*Unchangeableness of God*" in the "Jahrbücher für deutsche Theol. for 1856 and 1858, reprinted in his *Gesammelte Schriften aus dem Gebiet der system. Theol., Exegese und Geschichte,*" Berlin 1883, pp. 188–377; also his *Christl. Gl. lehre* Berlin, 1881, vol. II. 367 sqq. ROTHE: *Dogmatik,* II. 157 sqq. LIPSIUS: *Dogmatik,* Braunschweig, 2d ed. 1879, p. 481-485.

Dr. ALEX. B. BRUCE, Prof. in the Free Church College at Glasgow, gives the fullest account in English of the Kenosis theories in his able work, *The Humiliation of Christ,* Edinb., 2d ed., 1881, Lect. IV. Dr. CHARLES HODGE notices the Kenotic views of Thomasius, Ebrard, and Gess, but condemns them very severely, saying, "Any theory which assumes that God lays aside his omnipotence, omniscience, and omnipresence, and becomes feeble, ignorant, and circumscribed as an infant, contradicts the first principle of all religion, and, if it be pardonable to say so, shocks the common sense of men." *Syst. Theol.* II. 439. He also objects that the Kenosis destroys the humanity of Christ, since a being which never had a human soul and a human heart cannot be a man. But Gess maintains that the Logos *became* a true *human* soul.

CHRIST IN THEOLOGY. 109

the dogma of the Trinity and of the eternal Deity of Christ is concerned; but it likewise departs from the Chalcedonian dyophysitism, by holding to one divine-human Christ, with one consciousness and one will. It is based on the famous passage Phil. 2: 6-8,[1] and also on 2 Cor. 8: 9; John 1: 14;[2] Heb. 2: 17, 18; 5: 8, 9, and on the general impression which the gospel history makes of Christ as a truly human, yet divinely-human being, speaking of himself always as a unit.

The theory was suggested by Count Zinzendorf in the form of a devout sentimentalism, which brings the divine Christ down to the closest intimacy with men, and pervades the ascetic and hymnological literature of the Moravians. It was scientifically developed, though with various modifications, by a number of eminent divines of the Lutheran Confession (Thomasius, Gess, von Hofmann, Kahnis, Delitzsch, Liebner, Schöberlein, Luthardt, Martensen, Kübel), and several Reformed divines (Lange, Ebrard, van Oosterzee, Godet, E. de Pressensé, in Europe, Henry M. Goodwin, and Howard Crosby, in America).

These writers carry the *Kenosis* of the Son of God or the act of incarnation which coincides with it, much further than the Giessen Lutherans of the seventeenth century. They make it consist not only in a *non-use* (still less, like the Tübingen divines of the same period, in a *concealment* of the use[3]), but in an actual abandonment of the *possession*,[4] of the divine attributes of omnipotence, omniscience, and omnipresence, during the whole period of humiliation from the incarnation to the resurrection. They substitute a *genus kenoticum*, or *tapeinoticum*, for the *genus majestaticum* of the Lutheran Creed; in other words, they teach a communication of the properties of humanity to the divinity instead of a communication of the properties of the divine nature to the human nature. They proceed from the maxim, *infinitum capax est finiti*, which the old Lutheran theology rejected; while

---

[1] Ἑαυτὸν ἐκένωσεν, *he emptied himself*, etc., the subject of the Kenosis being the pre-existent, not the incarnate, Logos.
[2] The Logos *became*, ἐγένετο.   [3] Κρύψις.   [4] Κτῆσις.

the Lutherans held to the opposite maxim, *finitum capax est infiniti*, which the Calvinists rejected. Instead of raising the finite to the infinite, the modern Kenotic theory lowers the infinite to the finite. It teaches a temporary self-exinanition or depotentiation of the pre-existent Logos.[1] In becoming incarnate, the second Person of the holy Trinity reduced himself to the limitations of humanity. He literally emptied himself,[2] not only of his divine glory[3] and of his divine mode of existence,[4] but also of his divine being,[5] or at all events of some of his attributes, and assumed the conditions of a truly human being, subject to space and time, and the laws of development and growth. He ceased to be omnipotent and omnipresent: he became ignorant and helpless as a child. In one word (as von Hofmann expresses it), "he ceased to be God in order to become man." But he retained what Thomasius calls the *essential* attributes of truth, holiness, and love, and revealed them fully during his humiliation. The incarnation is not only an assumption by the Son of God of human nature, but also a self-limitation of the divine Logos; and both constitute one divine-human personality. Otherwise the infinite consciousness of the Logos could not coincide with the human consciousness of the historical Christ: it would transcend and outreach it, and the result would be a double personality. The self-limitation is to be conceived as an act of will, an act of God's love, which is the motive of the incarnation; and his love is absolutely powerful, even to the extent of the utmost self-surrender.

This is the view of THOMASIUS, a Bavarian Lutheran, and of LIEBNER. Both held at first, that the Logos actually became a rational human soul; but afterwards they assumed a truly human soul alongside with the Kenosis of the Logos (or a finite soul, together with an infinite but humanized soul); and thereby they lost the chief benefit of the Kenosis theory, namely the

---

[1] Godet calls the Kenosis *une espèce d'anéantissement volontaire.* "Revue chretienne," 1858, No. III.   [2] Ἑαυτὸν ἐκένωσε, Phil. 2: 7.
[3] Δόξα.   [4] The μορφὴ θεοῦ.   [5] Οὐσία or φύσις.

unity of the life of Christ as distinct from the dualism of the dyophysitic theory.

The most consistent development of the Kenosis theory is represented by GESS, a Swabian divine brought up under the influence of the school of Bengel, Oetinger, and Beck, and starting from a theosophic biblical realism. He carries the Kenosis to the extent of a suspension of self-consciousness and will.[1] He identifies it with the outgoing of the Son from the Father, or his descent from heaven, which resulted in a temporary suspension of the influx of the eternal life of the Father into the Son, and a transition from a state of equality with God into a state of dependence and need. He rejects a double soul in Christ and puts the divine Logos in the place of the human soul, like Apollinaris, but assumes, unlike him, an actual transformation of the Logos into a human soul to the extent that he surrendered even the attribute of holiness, became subject to temptation with the possibility of sinning, and had to work himself up by free action to holiness, like other men. The Logos *assumed* a human body from the flesh of the Virgin, but *became* a rational human soul, so that he had no need of assuming another soul. Consequently the soul of Christ was not derived from Mary: it was the result of a voluntary Kenosis, while an ordinary human soul derives its existence from a creative act of God. This view, therefore, is inconsistent with traducianism, and presupposes the theory of creationism.[2] It is very questionable whether such a soul, which is the result of a transformation, and which begins with divinity and ends with divinity, can be

[1] *Bewusstlosigkeit* and *Willenslosigkeit.*

[2] Gess (in the first ed. p. 330): "*Der Logos indem er in's Werden einging und Fleisch wurde, ist zur menschlichen Seele geworden, wie Geist des Lebens von Gott gehaucht in die durch Gottes Wunderkraft aus Staub bereitete Leiblichkeit zu Adams Seele, und wie Geist des Lebens von Gott gehaucht in die von unseren Eltern gezeugte Leiblichkeit zu unserer Seele wurde. Die Leiblichkeit aber, zu deren Seele der Logos wurde, indem er in's Werden einging und sich mit ihr vermählte, war durch den heiligen Geist in Mariens Schooss gezeugt.*" Dorner and Rothe object that such a soul is not a truly human soul: hence the charge of Apollinarianism against the Kenosis theory.

called a truly human soul any more than the Apollinarian Logos, who, remaining unchanged, occupied the place, and exercised the functions of the human soul. The bond of sympathy with Christ, on the ground of the identity of his mental constitution and condition, seems to be broken by this form of the Kenotic theory. Gess does not satisfactorily answer the question, how the Logos personally recovered his divine self-consciousness, whether by a recollection of his pre-existent state, or by a reflection on the Old Testament Scriptures, or by a direct revelation from the Father, or by the development of a native instinct.

EBRARD and GODET agree essentially with Gess in the extent of the *Kenosis*. Ebrard represents the Kenotic theory as a legitimate development of the orthodox Reformed Christology; but this is a mistake: it departs from the same as widely as from the Lutheran *Formula Concordiæ*.

MARTENSEN (d. 1884), a very able Lutheran divine of Denmark, who was brought up under the influence of Hegel's philosophy, Baader's theosophy, Schleiermacher's theology, and mediæval mysticism, teaches a real, but limited *Kenosis*, which is far less exposed to objection. He distinguishes between the Logos-revelation and the Christ-revelation, and confines the Kenosis to the latter. In the Logos-revelation the Son proceeds from the Father as God: in the Christ-revelation he returns to God as God-man, with a host of redeemed children of God. The eternal Logos continues in God and his general revelation to the world as the Author of all reason; while at the same time he enters into the bosom of humanity as a holy seed, that he may arise within the human race as a Mediator and Redeemer. He would, however, have become man even without sin, though not as Redeemer.[1] The Son of God leads a double life. As the pure

[1] "Are we to believe," asks Martensen (*Dogmatik*, p. 296,) "that the most glorious fact in the world was possible only through sin, and that without it there would be no room in history for the glory of the only-begotten of the Father?" He teaches, with several of the Fathers and modern German divines, that the incarnation is necessary for the highest revelation of God, and was only modified, not conditioned, by the fall.

divine Logos (*der reine Gottheitslogos*), he works in all-pervading activity throughout the kingdom of nature; as Christ, he works through the kingdom of grace, redemption, and completion, and he indicates his consciousness of personal identity in the two spheres by referring to his pre-existence, which, to his human consciousness, takes the form of a recollection. A similar distinction is made by the Reformed divines, that the Logos was simultaneously *totus extra carnem* and *totus in carne*.

SCHÖBERLEIN likewise assumes that the Son of God when he became incarnate, continued his world-ruling activity in heaven.

KAHNIS and LANGE limit the Kenosis substantially to an abandonment of the use, rather than the possession, of the attributes, and thus approach the Kenosis theory of Chemnitz and the Giessen divines, only making it fuller and more real. Lange's Christology abounds in fruitful and original hints for further and clearer development.

JULIUS MÜLLER (d. at Halle, 1879), the author of the great work on the *Christian Doctrine of Sin*, and one of the profoundest divines, whose humility and modesty induced him to forbid the publication of any of his valuable manuscripts, taught, likewise, a moderate Kenosis theory, which I am able to give from my notes of his Lectures on Dogmatics (1839 to 1840). "Paul contrasts," he says, "the earthly and pre-earthly existence of the Son of God as poverty and riches (2 Cor. 8 : 9), and represents the incarnation as an emptying himself of the full possession of the divine mode of existence (Phil. 2 : 6). This implies more than a mere assumption of human nature into union with the Son of God : the incarnation is a real self-exinanition (*Selbstentäusserung*), and a renunciation, not only of the use, but also of the possession, of the divine attributes and powers. . . . The Church is undoubtedly right in teaching a real union of the divine and human nature in Christ. But in the state of humiliation this union was first only potential and concealed; and the unfolded reality belongs to the state of exaltation. Only with the assumption of a self-exinanition can we fully appreciate the act of the self-denying condescension of divine love; while in the orthodox dogma God gives nothing in the incarnation, but simply receives and unites something with his person." Want of space forbids further extracts. This moderate Kenosis theory is the most plausible, and evades the chief objections.

GOODWIN, an American Congregationalist, differs from the German Kenoticists by assuming that the Logos is the human element in God which pre-existed in him from eternity, and became incarnate by taking flesh, and occupying the place of the soul.[1] No incarnation, he thinks, is possible without a humanization of the divine; and this implies a self-limitation, and true development from ignorance to knowledge and wisdom. The incarnation is not a synthesis or union of opposite natures, but a development of the divine in the form of the human. The Word did not *assume* flesh or human nature, but it *became* flesh. As the true idea of God includes humanity, so the true idea of man includes God. The divine and human differ only as the ideal differs from the actual, or the prototype from the copy. This essential unity is the basis of the possibility of the incarnation as a Kenosis.

Dr. CROSBY, a Presbyterian divine of New York, came to the Kenosis theory not from speculation, but from a purely practical motive. He reasons that Christ cannot be a real example for us in fighting temptation, if he was supported through all his earthly life by a full divinity, which made victory easy and certain. He holds, therefore, that the Son of God reduced himself to the dimensions of humanity, or as he calls it, to a state of "dormancy." The supreme Godhead of Christ is clearly taught in *words*, he says, but Christ nowhere showed it in *action*, from Bethlehem to Calvary; for his miracles,

---

[1] Isaac Watts believed in the pre-existence of the human soul of Christ, but as created, and distinct from the Logos. Swedenborg taught an eternal humanity of God himself, because he admits only one divine personality and identifies it with Christ. Keerl (*D. Gottmensch, das Ebenbild Gottes*, 1866) teaches the eternal preëxistence of Christ as the Son of Man, or ideal, antitypal man, in the glory of heaven.

like those of Moses, Elijah, and the apostles, were wrought by the power of God, by a delegated authority, and proved merely that he was *sent* from God, not that he *was* God. His Godhead was in a state of quiescency, or a sort of paralysis during his humiliation, and awoke with the resurrection, after which the divine overshadowed the human. Dr. Crosby goes apparently as far as Dr. Gess, but he declines to enter into speculations about the possibility of such self-reduction to a state of unconsciousness, which transcends human thought.

CRITICISM OF THE KENOSIS THEORY.

A Christology which arose almost simultaneously and independently in the minds of many devout and able evangelical divines must embody an important element of truth, and claims a respectful consideration. Dr. Dorner who has most thoroughly criticised the modern *Kenosis* theory, calls it a revival of Apollinarianism and Patripassianism. But while it resembles both in some features, it differs from them materially by assuming either a *human* soul along side with the Logos, or a *humanized* Logos, dwelling in the human body of Jesus; while Apollinaris taught that Christ had no rational human soul, and that the *unchanged* Divine Logos took the place of it.

The Kenosis theory furnishes a striking illustration of the inexhaustible mine of thought contained in the Scriptures. It was suggested by a single word of Paul, and has brought out its meaning more clearly and strongly than ever before. We cannot overestimate the amazing love of the Son of God in condescending to the lowest depth of man in order to raise him to the highest height. But we must not carry this to the extent of metaphysical impossibility, nor bring it into conflict with the essential immutability of God. And this is just the fault of the theory under consideration.

1. It is not sustained by a fair exegesis of Phil. 2: 7. The Pauline term for the incarnation: "*he emptied himself*" undoubtedly means far more than the English Version: "he

made himself of no reputation." Nor is it equivalent to: "he concealed himself," as the Kryptic theory of Tübingen taught.[1] It means: "he emptied himself," or "he made himself void."[2] So far Giessen was right against Tübingen. But of what did he empty himself? Merely of the *use* of the divine attributes? No; here the Giessen theory falls short of the force of the word which seems to imply the surrender of a *possession* as well as *use* of something which Christ had in his pre-existent state. What did he give up then? Not his divine essence,[3] for this would be self-annihilation or suicide, but according to the context (ver. 5), the divine form of existence,[4] which he voluntarily exchanged for the human form of existence.[5] This "form of God" is essentially the same with his pre-existent or pre-mundane divine glory,[6] of which he speaks in the sacerdotal prayer, John 17: 4: "And now, O Father, glorify thou me with thine own self with the glory which I had with thee before the world was." He abandoned the possession and enjoyment of the rights and prerogatives of the divine majesty, and assumed the condition and function of a servant.[7]

---

[1] This would require the verb, κρύπτω, which repeatedly occurs in the N. T., but never in connection with the incarnation.

[2] The verb κενόω (κενός, *empty*) means, first, *to empty* (the opposite of πληρόω, *to fill*), then, *to make void* or *vain*. It occurs twice in the Septuagint (Jer. 14: 2; 15: 9), and five times in the Greek Testament (always in Paul): Rom. 4: 14, κεκένωται ἡ πίστις, *faith is made void;* 1 Cor. 1: 17, ἵνα μὴ κενωθῇ ὁ σταυρὸς τοῦ χριστοῦ, *lest the cross of Christ should be made void;* 1 Cor. 9: 15, τὸ καύχημά μου ἵνα τις κενώσῃ, *that any man should make my glorying void;* 2 Cor. 9: 3, ἵνα μὴ τὸ καύχημα ἡμῶν τὸ ὑπὲρ ὑμῶν κενωθῇ, *that our glorying on your behalf may not be made void* (or *falsified*); and Phil. 2: 7, ἑαυτὸν ἐκένωσε, *he emptied himself*. The E. V. unnecessarily gives four different renderings in these five passages.   [3] Οὐσία, φύσις.   [4] Μορφὴ θεοῦ.   [5] Μορφὴ δούλου.   [6] Δόξα.

[7] Comp. our remarks on the exegesis of the whole passage on p. 61 and 62. The above interpretation is sustained by Meyer (*Br. an die Philipper*), 4th ed. 1874, p. 78): "*Er hat sich selbst entleert, und zwar, was der Context zweifellos macht, der göttlichen μορφή, welche er besass, nun aber mit einer μορφὴ δούλου vertauschte.*" Comp. p. 86: "*Was der göttliche Logos bei der Menschwerdung ablegte, war die μορφὴ θεοῦ, d. i. die göttliche δόξα als Existenzform, nicht aber das seine Natur wesentlich und nothwendig ausmachende εἶναι ἴσα θεῷ, welches er behielt.*" "Bishop Lightfoot (*in loc*): "He divested Himself, not of his divine nature,

CHRIST IN THEOLOGY. 117

The same is the meaning of the term Christ "became poor"[1] in the parallel passage 2 Cor. 8 : 9 ; that is he gave up his riches in order to enrich us. Self-impoverishment is not self-annihilation in whole or in part. A king in noble self-denial may lay aside or divest himself of his majesty and power, and condescend to the poorest of his subjects so as to put himself on a perfect equality of outward condition with him, without losing a single one of his intellectual or moral qualities; on the contrary he reveals thereby his love and mercy in the highest possible degree. In this way, and only in this way, can Christ be an example for our imitation. Paul exhorts the Philippians, not to empty themselves of their being or essential attributes, but to make them by self-denial and humility subservient and useful to others.

2. The Kenosis in the sense of an actual self-abandonment or self-reduction to an unconscious embryonic existence involves a metaphysical impossibility and moral monstrosity. God cannot do anything that is contrary to his rational and moral nature ; he cannot commit suicide, he cannot suspend himself, he cannot go to sleep. It is said that he gave up only some of his attributes which involve his relation to the world. But his attributes are not an outside appendix, they are inherent in the being itself and constitute it, so that the loss of all attributes (which Gess assumes) is an annihilation, the loss of some attributes (as Thomasius holds) is a mutilation, of the being itself.[2]

for this was impossible, but of the glories, the prerogatives, of Deity. This He did by taking upon Him the form of a servant. The emphatic position of ἑαυτόν points to the humiliation of our Lord as *voluntary, self-imposed.*" The μορφὴ θεοῦ is not equivalent to οὐσία or φύσις, although it is more than σχῆμα, a passing fashion. The difference of the two in the usage of Paul is well discussed by Lightfoot, in an Excursus, p. 125–131. Christ was ἐν μορφῇ θεοῦ, which means that he was the reflected image (εἰκών) of God. "We are transformed (μεταμορφούμεθα) into Christ's image" (not changed into his *essence,* transubstantiated); comp. 2 Cor. 3 : 18 ; Phil. 3 : 10 ; Rom. 8 : 29 ; 12 : 2 ; Gal. 4 : 19.

[1] Ἐπτώχευσε.

[2] Lipsius (*Dogmatik,* p. 484, 2nd ed.) objects to the Kenotic theory in either form (of Thomasius or Gess) that it destroys the very root of the idea of God. "*Ein Gott,*" he says, "*dem es nicht wesentlich ist absolut zu sein, ist eben kein wahrer Gott, sondern ein heidnischer Zeus. Absolutheit und Endlichkeit schliessen*

3. The Kenosis theory is inconsistent with the metaphysical unchangeableness of God. It is true that God is not unchangeable in the Stoic or Mohammedan sense of indifference, apathy, and immovable sameness. He is the God of history and revelation, he is a living God and ever moved by the deepest interest in his creatures, and undergoes changes in his relation to the world, as creator, redeemer, sanctifier. But he nevertheless remains metaphysically and morally the same yesterday, to-day, and forever. The creation, the incarnation, the atonement, justification, do not change his nature, but only reveal his eternal design. Even the hearing of prayer involves no change in the divine mind which foreknew and foreordained all free actions of the creatures.[1]

4. The last difficulty which presses against the Kenosis theory is its bearing upon the doctrine of the Trinity. It involves, as Gess admits, an actual suspension of the inter-trinitarian process and the trinitarian revelation for the thirty-three years of Christ's state of humiliation. The generation of the Son, the procession of the Spirit from the Father and the Son, and the government of the world through the Son ceased, and gave place to some unknown and unrevealed mode of divine operation. Such a suspension is inconceivable, and would be fatal to God and the world. It may be urged that it is the *person* of the Logos which became incarnate, and not the divine *essence* or

sich schlechthin aus und so wenig jene jemals zu dieser herabgesetzt werden kann, so wenig kann diese jemals zu jener gesteigert werden: ein vergotteter Mensch ist kein Mensch, sondern ein mythologischer Heros. Aber abgesehen hiervon wird mit allen Bemühungen die wahre Menschheit Christi nicht hergestellt. Ein in einen Menschen verwandelter Gott ist als ewig präexistentes, dereinst zur vollen Gottheit sich wieder hinaufpotenzirendes Subject uns Menschen eben nicht wesensgleich, auch dann nicht, wenn sein Incognito in der Welt, wie Gess will, für sein eignes Bewusstsein ein Incognito ist, und vollends nicht, wenn er, wie Thomasius lehrt, in jedem Augenblicke die Macht hat, diesem Incognito ein Ende zu machen."

[1] For a very profound discussion of this difficult subject in connection with the Kenosis, see the three articles of Dorner above referred to. In the second article he traces the history of the doctrine of the Unchangeableness of God from St. Augustin to Schleiermacher; in the third he endeavors to harmonize the ideas of God's *Lebendigkeit* and *Unveränderlichkeit.*

CHRIST IN THEOLOGY. 119

nature which he shares in common with the Father and the Holy Spirit. True, but we can not abstractly separate the person from the essence, and it is through the person of the Logos that God the Father made and preserves all things (John 1 : 3; Col. 1 : 15-17).

Martensen's theory escapes this objection by the distinction above mentioned between the Logos-revelation and the Christ-revelation, and by assuming that the former goes on without a break during the earthly life of Christ. But it raises another difficulty of two distinct Logoi, or a Logos with two heads, one infinite, and the other finite. And Martensen does not explain how this *Doppelleben* of the Logos can be reconciled with the unity of his personality any more than the two natures of the orthodox Christology. We fully agree with Martensen in asserting the uninterrupted integrity of the Logos in the life of the Trinity, but we substitute for his double Logos a gradual self-communication of one and the same Logos to the human consciousness of Jesus.

THE THEORY OF A GRADUAL INCARNATION.

The last attempt to promote the solution of this problem is the theory of a GRADUAL or PROGRESSIVE incarnation. It carries the divine Kenosis, or the motion of God's love to men, through the whole earthly life of Christ, instead of confining it to an instantaneous act when the Holy Spirit overshadowed the Blessed Virgin. When John says that the "Logos became flesh," he spoke as one of those who "beheld his glory, the glory of the only-begotten of the Father," as it manifested itself in his whole public life. This theory discards the impossible idea of an *essential* self-limitation of the Logos to a state of unconsciousness or dormancy, but assumes instead various degrees in the *self-communication* of the Logos to humanity. The being and actuality of the Logos remained metaphysically and morally unchanged in the holy Trinity and continued its activity throughout the world which is preserved and governed by him (Col. 1 :

17; Heb. 1–3); but Jesus of Nazareth possessed the Logos merely so far as was compatible with the truth of human growth and the capacity of his expanding consciousness. In other words, the eternal personality of the divine Logos entered into the humanity of Jesus measure by measure, as he grew, and became capable and worthy of receiving it. There were two corresponding movements in the life of Christ,—a descent of the divine consciousness, and an ascent of the human consciousness. There was a progressive self-communication of the divine Logos to Jesus, and a moral growth of Jesus in holiness keeping step with the former. The process of union began with the supernatural conception, and was completed with the ascension when he reassumed the glory which he had with the Father before the world was (John 17: 5).

The first act of the incarnation of the Logos was the beginning of the man Jesus, and both constituted one undivided personality. There was a personal unity and identity throughout the whole period, the same life of the divine-human personality, but in actual growth and development from germ to full organization, from infancy to ripe manhood. Christ became conscious of his Godhead as he became conscious of his Manhood; but the divine life always was the basis of his human life. The twelfth year of Jesus in the temple, and the baptism in the Jordan, mark two important epochs in the development of this divine-human consciousness. There was in connection with the gradual incorporation of the divine Logos into the humanity of Jesus an actual elevation of his humanity into personal union with the Godhead, as he grew in moral perfection; hence his exaltation is spoken of by Paul as a reward for his humiliation and obedience (Phil. 2: 9; comp. Heb. 5: 7–10).

This theory, in substance, is advocated by Dr. DORNER, who has devoted many years of earnest thought to the Christological problem and has written the fullest history of the doctrine.[1]

[1] Dorner was born June 20, 1809, and died July 9, 1884. He sums up his own view in his *Christliche Glaubenslehre*, 1881, vol. II. 431, as follows: "*Da*

CHRIST IN THEOLOGY. 121

The idea of a gradual incarnation is not free from objection (and which theory is not?), but it escapes the difficulties of the Kenotic theory, and is better reconcilable with the orthodox Christology of the creeds; the difference being only that the latter puts the end at the beginning, and ignores the intervening process by which the result is attained. Nearly all Christologists admit now the genuine growth and development of Christ's humanity, to which the Kenoticists add the impossible growth of the divine Logos from unconsciousness and impotence to omniscience and omnipotence. We maintain the former with-

der Menschheit das Werden geordnet ist, Christus aber die wahre Menschheit in einem wirklichen Menschenleben darstellt, so kommt ihm ein wahrhaft menschliches Werden zu. Da andererseits Gott in Christus erst dann kann volkommen offenbar sein, wenn die ganze Fülle des göttlichen Logos auch zur eignen Fülle dieses Menschen in Wissen und Wollen, also gottmenschlich geworden ist: so ist in ihm mit dem Werden der menschlichen Seite nothwendig auch ein Werden der Gottmenschheit gegeben und die Menschwerdung ist nicht als eine mit einem Male fertige, sondern als fortgehende, ja wachsende zu denken, indem Gott als Logos jede der neuen Seiten, die von der wahren menschlichen Entwicklung hervorgebildet werden, stetig ergreift und sich aneignet, wie umgekehrt die wachsende actuelle Empfänglichkeit der Menschheit mit immer neuen Seiten des Logos sich bewusst und wollend zusammenschliesst. Trotz dieses Werdens innerhalb der Unio ist aber der Logos von Anfang an mit Jesu im tiefsten Wesensgrunde geeinigt und Jesu Leben immerdar ein gottmenschliches gewesen, indem nie eine vorhandene Empfänglichkeit für die Gottheit ohne ihre Erfüllung blieb. Das menschliche Werden und die Unveränderlichkeit der Gottheit stimmt aber dadurch zusammen, dass Got als Logos ohne Selbstverlust in die Geschichte eingehen kann für den Zweck steigender Selbstoffenbarung in der Menschheit, diese aber fähig ist, immer mehr in die Unveränderlichkeit, wieder ohne Alterirung ihres Wesens, gestellt zu werden."

In the progress of his profound discussion (*Glaubenslehre*, II. 384), Dorner unfolds (1) the preëxistence of Christ according to his divine side, or the Eternal Word of God and his activity in creation and history; (2) Christ's presence on earth, or his parousia in the state of progressive humiliation and inner transfiguration, (*a*) The act of the incarnation of God in Christ, or his divine-human nature, (*b*) The ethical God-manhood (*Gottmenschlichkeit*), or the doctrine of the holy divine-human personality, (*c*) The official God-manhood of Christ, or his divine-human functions on earth, in which he presents himself as the Redeemer,—his prophetic, high-priestly, and kingly office; (3) The post-existence of Christ, or his person and work after his earthly life, the descent into Hades (*Hadesfahrt*), resurrection, exaltation to the right hand of God, and the continuation of his three-fold office in heaven till the completion of his work, and the judgment of the world.

out the latter, and thus save the continued integrity of the Logos.

There still remains the speculative problem felt by every theologian,— how the infinite consciousness of the eternal Logos can ever become *absolutely* coincident with the limited consciousness of the man Jesus, or how the whole fulness of the Godhead can dwell in a finite human nature. A difference of thirty-three years diminishes, but does not remove the difficulty. It must, however, be admitted in all fairness that this difficulty attaches to every theory which holds fast to the strict divinity of our Lord.

CONCLUSION.

We have briefly reviewed the train of thought and meditation which the profoundest minds of Christendom have bestowed upon this central truth of our religion. It began with Peter's answer to his Master's question: "Who say ye that I am;" it has gone on for these eighteen hundred years, and from every church and every school of believing divines sounds with ever growing force the echo of the same answer: "THOU ART THE CHRIST, THE SON OF THE LIVING GOD." Doubt has not shaken it, reflection and experience confirm it. Every Christological theory has furnished some contribution towards the solution, has opened some new avenue of thought, or discovered some hidden diamond in the crown of the Redeemer of the race.

The mystery still remains, but it is a mystery made manifest as the most glorious fact in history,—the blessed mystery of godliness, the inexhaustible theme of meditation and praise for all generations. How the whole fulness of uncreated divinity can be poured out into a human being passes our understanding, but not more, perhaps, than the familiar fact that an immaterial and immortal soul made in God's image, and capable of endless perfectibility, can inhabit and interpenetrate a material and mortal body. And deeper and grander than both mysteries is the infinite love of God which lies back of them in the very depths of eternity, and which prompted the incarnation and the death of his only-begotten Son for the salvation of a sinful world. Yet this love of God in Christ, whose " breadth and length and height and depth passeth knowledge " (Eph. 3: 18, 19), is more certain and constant than the light of the sun in heaven and the voice of conscience in man.

All honor to Christological speculation: it must and it will go on; and, under the inspiring guidance of the Gospels and Epistles, and with the aid of the creeds of the church, it will ascend still higher heights and fathom still deeper depths than heretofore. In the meantime the best *practical* knowledge of Christ, even for the profoundest theologian, is an humble and earnest imitation of his example, which can never lead astray and can never be surpassed.

PROTESTANTISM AND ROMANISM.

IT is impossible to reduce the fundamental difference between Protestantism and Romanism to a single formula without doing injustice to the one or the other. Nor should we forget that there are evangelical elements in Romanism, as there are legalistic and Romanizing tendencies in Protestantism. But if we ignore these exceptions and look at the prevailing character and the most prominent aspects of the two systems, we may draw the following contrasts.

Protestantism is the Christianity of the Bible; Romanism is the Christianity of tradition. The one directs the people to the fountain-head of divine revelation; the other to the teaching priesthood. The former freely circulates the Bible as a book for the people; the latter keeps it for the use of the clergy, and explains, supplements and overrules it by its traditions. Revelation is indeed older than the Bible, and made the Bible, not *vice versa;* but the Bible is the only clear mirror and unerring record of revelation. Moreover, the written word of Christ and the apostles is the same with their spoken word, and we can find out the latter only through the former. The New Testament, therefore, must ever be the standard and corrective of tradition.

Protestantism corresponds to the Gentile type of apostolic Christianity as represented by St. Paul, and laid down in the Epistles to the Romans and Galatians (the Magna Charta of the Reformation); Romanism corresponds to the Jewish type of Christianity, which, as far as it was true and historically necessary, had its chief representatives in St. James and St. Peter, the apostles of the circumcision. The temporary collision of Paul and Peter at Antioch (Gal. 2: 11) significantly anticipated and foreshadowed the great historical antagonism between Protestantism and Catholicism, which continues to this day. It should not be forgotten, however, that Peter, in his position at the Council of Jerusalem and in his first epistle, agreed in principle with Paul, and prophetically warned his readers against hierarchical pride, which is the fruitful germ and besetting sin of Popery and all popish tendencies in the church. He clearly taught salvation by the free grace of Christ through faith; and his conduct at Antioch was a temporary inconsistency of conduct, not an error of doctrine.

Protestantism is the religion of freedom (Gal. 5: 1); Romanism the religion of authority. The former is mainly subjective, and makes religion a personal concern; the latter is objective, and sinks the individual in the body of the church. The Protestant believes on the ground of his own experience; the Romanist on the testimony of the church (comp. John 4: 42).

Protestantism is the religion of immediate communion of the soul with Christ through personal faith; Romanism is the religion of mediate communion with Christ through the Church, and obstructs the intercourse of the believer with his Saviour by interposing an army of subordinate mediators and advocates. The Protestant prays directly to God in Christ; the Roman Catholic usually approaches him through the intercession of the Blessed Virgin and the saints.

Protestantism puts Christ before the Church, and makes Christliness the standard of sound churchliness; Romanism virtually puts the Church before Christ, and makes churchliness the condition and measure of Christliness. In other words, in Protestantism the Christian precedes and determines the churchman, in Romanism the churchman precedes and determines the Christian. This is, substantially, the meaning of Schleiermacher's famous formula.[1] "Protestantism makes the relation of the individual to the Church dependent on his relation to Christ;

[1] *Der Christliche Glaube*, vol. I. sec. 24.

Catholicism, *vice versa*, makes the relation of the individual to Christ dependent on his relation to the Church." His pupil and successor, Dr. Twesten, put the distinction in this way: "Catholicism emphasizes the first, Protestantism the second, clause of the passage of Irenæus: 'Where the Church is, there is the Spirit of God; and where the Spirit of God is, there is the Church and all grace.'" We may modify this and say with the same propriety: "Where Christ is, there is the Church:" this is the motto of Protestantism; "Where the Church is, there is Christ:" this is the motto of Romanism.

Protestantism proceeds from the invisible Church to the visible; Romanism, *vice versa*, from the visible to the invisible. This formula was suggested by Dr. Möhler, in his work on "Symbolics," and he thereby inconsistently admitted the essential truth of the Protestant distinction between the visible and invisible Church, which Bellarmin denied as an empty abstraction. But Möhler was quite familiar with the writings of the Reformers, and while studying in Berlin he heard, at a respectful distance, the lectures of Schleiermacher and Neander, who were then at the height of their usefulness.

Protestantism is the Christianity of personal conviction and inward experience; Romanism is the Christianity of outward institutions, sacramental observances, and obedience to authority. The one starts from Paul's, the other from James's doctrine of justification. The one lays the main stress on living faith, as the principle of a holy life; the other on good works, as the condition and evidence of justification.

Protestantism is the church of the Christian people; Romanism is the church of priests. The former teaches, with Peter, the general priesthood of believers; the latter teaches the exclusive priesthood of a class of ordained priests who stand as mediators between God and the laity.

Protestantism is the religion of evangelism and spiritual simplicity; Romanism is the religion of legalism, asceticism, sacerdotalism, and ceremonialism. The one appeals to the intellect and conscience; the other to the senses and imagination.

Protestantism is modern Christianity in motion; Romanism is mediæval Christianity in conflict with modern progress; while the Greek Church represents ancient Christianity in repose or stagnation.

Protestantism is progressive and independent; Romanism is conservative and traditional. The one is centrifugal; the other centripetal. The one is exposed to the danger of radicalism and endless division; the other to the opposite danger of stagnation, and mechanical and tyrannical uniformity.

Protestantism claims to be only one portion of the Church of Christ, and recognizes the Greek and Latin churches; Romanism identifies itself with the whole Catholic Church, and the Church with Christianity itself. The former claims to be the safest, the latter the only way to salvation.

Does this great antagonism, which has divided Christendom for more than three hundred and fifty years, admit of a final reconciliation? The threatening division between Jewish and Gentile Christianity in the apostolic age was avoided and healed by the Council in Jerusalem, on the principle of salvation by Christ alone, through faith (Acts 15: 11). If we make a distinction between Catholicism and Romanism, or Popery, as we must (similar to the distinction between the religion of the Old Testament and the later Judaism), a reconciliation with the former on the same apostolic principle is possible; but a union with Popery is as impossible as a union of apostolic Christianity with the Jewish hierarchy which crucified the Saviour under the plea of orthodoxy and zeal for the ancestral religion. By the Vatican decrees of 1870, Popery has proclaimed itself infallible, and therefore irreformable. It has thrown a new barrier in the way of reunion both with the Greek and the Protestant churches, and made it apparently impossible. But what is impossible with man is possible with God, who in His own way and time will overrule the sharpest discords for the deepest harmony.

THE PRINCIPLES OF THE REFORMATION.

[One of the seven Addresses of the Professors of the Union Theological Seminary, New York, delivered to the Students, Monday afternoon, Nov. 19th, 1883, at the celebration of the fourth Centennial of Luther's Birth, and printed for private distribution under the title "*A Symposiac on Martin Luther.*"]

Two years ago the New Testament was republished in a revised version to the English-speaking world, and read by more millions than in whole centuries before the Reformation. This year of our Lord eighteen hundred and eighty-three, the principles of evangelical Protestantism are republished in innumerable addresses and sermons not only in Eisleben, Erfurt, and Wittenberg, but throughout Christendom, in languages unknown to Luther, in countries which at the time of his birth were not yet discovered, and in nations which then were not yet born. No man has been so much honored, no man—save the apostles—deserves so much to be held in grateful remembrance as Martin Luther, remarkable alike as a man, as a Christian, as a husband and father, as a theologian, as a preacher and writer, as a Bible translator, catechist and hymnist, as the bold champion of the freedom of conscience, as the founder of the Lutheran Church, and as the chief leader of that Reformation which carried Christendom back to first principles and urged it forward to new conquests. Such a towering personality belongs not to a sect or school, not to one nation or country, but to the whole church of Christ and to the history of the world. Luther had great faults, but they were the shadows of great virtues; and even those who dissent from some of his favorite opinions, must say: " Luther, with all thy faults I love thee still." Zwingli gave expression to this feeling when, in the heat of the eucharistic controversy,

THE PRINCIPLES OF THE REFORMATION. 129

and with tears in his eyes, he offered him the hand of brotherhood at Marburg. Melanchthon, who suffered much from his overbearing temper, yet always revered him, and, in his funeral oration, compared him to Elijah, who had overthrown the worship of idols and set up again the pure word of God. And Calvin, Melanchthon's friend, and a mediator between the Lutheran and Zwinglian theories of the Lord's Supper, while keenly alive to the tempestuous violence of Luther, yet called him "a most eminent apostle of the Lord," who by "the sound of his trumpet" and by "thunder and lightning" aroused the world and the church from its fleshly security.

The principles of the Reformation for which Luther lived and was ready to die at any moment, are the propelling forces of modern church history. They have stood the test of more than three hundred years against persecution from without and corruption from within, and are still as vital as ever. They carry in themselves the possibility and guarantee of further reformation on the same immovable foundation of God's holy word, which, in the language of St. Augustin, has *haustus primos, haustus secundos, haustus tertios, haustus infinitos.* Christianity itself is perfect, but there is a progressive understanding and application of it in the history of the church.

FREEDOM IN CHRIST is the ultimate root of evangelical Protestantism; while bondage in the law is the essence of Romanism, and freedom *from* Christ, the essence of Rationalism. From that root of Christian freedom sprung three branches, which we may call the three principles of Protestantism: *the supremacy of the Bible, the supremacy of faith, the supremacy of the people.* These principles constitute a trinity in unity and a unity in trinity. The first is the objective principle, and relates to the source and rule of faith; the second is subjective, and belongs to the sphere of practical experience, or the religion of the heart; the third is social, and relates to the life and organization of the church.

1. The first principle is expressed in the statement: The *canonical Scriptures are the only infallible source and rule of the*

Christian faith and duty. The Word of God alone can bind the conscience, and every one has the right and duty to read, explain, and obey it to the best of his ability, and in full view of his personal responsibility to the Lord of conscience. This principle is opposed to the principle of traditionalism, which so overloads the Word of God with human afterthoughts as to hide it from the people and to make it of no effect. "The Bible, the whole Bible, and nothing but the Bible, is the religion of Protestants." Yet the Bible must be interpreted by the mind of the church as well as by the individual. No sound Protestant can despise the lessons of history, the value of doctrinal standards, the common teaching and experience of Christendom, but he subordinates them all to the oracles of the living God, who alone is infallible and who is wiser than all the wisdom of men. We honor the fathers, but still more the grandfathers. We go from enlightened reformers, schoolmen, and fathers to the inspired apostles, and from the apostles to Him who is not only a witness of the truth, but the Truth itself. We follow the river up to the fountain of the water of life. *Amicus Lutherus, amicus Augustinus, sed magis amicus Paulus, et maxime amicus Christus—Christus est veritas.*

> "*Es kommt der durst'ge Geist auf Wegen der Erfahrung*
> *Vom Ueberlief'rungsgrund zum Quell der Offenbarung.*"

With the Bible in his hand, head, and heart, Luther went forth to fight his battles against the pope and the devil, being assured that "one little word" of the Almighty can slay them. On this immovable rock the humble monk took his stand at the diet of Worms, *unus versus mundum*, strong in the sense of his weakness, independent in the sense of his dependence, free in his obedience to God and the voice of his conscience. And he conquered notwithstanding the pope's bull and the emperor's ban: he conquered not by money or favor or any worldly power, but by the force of truth and of faith, which rings so mightily through his battle hymn of the Reformation, "*Ein feste Burg ist unser Gott.*"

> "With our own strength we nothing can,
> Full soon we were down-ridden;
> But for us fights the proper Man
> Whom God himself has bidden.
> Ask ye, who is the same?
> CHRIST JESUS is his name,
> The Lord God Sabaoth
> He, and no other god,
> Shall conquer in the battle."

2. The second principle is *justification by grace through faith*, in distinction from justification by works or by faith and works as joint conditions. Faith is the pioneer of all great thoughts and deeds. It is the bond of confidence between man and man, between man and God. Christian faith is boundless trust in Christ, and lives and moves in Him. "The just shall live by faith," is the theme of the Epistle to the Romans. By faith Abraham became the father of a generation as innumerable as the stars in heaven; by faith Moses became the lawgiver of Israel; faith inspired the Psalms of David, and the prophecies of Isaiah; by faith the fishermen of Galilee were made fishers of men and pillars of the church. "Thy faith hath saved thee," we hear again and again from the lips of Christ in the Gospels, but never: "Thy works have saved thee;" or "charity has saved thee." "Whosoever believeth in me hath eternal life." We have it already here on earth; for faith makes us partakers of Christ, and Christ is life eternal. Faith, simple, childlike faith in Christ, as our all-sufficient Lord and Saviour, is the soul of true piety. This faith alone justifies, because it apprehends, appropriates and assimilates the grace of God in Christ, which is the only ground and cause of justification.

But faith, or rather the grace of God through faith, is also the root of sanctification. It overcomes the world and abounds in fruits of righteousness. In receiving Christ, faith receives a new life and a power of holiness which must at once manifest itself. Good works are necessary, not as conditions, it is true, but as evidences of justification, and a faith which shows no works is dead; it is no faith at all in the sense of Paul. The reformers insisted as strongly on a holy life as their opponents, and the moral condition of Protestant countries, to say the least, compares very favorably with any other. In the heat of polemics, Luther depreciated the Epistle of James, and could not reconcile him with his favorite Paul, who yet furnishes the key for the reconciliation in his pregnant phrase: "Faith working through love."[1] But in his best utterances, Luther did full justice to the working power of faith, which made him a reformer. "Faith," he says, in his Preface to the Epistle to the Romans, "faith is a living, busy, active, mighty thing, and it is impossible that it should not do good without ceasing. Faith does not ask whether good works are to be done, but before the question is put, it has done them already, and is always engaged in doing them. You may as well separate burning and shining from fire, as works from faith."

3. The third principle is the *general priesthood of believers*, in opposition to an exclusive hierarchy or priest-cast, which claims to be the indispensable mediator between God and man, and assigns to the laity the degrading position of passive obedience. Let us again quote from Luther, who always hit the nail on the head, and could say the deepest things in the plainest language. "It is faith," he says, "that makes men priests, faith that unites them to Christ, and gives them the indwelling of the Holy Spirit, whereby they become filled with all holy grace and heavenly power. The inward anointing—this oil, better than any that ever came from the horn of bishop or pope—gives them not the name only, but the nature, the purity, the power of priests; and this anointing have all they received who are believers in Christ." The general priesthood implies the right

---

[1] Πίστις δι' ἀγάπης ἐνεργουμένη, Gal. 5: 6.

and duty of every believer to read the Word of God in his vernacular tongue, to go directly to the throne of grace, and to take an active part in all the affairs of the church, according to his peculiar gift and calling. It makes the whole congregation an active, working, evangelizing power, and utilizes every member for the general good.

The saints of the Roman catholic church are an aristocracy or nobility of ordained priests, monks and nuns. But the New Testament calls all Christian believers "saints," whether ordained or not, whether married or single, because they are all consecrated by the same Holy Spirit and called to be perfect, as their Father in heaven is perfect. They are " an elect race, a royal priesthood, a holy nation, a people for God's own possession," that they and every one of them " may show forth the excellences of Him who called them out of darkness into his marvellous light."

The principle of the general priesthood of the Christian people is the true source of religious and civil freedom. It has never yet been fully realized in Europe, but has its widest prospects in the virgin soil of this vast republic under the sunshine of liberty, if we are true to our trust and avoid the dangers that threaten us. What else is universal suffrage but the application of that principle to the political and civil sphere? The true Christian is not only a priest, but also a king. He partakes of the threefold office and dignity of Christ, the prophetic, the priestly, and the kingly. As a king he has a share in the government of the people by the people and for the people.

But let us not forget that, as the general priesthood is based on faith in Christ, our only high-priest, so the general kingship is based on the moral power of self-government and discipline. Only he is truly free whom the truth has made free. That freedom alone can stand the test of time, and be a blessing to the people. A republic without the Bible, without the Lord's Day, without the Lord's Church, is an empty shell and will be broken to pieces.

4. These three great principles were in Luther not mere notions or scholastic formulas, but vital truths. They were the ripe fruits of his profound study of the Scriptures, and his severe ascetic self-discipline in the convent at Erfurt. He passed through that intense moral struggle described by St. Paul in the seventh chapter of the Romans. As St. Paul was a Pharisee of the Pharisees, so Luther was a monk of the monks, and law was to both a schoolmaster which led them to the freedom of the gospel. Hereafter he devoted his whole energy to the defense of that freedom, yet without running into the excesses of lawlessness. He became the chief expounder of the Epistle to the Galatians both in its protest against legalistic bondage and against antinomian license. He held fast to that "liberty wherewith Christ hath made us free." The great fundamental truths of the gospel continued to be his very life, his strength, his comfort, his joy. The Bible was his daily food, faith was the element in which he moved, and prayer was the breath of his soul and the last utterance from his lips.

Let us then, my fellow-students, learn this practical lesson from the Luther-celebration. Let us vitalize and individualize those great principles of which he stands out as a typical representative. Let us follow him as far as he followed Paul, and no further, and let us follow Paul as Paul followed Christ, the Lord and Master of all. Let us be theologians after God's own heart, mighty in the Scriptures, full of faith and good works, and fervent in prayer. Let us, as true priests, live in daily communion with God and consecrate our persons to His service which is perfect freedom.

Thus will you become a blessing to your generation, and help to prepare the way for that grander reformation and reunion of divided Christendom which the Lord of the Church will surely bring about in His own good way and time.

CREEDS AND CONFESSIONS OF FAITH.

THE BIBLE AND THE CREED.

THE Bible is the Word of God to man; the Creed is the answer of man to God. The Bible is the book to be explained and applied; the Creed is the Church's understanding and summary of the Bible. The Bible contains the truth itself, fresh, unerring, and unalterable, from the mouth of its author; the Creed is a human statement of the truth, more or less imperfect, fallible, and subject to improvement with the progressive knowledge of the Church. The Bible is the truth in the form of life and fact; the Creed is the truth in the form of logic and dogma. The Bible is the only and sufficient rule of faith (*norma credendi*); the Creed is the rule of public teaching (*norma docendi*) derived from the Bible, and guarding it against heretical perversion and corruption. The Bible contains all that is necessary to salvation; the Creed ought not to contain any article that is not clearly revealed. The authority of the Bible is divine and absolute; the authority of the Creed is ecclesiastical and relative. The Bible is the rule and corrective of the Creed, and must forever remain the final tribunal for the settlement of differences of creeds.

Christianity stands above both, for it made them both. The Creed is a mirror which reflects the Bible, and the Bible is a mirror which reflects Christ, who is the Way, the Truth, and the Life. We must not look *at* the mirror, but *through* the mirror to the glorious object which it reveals.

In the present divided state of Christendom there are as many creeds as there are churches and sects. They all profess to be derived from the Bible, or at all events to be consistent with it; while yet they differ, and in part are antagonistic and apparently irreconcilable. Let us first briefly review them in their historical order, and then see how far they agree and disagree, and how they may be harmonized.

THE CONFESSION OF PETER.

The first and fundamental creed, which must ever constitute the beating heart of every other, is Peter's answer to his Master's question, "Who say ye that I am?" It is the confession of his personal faith that the man Jesus of Nazareth is "the Christ, the Son of the living God." He saw in Him the promised Messiah, the Saviour from sin, and the highest revelation of the infinite Jehovah.

This confession came not from flesh and blood, but was revealed to the mind and heart of Peter by our heavenly Father, through the Holy Spirit. This confession, as proclaimed by Peter, is the immovable rock on which Christ, the divine architect, built his Church on the day of Pentecost when Peter fulfilled the prophecy of his new name and converted three thousand souls to his Lord. This confession is the standard and rule of every creed, which is true or false in proportion as it agrees with or departs from its spirit. Christ, the God-Man, the Lord and Saviour, is the beginning, the middle, and the end of our Christian faith and spiritual life. Every other article must cluster around this Christological centre. The creed of the reunited Church of the future will be but an expansion of the confession with which it started. Gold and silver, and many precious stones of divine truth, have been built upon this foundation, and they will remain; but the hay and stubble of error will be burned (1 Cor. 3: 12–15).

THE BAPTISMAL CREEDS OF THE ANCIENT CHURCH.

From the confession of Peter, in connection with the baptismal formula, have legitimately grown the rules of faith or

CREEDS AND CONFESSIONS OF FAITH. 137

baptismal creeds of the ante-Nicene Church. We find them incidentally mentioned in the writings of Irenæus, Tertullian, Novatian, Cyprian, Origen, Gregory Thaumaturgus, Eusebius, Cyril of Jerusalem, Ambrose, Rufinus, Augustin, Jerome, and others, as expressing the general faith of Catholic Christendom in distinction from Judaism and Heathenism, and the pseudo-Christianity of heretics. They were at first not committed to writing, but orally transmitted, and taught the catechumens shortly before baptism, as a part of "the secret discipline," which concealed the sacraments of baptism and the eucharist from the profanation of the heathen. They vary considerably in form and extent, but they all substantially agree, and resolve themselves into three articles in conformity to the Trinitarian basis of the baptismal formula, viz., belief in

God the Father Almighty,
And in Jesus Christ His Son, our Lord,
And in the Holy Ghost.

The other articles are arranged under these three heads; to the Father being ascribed the creation, to the Son the redemption, and to the Holy Ghost the sanctification, which will be completed in the resurrection of the body and the life everlasting. In all these forms the second article is made the most prominent, and includes the principal facts in the life of Christ from His supernatural conception to His ascension and return from heaven to judge all men.

THE ŒCUMENICAL CREEDS.

The Œcumenical Creeds are an expansion of the ante-Nicene rules of faith, and superseded them for public use. The Western or Latin forms matured in what is called the APOSTLES' CREED, the Eastern or Greek forms culminated in the NICENE CREED. They are likewise Trinitarian and predominantly Christological; they profess the same faith—in one God, the Father Almighty, Maker of heaven and earth; and in Jesus Christ his Son, our Lord, who became man for our salvation, suffered and died on the cross, rose again from the dead, and ascended to heaven, from whence He shall come to judge the quick and the dead; and in the Holy Ghost, who applies to the believer the benefits of Christ in the Holy Catholic Church and the communion of saints through the means of grace.

The Nicene Creed differs from that of the Apostles only in this: it is more theological, and emphasizes more clearly and forcibly the divinity of Christ and His essential coëquality (*homoousia*) with the Father, in opposition to the Arian heresy which agitated the Eastern Church for half a century, and was the occasion of the first two Œcumenical Councils held in the East (325 and 381).

These two venerable Creeds are to this day the common doctrinal bond of union between the three great branches of Christendom—the Greek, the Latin, and the Evangelical—and between the different ages of the Church. They can never be abolished or superseded. They carry with them an authority and force as no other confession.

It is true the famous clause *Filioque*, inserted in the Latin text of the Nicene Creed since the year 589, is still a bone of contention between the Eastern and Western Churches; the former, looking chiefly to the divine unity and the dignity of the Father, strictly adheres to the single procession of the Holy Spirit; while the latter, in her zeal for the equality of the Son with the Father, teaches the double procession. This insertion ought never to have been made, as even Pope Leo III., in 809, admitted (herein differing from his infallible successors).[1] The difference should be left to the school, and should not disturb the unity and peace of the Church.

Besides the Apostles' Creed and the Nicene Creed, two other

[1] When appealed to by the delegates of Charlemagne in behalf of the *Filioque*, Leo caused the original Nicene-Constantinopolitan Creed, in Greek and Latin, to be engraved on two tablets of silver and suspended in the Basilica of St. Peter, as a perpetual protest against the innovation, although he approved the doctrine of the double procession.

CREEDS AND CONFESSIONS OF FAITH. 139

documents claim Œcumenical authority, at least in a secondary degree, namely, the Christological decision of CHALCEDON, 451, asserting against the Nestorian and Eutychian errors the inseparable and yet unmixed unity of the divine and human natures in the one Person of our Lord; and the so-called ATHANASIAN Creed of much later origin, which is the clearest and fullest creed statement of the doctrine of the Holy Trinity and the Incarnation, but has never been adopted by the Eastern Church, and is very seriously marred by three warning or damnatory clauses.[1]

THE GREEK CREED.

We now come to the conflicting Creeds of the Greek Catholic, the Roman Catholic, and the Evangelical Protestant Churches, which have grown up during the middle ages and modern times.

The Greek, or Oriental Creed, to which also the Orthodox Church of Russia adheres, embraces, first of all, the doctrinal decisions of the seven Œcumenical Councils—from 325 to 787 —and more particularly the Nicene Creed, which is made the basis of all catechetical instruction; in the next place, a number of confessions and catechisms, drawn up since the Reformation period, in opposition both to Romanism and to Protestantism. The most important of these are the orthodox confession of Peter Mogila, 1643, the Eighteen Decrees of the Synod of Jerusalem, 1672, and the Larger Catechism of Philaret, sanctioned by the Holy Synod of Russia, 1839.

The Greek Church dissents from the Roman Catholic mainly in the doctrine of the double procession of the Holy Spirit (the

---

[1] These damnatory clauses at the beginning, middle and end, make salvation depend on faith in the doctrine therein set forth, and have from time to time roused strong opposition to the public use of that creed in the Church of England, though thus far without effect. The Episcopal Church in the United States escapes the difficulty by omitting the Athanasian Creed from the Prayer Book altogether. Other Protestant churches (the Lutheran, Dutch, and German Reformed), although they expressly approve its doctrine, have never prescribed its use in public worship.

clause *Filioque*), and the doctrine of the Papacy. In rejecting the claims of the Papacy she sides with Protestantism, but from a different standpoint. In all other distinctive doctrines she is much nearer the Roman than the Protestant Church. The Greek Church teaches, in common with the Roman, *tradition* as the joint rule of faith with the Scriptures (but rejecting Papal infallibility); justification by faith *and works;* seven sacraments or mysteries (with minor differences on confirmation and extreme unction); transubstantiation (less clearly defined) and the unbloody sacrifice of the mass; a middle state and place of purification (though excluding the idea of material fire), with prayers for the dead; the worship of saints, angels, images, and relics, and especially of the Virgin Mary (though protesting against the Papal dogma of the Immaculate Conception).

The Greek and Russian Creed, then, is essentially un-Protestant. It includes many post- and extra-Scriptural additions, which we can never accept. But the Eastern Church, while she is considerably behind the Roman in culture, vitality, and energy, is not so fully committed to some of these traditions and to the condemnation of Protestantism, is less intolerant, and allows and encourages—at least in Russia—the circulation of the Bible in the vernacular. Moreover, by disowning infallibility (except in a general way), she leaves the door open for possible self-correction and improvement.

THE ROMAN CREED.

This is the most fully developed and clearly defined of all creeds. It rises from deep and strong foundations, like a Gothic cathedral, with a forest of turrets and statues, with painted windows, lofty pillars, side-naves, chapels and altars, and many strange mythological figures of idols and demons. Fathers, schoolmen, mystics, popes, and councils helped to rear the imposing structure until it finally reached its completion in the Vatican dogma of Papal infallibility. It has the tenacity and durability of the *urbs æterna*. It has its infallible interpreter in the oracle of the Vatican. It claims universal and absolute authority equal to the Word of the living God.

The doctrinal standards of the Roman church may be divided into two classes—the Tridentine and the Vatican.

The Tridentine symbols are the decrees and canons of the Council of Trent, the Profession of Pius IV. (or Profession of the Tridentine Faith), and the Roman Catechism. They date from the middle of the sixteenth century, and are directed against the Protestant Reformation. They fix the dogmas of Scripture and tradition as joint rules of faith, the extent of the Scripture canon including the Apocrypha, the authority of the Latin Vulgate, the primitive state and original sin, justification by works as well as faith, meritorious works, seven sacraments, transubstantiation, the withdrawal of the cup from the laity, the sacrifice of the mass for the living and the dead, auricular confession and priestly absolution, extreme unction, purgatory, indulgences, and obedience to the Pope as the successor of Peter and Vicar of Christ. All these dogmas were previously prepared by patristic and scholastic speculations, but more or less disputed in the Latin communion itself, until they received the solemn sanction of the Council of Trent.

The Vatican symbols are the definition of the Immaculate Conception (1854), the Papal Syllabus (1864), and the decrees of the Vatican Council (1870). They were issued under Pope Pius IX., either alone or in connection with his Vatican Council, just three hundred years after the Tridentine standards. They are directed partly against the infidelity of the nineteenth century, which has affected the Roman Church even more than the Protestant, partly against Liberal Catholicism (Gallicanism). They declare war against civil and religious liberty and the reigning spirit of modern civilization, and proclaim the dogma of the sinlessness of Mary, Papal absolutism, and Papal infallibility, which had hitherto been open and disputed questions among Romanists. They have occasioned the secession of the Old Catholics—the largest since the sixteenth century, and vastly outnumbering the previous Anglo-Catholic secession to Rome. They have provoked a new conflict between the Empire and the Papacy, between the civil and the ecclesiastical power. Vaticanism consolidates and intensifies Romanism, and widens the breach which separates it from the Eastern Church and from Protestantism.

THE EVANGELICAL CREED.

The Evangelical Creed is the result of the great Reformation of the sixteenth century in its conflict with the unscriptural doctrines and usages of the mediæval Papacy. It produced a split in the Western Church deeper and more comprehensive than the previous separation of the Latin and Greek Churches. It stands on the common basis of the Œcumenical Creeds, and expressly asserts its hearty consent to the ancient doctrines of the Trinity and the Incarnation. But it opened a new chapter in anthropology and soteriology, especially in those doctrines which relate to the subjective application of the Christian salvation, which had not yet been symbolically settled. Here the Reformers followed the lead of Augustin, the greatest among the fathers, in his views on sin and grace in opposition to the Pelagian and semi-Pelagian views which, though condemned, came practically to prevail in the mediæval Church.

But the Reformers went beyond the teaching of the ancient Church to the fountain-head of Christianity itself, and derived their creed directly from the New Testament, which was now more deeply and clearly understood and apprehended than ever before. Luther and Calvin republished the gospel of a free and full salvation, and renewed the protest of the Apostle of the Gentiles against the Roman Judaism, which depended upon outward observances and human performances, and by its innumerable traditions obscured and almost neutralized the word of the living God and the all-sufficient merits of Christ, as the traditions of the Pharisees had obscured the Old Testament.

The Evangelical Creed, in all its essential features, is identified with the Bible, from which it is derived; and hence it can never be destroyed. Protestantism encourages, while Romanism discourages, the popular distribution of the Scriptures, and this fact can be rationally explained only from the congeniality of Evangelical Christianity with Bible Christianity, and the want of harmony of Roman traditionalism with the same. The British and Foreign Bible Society, and the American Bible Society, circulate probably a greater number of copies of the Scriptures in one year than the entire Roman Church has done within the last three centuries. The Popes have more than once denounced Protestant Bible Societies as pests of society.

The fundamental doctrines of the Evangelical Creed, as distinct from the Greek and the Roman, are these three:—

First, The sovereign authority of the Word of God, as the only and sufficient rule of the Christian faith, to which all ecclesiastical traditions must be subordinated. This is the objective (usually called the formal) principle of Protestantism.

Secondly, Justification by the sole merits of Christ, as apprehended by faith, without works of our own, which are indeed necessary as fruits or evidences, but not as conditions, of justification. This is the subjective (or material) principle.

Thirdly, The general priesthood of believers, and their right and privilege of direct access to God in Christ and to His Word, without the restraining intervention of a special priesthood, the intercession of saints, and the teaching of tradition. This may be called the ecclesiastical or social principle.

From this common positive basis the Evangelical Creed protests against the tyranny and misbelief of the Papacy, on the one hand, and the licentiousness and unbelief of ancient and modern heresies on the other. But it claims no perfection and infallibility—hence it requires no blind and absolute submission. It bows before the sovereign authority of God's revelation, and, believing in a progressive understanding and application of the Bible, it keeps itself open to new and better light.

LUTHERANISM AND REFORM.

The Evangelical Creed is divided into the Evangelical Lutheran and the Evangelical Reformed. They differ on the doctrines of the Lord's Supper and Predestination, but agree substantially in almost every other article of faith, and hence they admit of a union (which was actually introduced in Prussia and other German states). The Lutheran Creed is mainly laid down in the Augsburg Confession of 1530, Luther's Small Catechism of 1529, and the Formula of Concord, 1577; that of the Reformed Churches in the Second Helvetic Confession of 1566, the Heidelberg Catechism, 1563, the French, Belgic, and Scotch Confessions, all of the same age, the Thirty-nine Articles of the Church of England, the Decrees of the Synod of Dort, and the Westminster Confession and Catechisms. The Reformed Confessions, owing to the many geographical and national divisions they represent, are more numerous than the Lutheran; but they agree as fully in every article. This was shown long ago in an interesting work, "The Harmony of the Orthodox and Reformed Churches," which was prepared under the direction of Theodore Beza, and appeared at Geneva, 1581.[1]

LATER EVANGELICAL CREEDS.

The Reformation has proved a fruitful mother of many daughters; and, with her elastic notions of Church unity, she

---

[1] "*Harmonia Confessionum Fidei Orthodoxarum et Reformatarum Ecclesiarum quæ . . . . sacram evangelii doctrinam pure profitentur,*" etc. An English translation was published at Cambridge, 1586, then at London, 1643, and a revised edition by Peter Hall in London, 1842. The work grew out of a desire for one common creed of the Reformed Churches, but took the shape of a selected harmony, which presents, under nineteen sections, full extracts from all the leading Reformed, and also from three Lutheran Confessions (viz., the Augsburg, the Saxon, and the Würtemberg Confessions), with a view to show their agreement on all the important articles of faith. It is the first attempt at a system of comparative symbolics and Evangelical irenics. It was intrusted to Beza, Daneau, and Salnar, and executed mainly by Salnar. The same irenical aim prompted the collection and publication of the *Corpus et Syntagma Confessionum Fidei*, Geneva, 1612; second ed. 1654.

allows them to set up independent households. We must admit, however, that every Protestant Church establishment has shown more or less intolerance against dissenters, which crops out of selfish human nature wherever it has the power.

Since the sixteenth century there have grown up within the Protestant communion, especially in England, a number of separate denominations, such as Congregationalists, Baptists, Arminians, Quakers, Methodists, Moravians, which hold fast to the supreme authority of the Bible and the principles of the Reformation, yet differ from the Lutheran and Calvinistic Creeds in minor points of doctrine or discipline, and are fulfilling an important and useful mission of their own. God has blessed them just as much as he has blessed the older communions, from which they either voluntarily seceded or have been expelled. Their growth and success entitle them to a full recognition among the regular divisions of Christ's army, and demand a revision of the traditional terminology in ecclesiastical geography and statistics. The Continental division of all orthodox Christendom into three Churches—the Catholic (Greek and Roman), the Lutheran, and the Reformed—and the odious designation of all the rest as mere *sects*, will answer no longer. The English distinction between Churchmen (or Episcopalians) and Dissenters (or Nonconformists) has no meaning in the United States, where all Christian denominations are independent of the civil government, and on a perfect equality before the law. For any one of these Protestant denominations to call itself *the Church*, and all the rest *sects*, is simply absurd, and implies presumption, or ignorance, or both. Such exclusiveness may do for Romanists, with whom it is natural and consistent; but among Protestants it is a solecism and barbarism.

We must recognize, then, in our common Protestant Christianity, a number of distinct types, which are equally Protestant and Evangelical, and equally necessary and useful in the particular fields of labor which the Great Head has assigned them.

There is an abundance of work for them all both at home and in heathen lands.

THE PROBLEM OF REUNION.

How shall these conflicting creeds be harmonized, and a reunion of divided Christendom be brought about?

This question has challenged the attention of Melanchthon, Calixtus, Grotius, Leibnitz, Bossuet, Schleiermacher, Schelling, Döllinger, and other eminent divines and philosophers. It has called forth many conferences between Greeks and Latins, Protestants and Catholics, Lutherans and Calvinists, Calvinists and Arminians, Anglo-Catholics and Russo-Greeks. So far all the attempts at a reunion have failed, or resulted in greater alienation, or in partial and temporary compromises. They have been, at best, only noble efforts in a noble cause. The Old Catholics, under the lead of Dr. Döllinger, who, before the Vatican Council, was esteemed the first divine among the Roman Catholics of Germany, took up the mighty problem as a part of their peculiar mission, and held two union-conferences with Greek Catholics and Anglicans, in Bonn, 1874 and 1875, which resulted in a tentative formula of agreement on fourteen disputed articles; but so far this formula has no sort of official sanction or ecclesiastical authority, and is not likely to be recognized by the Greek or Anglican church. The problem therefore remains and is apparently as far from solution as ever. It is even increasing with every new division which springs up in the Protestant camp.

DIFFERENT KINDS OF UNION.

The different modes of attempting a doctrinal consensus of Christendom may be reduced to four:—

1. An *absorptive* union of all creeds in one.

This is the only kind of union which the Roman Catholic Church admits and aims at. She claims the monopoly of Christian truth, and regards all other creeds as heretical and schismatical. She will never yield an iota of her teaching, and cannot do it without giving up her claim to infallibility. There are also narrow-minded sectarians among Protestants, who hold up their own creed as the standard which all other Christians ought ultimately to adopt.

But it is an idle dream to suppose that the Greeks and Protestants will ever submit to the authority of the Pope, or that Romanists, *en masse*, will ever become Protestants, or that all Protestants will become either Lutherans, or Episcopalians, or Presbyterians, or Congregationalists, or Methodists, or Baptists. Some minor sects, which have no historical basis and no special mission, will no doubt disappear—the sooner the better; but the leading denominations will last to the millennium.

2. A *negative* union, which would give up all distinctive creeds, and adopt the Bible alone.

This scheme would resolve the holy Catholic Church into a Bible Society. It would undo the whole history of Christianity, which is impossible. It would require a reconstruction and repetition of the whole process of the past, with no prospect of a better result, unless human nature and the laws of historical development were radically changed. For as soon as we begin at the beginning and explain the Bible, the same questions of interpretation which led to different theological schools, denominations, and creeds, will come up again, one by one, and produce the same divisions. History is no child's play, but a steadily-progressing development of God's own plan, and the great storehouse of wisdom and experience for all time to come.

3. An *eclectic* creed, composed of fragments from all creeds.

This would be a syncretistic patchwork or mechanical compound of heterogeneous elements, and satisfy no party. A creed must be an organic growth, a living unit, and the product of inspiration by the spirit of truth.

4. A *conservative* union, which recognizes, from a broad and comprehensive evangelical catholic platform, all the creeds in their relative rights as far as they represent different aspects of

divine truth, without attempting an amalgamation or organic union of denominations. This seems to us the only view which consists with a proper respect for God's work in the history of the past.

THE DOCTRINAL CONSENSUS ALREADY EXISTING.

We must recognize, first of all, an already existing and well-established historical basis of concord among Christians. All true believers are one in Christ, their common Lord and Saviour, one in saving faith, one in love, one in hope, one in their spiritual life. This unity existed from the beginning in all ages, and is only marred and interrupted, but not destroyed, by ecclesiastical and sectarian divisions. The nearer we approach to Christ in prayer and devotion, the nearer we approach one another. The more Christ-like we become, the more we esteem and love the brethren. All Christians read the same Bible, drink from the same spiritual rock, can join in the same Psalms and the same *Te Deum* and *Gloria in excelsis;* Calvinists and Arminians forget their theological quarrels when they sing "Rock of Ages," of the Calvinist Toplady, and "Jesus, lover of my soul," of the Arminian Wesley. Moreover, there is not only a union of life and sentiment, but also a doctrinal union already at hand, which we must never lose out of sight.

1. In the first place we have, as already remarked, a common *œcumenical* basis in the *Apostles' Creed* and the *Nicene Creed* (waiving the disputed *Filioque*), which we hold and profess even with Greek and Roman Christians in distinction not only from all followers of false religions, but also from heretics and unbelievers. In our controversy with Rome, we should ever remember that we believe in the same Father, Son, and Holy Ghost, the same Divine-human Christ, and all those fundamental facts of our salvation which are set forth so plainly and forcibly in the venerable creeds of the undivided Church, our common mother. It is of the utmost importance to emphasize this fact in opposition to the fearful power of infidelity which has of late grown up in all sections of nominal Christendom, and

CREEDS AND CONFESSIONS OF FAITH. 149

threatens to overthrow the very foundations of our holy Catholic faith.

It is true, as *Protestant* Christians, we can never cease to protest against the spiritual tyranny and the unscriptural and dangerous innovations and corruptions of Popery. Yet even in this righteous and necessary warfare we should keep in mind that there is a material distinction between Catholicism and Popery, as there was between the Old Testament religion and the Jewish hierarchy at the time of Christ. There is no Roman error without an underlying truth from which the error derives its vitality and force, and which must be truly appreciated, in order successfully to refute the error. The great fault of Romanism is not that it denies the Bible, but that, like Pharisaism of old, it obscures and weakens its force by the human traditions accumulated upon it.

2. In the next place there is an *evangelical* consensus in all the Protestant creeds. All believing Protestants profess, as we have seen, the same fundamental principles, the supremacy of the Bible, justification by faith, direct communion with Christ, the universal priesthood of believers, and other important doctrines, with a corresponding negation of errors which are inconsistent with them. This consensus can easily be ascertained by a comparison of the different Lutheran and Reformed confessions, which agree much more than they disagree.

It is very desirable that this evangelical consensus should be clearly and briefly formulated in a way that could be adopted by the Protestant Churches as a bond of intercommunion, as an act of faith and worship, and would answer the same purpose for all Protestants as the Apostles' Creed does for all Christians. But such a creed would require the combined wisdom and charity of all the churches under the direction of the Spirit of Christ.

PRACTICAL SUGGESTIONS FOR PROMOTING A FREE UNION.

1. We must dismiss all idea of a perfect uniformity of belief. This, even if it were possible, would not be desirable. God's

truth is infinite, and cannot be fully comprehended by any one church or denomination, much less by an individual. God has constituted men's minds differently. No two are precisely alike. Every disciple reflects a peculiar lineament of the Great Master of all. Unity is not uniformity, but implies freedom and variety. It takes many sounds to produce a harmony, and many flowers of different shape, color, and flavor to make a garden.

The New Testament itself exhibits great variety in the unity of spirit. Every one of the four Gospels has a marked individuality in conception, plan, and style, and presents some peculiar aspects of the image of Christ. How different from Matthew, Mark, and Luke, is John who leaned on the Master's bosom; and yet his incarnate God is the same person with the Divine Man of the Synoptists. And if we examine the Epistles, we can clearly discern three distinct types of doctrine: the conservative Jewish Christian type of James and Peter, the progressive Gentile Christian type of Paul, and the higher union of the two in John. There is an apostle of hope, an apostle of faith, and an apostle of love. The harmony and the difference of the Old and New Testaments, the principle of authority and the principle of freedom, divine sovereignty and human responsibility, justification by grace and the necessity of personal holiness, are alike set forth in the apostolic writings, not as contradictory but as supplementary truths.

2. We must distinguish between truth and dogma. Truth is the divinely-revealed substance, dogma is the human form and logical statement of truth. Many may sincerely believe the truth as exhibited in the Word of God, and yet feel unable to accept as binding any dogmatic formula. Truth alone can save, not dogma. Theoretical orthodoxy is not always connected with living piety. It may be dead and worthless before God. "The devils also believe, and shudder." To feel right and to act right is as important as to think right and to believe right.

3. Another important distinction must be made between religious and theological differences. Learned Christians of

different denominations, or of the same denomination, may be at perfect harmony in their inward spiritual life, and yet they may widely dissent in their theology. Most of the differences of the orthodox creeds are not religious, but theological, and hence secondary or non-fundamental. It was a serious mistake of an intensely theological age to introduce so much logical and metaphysical theology into the creeds, and thus to intensify and perpetuate controversy, bigotry, and hatred. A creed is not a system of scientific theology. Many of the Confessions of the sixteenth and seventeenth centuries would be far better for being shorter, simpler, and more popular. But changes in public documents, once accepted, are inexpedient, and lead to endless trouble and confusion, as the history of the *Filioque*, and the *altered* Augsburg Confession, abundantly prove.

4. We must cultivate a truly evangelical catholic spirit, a spirit of Christian courtesy, liberality, and charity towards all, of whatever creed, who love our Lord and Saviour. We must subordinate denominationalism to catholicity, and catholicity to our common Christianity. We must be Christians, or followers of Christ, first and last, and followers of Luther, Calvin, Knox, Wesley, only so far as they themselves follow Christ. *Christianus sum, Christiani nihil a me alienum puto*. We are saved not by our human notions of divine truth, but by the divine truth itself—not by what separates us, but by what we hold in common, even Him who is above us all, and for us all, and in us all.

In the present divided state of Christendom, we must belong to a particular denomination, and are bound to labor for it with honest loyalty, zeal, and energy. But our steady aim should be, through our denomination, to serve and promote the kingdom of Christ alone. While living in one story and in one apartment of the great temple of God, as we must do if we are to live in the temple at all, we may maintain the most friendly and fraternal relations to our neighbors who occupy different apartments, yet worship and glorify the same God and the same

Saviour. It is wicked to hate and curse those whom God loves and blesses. We should rejoice in every victory won for Christ, in the erection of every new church or chapel, whatever name it may bear. If we love Christians of other creeds only as far as they agree with us, we do no more than the heathen do who love their own. We should love them also *because* of their peculiarities and differences, as far as these represent aspects of truth, and are prospered by God. Man admires and loves a woman for her *womanly* qualities, and woman admires and loves a man for his *manly* qualities. We must rise to a higher platform, from which we can recognize and bid God speed to every corps and division of the army of the great Captain of our salvation. Let our theology be as broad as God's truth and God's love, and as narrow as God's justice. Let us think more highly of others than of ourselves. Let humility and love be our cardinal virtues. Thus shall we prove true disciples of Him who died and rose for us all, and whose first and last command is to love God with all our heart, and our neighbor as ourselves.

Neither circumcision nor uncircumcision, neither Lutheranism nor Reform, neither Calvinism nor Arminianism, neither Episcopacy nor Presbytery, nor any other human distinction, availeth anything before God and at His judgment-seat, but a new creature in Christ Jesus. To Him we belong. In His name we are baptized, by His blood we are saved, Him alone let us love and serve as long as life lasts; and when we shall see Him as He is, not in a mirror darkly, but face to face, in all His loveliness and majesty, we shall reach in Him the solution of all perplexing problems on earth, the divine harmony of all discordant human creeds.

God speed the blessed time when we shall no more see Peter and Paul and Apollos standing in the foreground, but "Jesus alone," and be in Him and have Him in us, even as He is in the Father and the Father in Him!

THE CONSENSUS OF THE REFORMED CON-
FESSIONS,

AS RELATED TO THE PRESENT STATE OF EVANGELICAL
THEOLOGY.

[Read by appointment at the first session of the First General Presbyterian Council in Edinburgh, July 4, 1877].

CRANMER'S PROPOSAL OF A REFORMED CONSENSUS.

IN the year 1552, while the Council of Trent was framing its decrees against the doctrines of the Reformation, Archbishop Cranmer invited Melanchthon, Bullinger, Bucer, and Calvin to a conference in London, for the purpose of framing an evangelical union creed. To this letter Calvin replied that for such an object he would willingly cross ten seas, and that no labor and pain should be spared to remove, by a scriptural consensus, the distractions among Christians, which he deplored as one of the greatest evils.[1]

In this noble sentiment Calvin expressed the true genius of the Reformed Church, which has always been in favor of union on the basis of truth, and willing to cherish Christian fellowship with other evangelical Churches, notwithstanding minor differences in polity, worship, and even in dogma. Zwingli struck the key-note of this catholic spirit at the conference in Marburg when, with tears in his eyes, he offered the hand of brotherhood to Luther, though he could not agree with him on

[1] " *Quantum ad me attinet, si quis mei usus fore videbitur, ne decem quidem maria, si opus sit, ob eam rem trajicere pigeat. Si de juvando tantum Angliæ regno ageretur, jam mihi ea satis legitima ratio foret. Nunc cum quæratur gravis et ad Scripturæ normam probe compositus doctorum hominum consensus, quo ecclesiæ procul alioqui dissitæ inter se coalescant, nullis vel laboribus vel molestiis parcere fas mihi esse arbitror. . . . Mihi utinam par studii ardori suppeteret facultas !* " See the Correspondence in Cranmer's Works (Parker Soc. ed.), vol. II. p. 430-433.

the mode of Christ's presence in the Eucharist. Calvin once declared, that even if Luther should call him a devil, he would still revere and love him as one of the greatest servants of God.

Cranmer, the moderate and cautious reformer and martyr of the Church of England, the chief framer of its Liturgy and Articles of Religion; Melanchthon, "the preceptor of Germany," the gentle companion of the heroic Luther, the author of the Augsburg Confession, and the surviving patriarch of the German Reformation; Bullinger, the friend and successor of Zwingli, the teacher and benefactor of the Marian exiles, and the author of the most œcumenical among the Reformed Confessions; Bucer, the indefatigable, though unsuccessful, peacemaker between the Lutherans and Zwinglians, and the mediator between the Anglican and the Continental Reformation; Calvin, the master-theologian, commentator, legislator, and disciplinarian, who was then just in the prime of his power, and (in the language of John Knox) at the head of "the most flourishing school of Christ since the days of the apostles"—these representative men, assembled in Lambeth Palace or the Jerusalem Chamber, would have filled an important chapter in church history and challenged the assent of the Reformed Churches for a common confession of faith that embodied their learning, wisdom, and experience.

But the conference was frustrated by political events, and a Reformed union creed remains a *pium desiderium* to this day. "*Deus habet suas horas et moras.*" It was the will of Providence that the Continental and the English and American branches of the Reformed family should grow up independently, and fulfil their special mission to their age and country. Each shaped its own creed, polity, and worship. Thus, instead of one confession and one catechism which might have answered for all, we have as many confessions and catechisms as there are national and independent Churches, and even more.

THE REFORMED CONFESSIONS.

The Reformed Confessions may be divided into three classes —the ante-Calvinistic or Zwinglian, the Calvinistic, and the post-Calvinistic. The first represent the preparatory stage, and acquired only local authority in Switzerland. The second class were framed under the influence of Calvin's theology after the middle of the sixteenth century, simultaneously with the Tridentine standards of the Roman Church, and in vindication of the protest against Rome. The third class were made in the seventeenth century, and arose from theological controversies within the Reformed Church.

The confessional development of the Lutheran Church began with the Augsburg Confession in 1530, and was completed, after stormy controversies, in the Formula of Concord, 1577. The Roman Catholic system of doctrine received its pyramidal apex only in our age under the long reign of the first infallible pope by the decrees of the Vatican Council (1870). The symbolic tendencies of Romanism and Protestantism are opposite—the former may indefinitely increase the number of dogmas to the maximum of traditional orthodoxy, and can never give up or revise a single article without destroying its claim to infallibility; the latter diminishes the number to the minimum of scriptural belief, and allows a correspondingly larger freedom to private judgment and theological progress.

The chief Reformed symbols of the sixteenth century are— The *Gallican Confession*, for the Protestants of France (1559); the *Belgic Confession*, for the Netherlands (1561); the *Second Helvetic Confession*, for Switzerland and other countries (1566); the *Heidelberg Catechism*, for Germany and Holland (1563); the two *Scotch Confessions* (1560 and 1581), which were subsequently superseded by the Westminster standards; and the *Thirty-Nine Articles* of the Church of England (1563), which likewise belong to the Reformed type of doctrine, especially as explained and supplemented by the Lambeth Articles (1595), and the Irish Articles of Archbishop Ussher (1615), which prepared the way for the Westminster Confession.

The chief symbols of the seventeenth century are the *Canons of the Synod of Dort* (1619), which give the results of the Arminian controversy on the five knotty points of scholastic Calvinism, and the *Westminster Confession* and *Catechisms* (1647), which grew out of the mighty conflict between Puritanism and semi-Romanism, and sum up the results of what may be called the second Reformation of England. The Westminster standards present the ablest, the clearest, and the fullest statement of the Calvinistic system of doctrine. Although least known on the Continent, and given by Niemeyer merely as an appendix to his Collection of Reformed Confessions, they are the most important of the Reformed symbols, and have shown the greatest vitality. It is a remarkable fact that they were made by English divines for three kingdoms under the shadow of Westminster Abbey, and around the warm hearth of the historic Jerusalem Chamber, where churchmen and dissenters are now engaged in the revision of the English Bible for the use of English speaking Christendom. These standards were rejected in the land of their birth, but became the corner-stone of the Churches of Scotland and of Churches beyond the Atlantic and Pacific. Failing in England, they have shaped the theology and religion of countries and nations unknown to the authors. They have been adopted not only by Presbyterians, but also — with modifications on church polity and the doctrine of baptism, and with a reservation of greater freedom — by the orthodox Congregationalists, and the Regular or Calvinistic Baptists in Great Britain and America.

These Reformed Confessions form a very remarkable body of literature. They were composed by confessors and martyrs of the Reformed faith in times of the deepest intellectual and religious commotion, and in the face of cruel persecution. They are fraught with the memories of the most important period of church history, next to the creative period of the apostles.

CONSENSUS OF THE REFORMED CONFESSIONS. 157

They embody the biblical and theological learning and wisdom of the Reformers, and the ripe fruit of the gigantic struggle with the papal power which had kept the Christian world under discipline and in bondage for many centuries. They set forth, not abstract doctrines, but vital truths for which the confessors were ready to suffer exile, imprisonment, torture, and death. Some are indeed systems of theology rather than popular summaries of faith; but all are full of faith and enthusiasm for the truths of the gospel. They have fashioned the religious opinions and lives of many generations, and trained the most heroic races of Christians and the pioneers of civil and religious freedom—the Huguenots of France, the Burghers of Holland, the Puritans of England, the Covenanters of Scotland, and the Pilgrim Fathers of America. They will ever remain venerable monuments of a pure and heroic faith from the creative period of the evangelical Churches.

The Reformed (as also the Lutheran) Confessions were not intended by their framers to be binding formulas for subscription and checks upon theological progress. Otherwise they would have been made much shorter and simpler. They were originally apologetic documents or vindications of the evangelical faith against misrepresentation and slander. Hence some of them embody a large amount of controversial and metaphysical matter, and are too long and minute for popular use. They resemble the early Christian Apologies, with this difference, that they were directed against Romanism instead of Paganism, and represent a more advanced and mature stage in the development of Christian doctrine. Their official character and their intrinsic merits clothed them gradually with an ecclesiastical authority inferior only to that of the Holy Scriptures. They became the rule of all public teaching in the pulpit and the university. They were a sort of secondary rule of faith (the *norma normata*), derived from the primary rule of the Scriptures (the *norma normans*). They continued in force during the seventeenth and eighteenth centuries, and though since partly displaced in the Churches on the Continent, they still express the faith of some of the most enlightened and active sections of the Christian world.

THE HARMONY OF THE REFORMED CONFESSIONS.

The Reformed Confessions present the same system of Christian doctrine. They are variations of one theme. There is fully as much harmony between them as between the six symbolical books of the Lutheran Church, or between the Tridentine and Vatican decrees of Rome. The difference is confined to minor details, and the extent to which the Augustinian and Calvinistic principles are carried out; in other words, the difference is theological, not religious, and logical rather than theological.[1]

The Reformed Confessions are Protestant in bibliology, œcumenical or old catholic in theology and christology, Augustinian in anthropology and the doctrine of predestination, evangelical in soteriology, Calvinistic in ecclesiology and sacramentology, and anti-papal in eschatology.

Let us briefly explain this.

1. BIBLIOLOGY OF THE RULE OF FAITH.—The Reformed symbols unanimously teach, as a fundamental principle of Protestantism, the divine inspiration and absolute and exclusive authority of the canonical Scriptures of the Old and New Testaments in all matters of the Christian faith and morals, in opposition to the Roman Catholic doctrine of ecclesiastical traditions, as a co-ordinate rule of faith and infallible interpreter of the Scriptures. This doctrine is most clearly and fully set forth in the first chapter of the Westminster Confession, which is an acknowledged masterpiece of symbolic statement.

The Lutheran Church and the Anglican Church maintain the

---

[1] The documentary proof of this agreement was furnished long ago by extracts from the Confessions themselves, in the *Harmony of Confessions*, prepared and published under the direction of Beza at Geneva, 1581, in Latin, and translated into English (Cambridge, 1586, also London, 1643, and 1842)

same principle, but in practice they allow tradition and the voice of the early fathers and councils a greater authority and influence than the Calvinistic Churches, especially in matters of church polity and worship.

2. THEOLOGY and CHRISTOLOGY.—The œcumenical articles of the unity and tripersonality of the Godhead, the incarnation and the theanthropic constitution of Christ's person, were expressly endorsed by all the Reformers; and hence the Apostles' Creed and the Nicene Creed (to a less extent also the Athanasian Creed so-called) were retained in the Protestant Churches.

Herein the Protestant symbols agree with the orthodox Greek and the Roman Catholic standards, in opposition to ancient and modern Trinitarian and Christological heresies. A difference sprung up between the Lutheran and Reformed Christology, in connection with the Eucharistic controversy, concerning the extent of the *communicatio idiomatum* and the ubiquity of Christ's body, but this subject belongs to the obscurest corner of theological metaphysics, and does not affect the great truth of God manifest in the flesh, which is taught by both Churches with equal emphasis. The Reformed Christology is more simple and natural than the Lutheran, and accords better with the historical Christ of the Gospels.

3. ANTHROPOLOGY and SOTERIOLOGY.—The Reformed symbols teach the Augustinian views of sin and grace, that is, the total depravity and condemnation of the whole human race in consequence of Adam's fall, and the absolute sovereignty and sufficiency of divine grace in the work of salvation. They strongly emphasize these doctrines in opposition to the then prevailing Semi-Pelagianism of the Latin Church, with its mechanical legalism and meritorious works on which salvation was made to depend. The Reformers passed through the experience of St. Paul; they felt the operation of the law upon the heart and conscience, as a schoolmaster leading to Christ. They started with an overwhelming sense of the awful fact of sin and the absolute need of redemption. Their theology was

intensely practical, and turned on the question, What shall a man do to be saved, and how shall a sinner be justified before a holy and righteous God? To this the New Testament, and especially the Epistles to the Romans and Galatians, returned the answer, "Not by any works and institutions of man, not by any outward observances and performances, but solely by the free grace of God in Christ, which is the beginning, the middle, and the end of spiritual life." Thus salvation by grace became the central doctrine, the experimental or subjective principle of evangelical Protestantism, and a fountain of comfort and peace in life and in death.

The Reformed system went back to the ultimate source of free salvation in the pre-mundane eternal act of election, upon which the historical process of salvation in all its stages depends; while Luther made the experimental fact of justification by faith alone, the article of the standing or falling Church. The Reformed system, moreover, lays greater stress on holiness and good works, as the necessary manifestation of justifying faith.

In anthropology, the Reformers were entirely under the spell of the anti-Pelagian writings of St. Augustin, whom they revered as the greatest, soundest, and most evangelical among the fathers. But his anti-Manichæan and anti-Donatist writings are more on the Roman Catholic than on the Protestant side of the controversy. Zwingli, with his classical rather than mediæval training, was independent of patristic authority, and taught a milder view of hereditary sin and guilt than either Luther or Calvin. The Augustinian system always had some able advocates in the Latin Church, but was overshadowed by hierarchical, sacramentarian, and ascetic tendencies; while the Greek Church adhered to the less definite, we might say, semi-Pelagian views of the older Fathers, and lays great stress on the freedom of will.

The Protestant soteriology differs from the Augustinian, at least in form, and is more evangelical. Augustin, who was poorly acquainted with Greek and Hebrew, and followed the Latin version of the Bible, had the Roman Catholic conception of justification, understanding it to be a gradual process of making just (which virtually identifies it with sanctification); while the Protestant divines, in accordance with the Hellenistic usage of the corresponding Greek terms[1] viewed justification as a forensic or declaratory act of acquittal from the guilt and condemnation of sin, on the ground of the merits of Christ, and on condition of faith apprehending Christ, to be necessarily followed by gradual growth in holiness. Justification is the beginning of sanctification, yet distinct from it as a single act is from a gradual process, as birth is from the life which follows.

4. PREDESTINATION.—The symbols teach the positive decree of an eternal and unchangeable *election* of believers to holiness and blessedness, and the perseverance of saints as a necessary means to that end; while the rest are left to the consequences of their sin. All men are justly condemned, but God in his sovereign mercy chooses to elect a part from this mass of corruption, and to reveal in them the boundless riches of his grace in Christ. This is the amount of the Reformed dogma of predestination as far as it has any practical religious value, and is taught directly or indirectly in all symbols. The negative decree of *reprobation* is either wisely passed by in the Confessions (as in the second Helvetic Confession, the Thirty-Nine Articles, and the Heidelberg Catechism), or is mentioned only as a judicial act in view of foreseen sin and guilt. The fall of Adam is put under a *permissive* (not an *efficient* or *causal*) decree, and the blasphemous doctrine that God is in any sense the author or approver of sin, is expressly and emphatically condemned by all the Reformed Confessions and theologians.

This is the infralapsarian scheme of redemption which Augustin taught as a necessary consequence of his doctrine of universal damnation in Adam, and the total moral inability of man. The supralapsarian scheme, which differs from the former in

[1] Δικαίωσις and δικαιόω.

the order of the decrees, and, with a severer but terrible logic, includes the fall as a necessary negative condition for the manifestation of God's redeeming mercy on the elect, and his punitive justice on the reprobate, was held as a private opinion by some eminent Calvinists such as Beza, Gomarus, Twiss, but it is not taught in any Confession; even the Canons of Dort, the Westminster Confession, and the Helvetic Consensus Formula, which are most pronounced on the doctrine of decrees, stop within the limits of infralapsarianism. And it should be noticed that the Westminster Confession expressly teaches the freedom of will as well as foreordination, and leaves the solution of the apparent antinomy to scientific theology.[1] It is also a remarkable fact, that in the Westminster Assembly, as the recently published Minutes show, the scheme of a universal offer of salvation or hypothetical universalism found advocates among the ablest and most influential members, such as Calamy, Arrowsmith, Vines, and Seaman.[2]

The subject of election holds a prominent, and, we may say, a disproportionate place in the Calvinistic system. It was a necessary and wholesome reaction against the papal doctrine of human merit. It was considered as the backbone of the doctrines of free grace, and was death to all pride and self-righteousness. It furnished an immovable basis in eternity for the salvation in time, and the most solid comfort to the believer in seasons of despondency and temptation. Hence we find it among all the Reformers. Luther, in his tract on *The Slavery of the Human Will*, which he never recalled, but regarded as one of his best books, goes even further in this direction than Calvin ever did. Melanchthon was at first almost a fatalist (tracing the fall of Adam, the adultery of David, and the

---

[1] Chapter III. 1: "God from all eternity did, by the most wise and holy counsel of his own will, freely and unchangeably ordain whatsoever comes to pass; yet so as thereby neither is God the author of sin, nor is violence offered to the will of the creatures, nor is the liberty or contingency of second causes taken away, but rather established.'

[2] See my work on the *Creeds of Christendom*, vol. I. p. 770

treason of Judas to the will of God), but afterwards he suggested what is called the system of Synergism (an improved evangelical form of Semi-Pelagianism and an anticipation of Arminianism). The Formula of Concord, however, rejected it, and teaches total inability and unconditional election, yet at the same time also universal vocation, or the sincere will of God to save all men, and the resistibility of divine grace.[1] The difference between the Calvinistic and the Lutheran symbols is, that the former are more consistent with the Augustinian anthropology, and give greater prominence to election, while the latter emphasize baptismal grace and a universal call to salvation. But, in point of fact, the vast mass of mankind never hear the sound of the gospel within the limits of the present life, to which all orthodox systems confine the possibility of salvation. Calvinism reckons with actual facts as they appear to all observers, and traces them back to the inscrutable will of God, which is holy and wise, though we cannot fathom it.

5. ECCLESIOLOGY.—The Reformed symbols make an important distinction between the visible (actual) Church, which is manifold and exists in various organizations or denominations, and the invisible (ideal) Church, which is one and universal, and embraces all the elect or true believers of whatever denomination or sect. They also distinguish in each visible church or congregation between communicant members which constitute the church proper, and the nominal members or hearers. They lay stress on the necessity of discipline for the preservation of the purity and dignity of the Church. They maintain the right of ecclesiastical self-government, as distinct from the power of

---

[1] The later Lutheran divines since Hunnius endeavored to solve this contradiction of the Formula of Concord by a distinction between the single *voluntas antecedens* by which God, from eternity foreseeing (not foreordaining) the fall of Adam, resolved to save *all* men, and the double *voluntas consequens* whereby, foreseeing that some would believe and some would not believe, he resolved (likewise from eternity) to save those who would believe, though not *propter fidem*, but *per fidem* or *ex prævisa fide*, and, on the other hand, to condemn those who would not believe.

the Civil Magistrate; although in practice this right is more or less abridged wherever the Church is united to the State and supported by the State. (For self-government and self-support go together; and he who pays claims the right to rule.) The Reformed standards teach the parity of ministers, the institution of lay-elders and deacons representing the people, and presbyterial and synodical legislation and administration. The presbyterian form of government was born in Geneva, but fully developed in Holland, Scotland, and the United States.

Herein the Presbyterians differ from Episcopalians on the one hand, who maintain episcopacy and three orders of the ministry, and from Congregationalists on the other, who deny the legislative authority of presbyteries and synods, and teach the independence of each congregation properly constituted according to the Word of God. But the questions of presbytery, episcopacy, and independency are questions of polity, not of dogma. Moreover, the Church of England in her early standard writers (as the Reformers, and Hooker) holds that episcopacy is the best, not the only, form of government, and necessary for the well-being, but not for the being, of the Church. She never officially denied the validity of non-episcopal orders, and even expressly acknowledged them in various ways down to the period of Laud, the first typical high-churchman, who, when he defended the principle of exclusive episcopacy was censured by the authorities of the University of Oxford. The unwise and unrighteous attempts of the Stuarts to force episcopacy upon the reluctant people of Scotland have made the difference much greater than it originally was in the mind, of Calvin and Knox, as well as of Cranmer, Latimer, and Ridley.

6. SACRAMENTOLOGY.—The two sacraments of the New Testament are significant sealing ordinances, whose efficacy depends on the faith of the recipient. The *opus operatum* theory, the necessary connection of water baptism with moral regeneration, and all materialistic conceptions of the real presence,

CONSENSUS OF THE REFORMED CONFESSIONS. 165

whether in the form of transubstantiation or consubstantiation, are rejected.

Here lies the only serious doctrinal difference between the Calvinistic and the Lutheran symbols. The former make spiritual regeneration independent of water baptism, so that it may either precede or succeed it or coincide with it, according to the divine pleasure; and they teach a spiritual real or dynamic and effective presence of Christ in the Eucharist for believers only, while unworthy communicants receive no more than the consecrated elements to their own judgment. The latter teach unconditional baptismal regeneration, and a corporeal real presence of the true body and blood of Christ in, with, and under the visible elements, for all communicants, unworthy as well as worthy, though with opposite effects. The Lutheran theory of the real presence and oral manducation requires for its dogmatic support either a perpetual miracle (as the Roman theory of transubstantiation), or the hypothesis of the ubiquity of Christ's body (taught by Luther and the Formula of Concord). This hypothesis is rejected by all branches of the Reformed Church as being inconsistent with the limitation of all corporeal substances, and with the facts of Christ's visible ascension to heaven and future return from heaven. Some of the ablest Lutheran divines, however, sustain on purely philological grounds the Reformed or figurative interpretation of the words of institution, and admit that a literal interpretation of them would lead rather to transubstantiation, which they reject.

The Church of England teaches in her formularies the Calvinistic theory of the sacraments in general, and of the Lord's Supper in particular; but in the baptismal service of the Book of Common Prayer she renders thanks for the regeneration of every baptized infant,[1] and in practice she gives larger scope than the Presbyterian Churches to the sacramentarian principle.

---

[1] "We yield thee hearty thanks, most merciful Father, that it hath pleased thee to regenerate *this infant* with the Holy Spirit, to receive *him* for thine own *child* by adoption, and to incorporate *him* into thy holy church." Many

7. ESCHATOLOGY.—The Reformed (as well as all other Protestant) symbols recognize but two places and states in the invisible world—heaven for believers and hell for unbelievers, with different degrees of bliss and misery, according to the degrees of holiness and wickedness. They unanimously reject the mediæval fiction of an intervening purgatory for imperfect believers, with its gross superstitions and abuses. But the doctrine of the middle state of all departed spirits between death and resurrection, which is distinct from the question of purgatory, was left unsettled, and is to this day a matter of theological speculation rather than positive doctrine. It is characteristic that the scriptural distinction between Sheol or Hades, and Gehenna or Hell, is obliterated in the Lutheran, the English, and other Protestant versions.

THE THEOLOGICAL REVOLUTION.

This body of doctrine laid down in the Confessions, maintained its hold upon the Reformed Churches of Switzerland, Germany, France, Holland, England, and America for more than two centuries, and is still a living power in those Churches. It was analyzed, systematized, and developed in all its details by the scholastic theology of the seventeenth century, which forms a worthy parallel to the mediæval scholasticism of the Latin Church in its relation to the patristic doctrines, being nearly equal to it in metaphysical subtlety, and superior in solid scriptural learning. But all forms of scholasticism are apt to degenerate into a dry and sterile intellectualism, and to provoke a reaction.

After the middle of the eighteenth century, which may be called the century of revolution, a destructive tornado swept over the Churches of the Continent, and threatened to carry away the very foundations of Christianity. It began with

Anglican divines, however, make a proper distinction between baptismal and moral regeneration, as also between regeneration (as the act of God) and conversion (as the act of man).

Deism in England, which substituted a meager skeleton of natural religion for the revealed religion of the Bible; but the progress of Deism was checked by the Methodist revival, and the apologetic works of Butler and Lardner. In France Deism degenerated into blasphemous Atheism. Voltaire and Rousseau, the apostles of infidelity and architects of ruin, undermined the foundations of Romanism which, by cruelly persecuting the Huguenots and casting out the Jansenists, provoked the Revolution with its reign of terror and insane attempt to destroy the Christian religion. In the Lutheran Church of Germany the negative movement assumed the more serious form of Rationalism which, in its various phases and stages, revolutionized exegetical, historical, and systematic theology. The Reformed Churches of Great Britain and North America, owing to their isolation and their better organization, remained, upon the whole, faithful to their doctrinal and disciplinary standards; but in the Reformed Churches of the Continent the symbolical books were nearly all abolished or reduced to a dead letter, and it seems impossible to restore them to their former authority.

This theological revolution or pseudo-reformation has done, and is still doing, an incalculable amount of harm; but it was a revolt of reason against the tyranny of symbololatry, and proved a wholesome purgatory of orthodoxy. It dispelled old prejudices, and stimulated new and deeper inquiry; it advanced biblical philology and criticism, and enriched the stores of historical knowledge. It compelled the investigation and recognition of the human aspect and fortunes of Christianity in opposition to the exclusive consideration of its unchangeable divine aspect. Thus error is always providentially overruled for the progress of truth.

THE REVIVAL OF EVANGELICAL THEOLOGY.

The nineteenth century may be characterized as the century of revival and reconstruction. Rationalism, indeed, is by no means dead; it continues, in the name of biblical criticism, speculative philosophy, natural science, and humanitarian culture, to undermine the historical foundations of Christianity and all faith in a supernatural revelation; it penetrates the masses by the endless ramifications of the periodical press, which has become a formidable rival of the pulpit. But the antidote is also at hand. An evangelical theology has sprung up which is successfully combating error in all its forms. There is more general intelligence, more vital energy and activity, and a great deal more charity and catholicity in Protestantism than ever before. Bible distribution, home and foreign missions, literary and benevolent institutions are steadily increasing. Germany has taken the lead in the theoretical part of this work of reconstruction, and has been for the last fifty years the chief workshop of evangelical theology, as it has been of Rationalism; while England and America have carried on mainly the practical work of religion, and are above all other nations intrusted with the preservation and spread of Bible Christianity to the ends of the earth. Both are coming nearer and nearer together through their literature and personal intercourse, to their mutual benefit. The Teutonic and the Anglo-Saxon races united are a match for the world. We need not fear the final issue of the present conflict with scepticism and infidelity. What the great Athanasius said of the short and abortive reign of Julian the Apostate, may be applied to every phase of error and unbelief: "It is a little cloud, it will soon pass away." Christianity, which has overcome so many foes, and grown stronger in every battle, will no doubt survive; its past is secure, and affords the best guarantee for the future.

THE RELATION OF MODERN EVANGELICAL THEOLOGY TO THE REFORMED CONFESSIONS.

The religious revival of the nineteenth century in the Protestant Churches is a return to the faith of the Reformation as laid down in the Bible and the symbolical books. But it is not a mere restoration of the old, it is also a free reproduction and an advance. The faith is the same, the theology is different. It is different in the form of statement and the relative importance and arrangement of topics. Every age must produce its own theology adapted to its peculiar condition and wants.[1] Thus we have a patristic theology, a scholastic theology, a Reformation theology, and a modern evangelical theology, not to speak of the various shades of denominational theologies. Divine truth, as revealed in the Scriptures, is unchangeably the same yesterday, to-day, and forever; but it must be ever reproduced, newly appropriated, and represented in all its phases. The human understanding and exposition of the truth is steadily progressing with the Church itself, though passing through many obstructions and reactions. Every true progress in theology is conditioned by a deeper study and understanding of the Word of God, which is ever new, and renewing the Church, and will ever remain the infallible and inexhaustible fountain of revealed truth. The Scriptures may have been studied more intensely and devoutly in former ages, but they were never studied so extensively and with such an array of facilities and advantages as at the present age. Every progress in exegesis must have its effect upon systematic theology and the symbolic statement of truth.

Let us endeavor to indicate the points of difference between the modern and the old theology of the Reformed Churches as viewed from an œcumenical point of view, and leaving room for some qualifications in detail. Upon the whole, the Anglo-American theology is more orthodox in the historical sense than the Continental, but in some points it is more liberal. I have to take an average view before this Assembly which represents all sections of the Reformed Church, and I may be permitted to

[1] [In the discussion which followed, Dr. Begg of Edinburgh took exception to this statement, and said that "all theology was contained in the first promise given in Paradise." To this Dr. Ormiston of New York (himself a native of Scotland, "brought up on oat cakes and the Shorter Catechism") aptly replied: "Very true. In like manner the human race was also contained in Paradise, but it has been wondrously developed since."]

say that, within the last six months of travel through Europe and the East, I had special opportunities to ascertain the state of theological sentiment on all the leading questions on which I shall touch.

I. BIBLIOLOGY. — On the fundamental and preliminary question of the divine authority and absolute sovereignty of the canonical Scriptures as the only infallible rule of faith, the position of the Reformed Confessions after an experience of three centuries stands unaltered and impreguable. This is to-day, as it was in the sixteenth century, the *articulus stantis vel cadentis ecclesiæ evangelicæ*, as the article of the divinity of Christ is the *articulus stantis vel cadentis ecclesiæ Christianæ*. "The Bible, the whole Bible, and nothing but the Bible," said Chillingworth, "is the religion of Protestants." Since the rise of Rationalism and the development of Vatican Romanism, it is all the more important to maintain our stand upon the immovable rock of God's truth, without deductions or additions. Christ and his gospel are the sum and substance of evangelical Protestantism, as the Church and her traditions are the sum and substance of Roman Catholicism. Protestantism stands or falls with the Bible, Romanism stands or falls with the papacy. We cannot go back to Romanism; still less can we surrender ourselves to the icy embrace of Rationalism. We should, indeed, honor and consult the universal voice of Christendom, and allow it full weight in the interpretation of the Bible; nor should we despise reason, which God has given us as the organ for ascertaining and understanding his revealed truth; but the final appeal must always be to "the Law and the Testimony." Tradition and reason are not the divine Light itself, but, like John the Baptist, they "bear witness of that Light," that "all men through them might believe." *Amicus Calvinus, amicus Lutherus, amicus Augustinus, sed magis amica veritas, et verbum Dei est veritas.*

If the Holy Spirit himself could not clearly and unmistakably point out the way of salvation, it is not likely that popes and councils, composed of sinful and erring mortals, can do it any better. If the teaching of our Lord in the Gospels and Epistles does not contain the pure Christianity, we look in vain for it in the whole domain of ecclesiastical literature.

We must therefore maintain the true infallibility of God's Word against the pretended infallibility of the Vatican, which, like Phariseeism of old, obscures and paralyzes the Bible by human additions; and against the fallibility of pseudo-Protestant Rationalism, which, like Sadduceeism, mutilates the Bible, and substitutes for it the uncertain guidance of human reason.

The divine authority of the Scripture implies, of course, its divine inspiration, and has no sense without it. But as regards the *mode* of inspiration, which must be distinguished from the *fact* of inspiration, a considerable change has taken place among Protestant scholars. The mechanical or magical theory of the seventeenth century, which looked exclusively at the divine aspect of the Bible, and reduced the sacred writers to passive penmen of the Holy Ghost, has been abandoned for an organic theory which does full justice to the human and historical character of the Bible, and regards the authors as the free organs of the Spirit of God, representing the unity and harmony of eternal truth in a variety of gifts and modes of thought and style. The written Word is all divine and all human, and reflects the theanthropic character and glory of the personal Logos who became flesh for our salvation. As the recognition of Christ's full humanity, yet without sin, brings him nearer to us, so the recognition of the human element in the Bible, yet without error, ought to make it clearer to our understanding and dearer to our heart.

This view of inspiration was anticipated by Luther and Calvin, who, with the profoundest reverence for the divine substance of the Bible, had a very liberal view of its human form; it is not inconsistent with the Reformed Confessions, which simply assert the fact of the divine inspiration, without committing themselves to any particular theory of its mode. (The

Helvetic Consensus Formula, which teaches even the inspiration of the Hebrew vowel-points, makes an exception, but never acquired general authority.) The Westminster statement on this subject is as cautious and circumspect as it is clear and strong.

2. THE THEOLOGICAL STANDPOINT.—The theology of the Confessions was anti-Romish, and directed against the unscriptural traditions and additions of superstition or misbelief; the modern evangelical theology is anti-rationalistic, and directed against the deductions and negations of unbelief. The former had to deal with an excessive supernaturalism, the latter with the denial of the supernatural and miraculous. The former was chiefly concerned with anthropological and soteriological problems; the latter has to vindicate the authenticity and integrity of the Bible against negative criticism, the existence and personality of God against Atheism and Pantheism, and the true divinity and historicity of Christ against the mythical, legendary, and humanitarian pseudo-Christologies of the nineteenth century.

Hence some doctrines which were most prominent in the Reformation period must give precedence to others which were then not disputed by the contending parties. Modern theology is neither solifidian, nor predestinarian, nor sacramentarian, but Christological. The pivotal or central doctrine round which all others cluster, is not justification by faith, nor election and reprobation, nor the mode of the eucharistic presence, but the great mystery of God manifest in the flesh, the divine-human personality and atoning work of our Lord. In this respect modern theology goes back to the primitive confession of Peter (Matt. 16 : 16), and the criterion of John concerning the mark of Antichrist, who denies that "Jesus Christ is come in the flesh" (1 John 4 : 2, 3). The great question on which the very existence of Christianity depends is again asked: "Who do men say that I the Son of Man am?" And to this question the experience of eighteen centuries returns the answer of the first confessor: "Thou art the Christ, the Son of the living God." All evangelical denominations in their ablest divines are verging toward a Christological theology, in which alone they can ultimately adjust their differences. For the nearer they approach Christ, the nearer they will come to each other. Christ is the true concord of ages, the divine harmony of human discords.

3. CATHOLICITY.—The old theology was intensely polemical, denominational, and exclusive. It grew out of the gigantic struggle with the papacy, and in the heat of controversy did great injustice to the mediæval Church, which after all was the cradle of the Reformation, as Judaism was the cradle of Christianity. The war with Rome was followed by internal wars of equal bitterness between Lutheranism and Calvinism, Calvinism and Arminianism, Episcopacy and Presbytery, Presbytery and Independency. Disproportionate importance was attached to minor points of difference, and the elements of truth on the side of the opponent were ignored or denied.

There is still, and ever will be to the end of the world, a great deal of sectarian bigotry with which even the gods fight in vain, but it has lost its former hold upon the Christian people. The experience of three hundred years, and the vast increase of our knowledge of church history, with its lessons of wisdom and charity, have widened the theological horizon. Denominations which formerly stood in battle-array against each other have forgotten their old animosities and learnt to co-operate freely and heartily in catholic enterprises, and against the common enemies of Christianity. The articles of agreement are magnified above the articles of disagreement. The Old and New School Presbyterians of the United States, after a thirty years' theological war, have concluded a peace which it is hoped will never be broken, and the result so far has been increased vitality and energy. A similar union has taken place among Presbyterians in England, in Scotland, and in Canada, and will we trust extend still further, until all family feuds of the past shall be healed. The Evangelical Alliance has done much toward individual Christian union, and I trust that the

Presbyterian Alliance, while aiming to promote ecclesiastical or confederate union among the branches of the Presbyterian family, will not weaken but strengthen Christian union among believers of every denomination. Both Alliances were chiefly founded and are promoted by the same class of men, and are animated by the same spirit. The problem of Christian union and brotherhood is one of the great problems of the nineteenth century, and will work itself out in various ways until the great prophecy of the one Shepherd and one flock be fully realized.

4. MODERATION OF HIGH CALVINISM.—The scholastic Calvinists of the seventeenth century mounted the alpine heights of eternal decrees with intrepid courage, and revelled in the reverential contemplation of the sovereign majesty of God which seemed to require the damnation of the great mass of sinners, including untold millions of heathen and infants, for the manifestation of his terrible justice. Inside the circle of the elect all was bright and delightful in the sunshine of infinite mercy, but outside all was darker than midnight. This system of doctrine commands our respect, for it has produced a race of most earnest and heroic Christians, but it is nevertheless austere and repulsive; it glorifies the justice of God above his mercy; it savors more of the Old Testament than of the New, and is better at home on Mount Sinai than on Calvary. "God is love," and love is the only key that can unlock the deepest meaning of his words and works.

The greater liberality of modern Calvinism shows itself especially in the doctrine of predestination and infant salvation.

(*a*) The problem of *predestination* and of the relation of divine sovereignty to human responsibility is not yet solved, either philosophically or theologically, and will perhaps never be solved theoretically until we see face to face. But there is a practical solution in which all true Christians can agree, namely, that all who are saved are saved by the free grace of God without any merit of their own—and this is Calvinism; and

CONSENSUS OF THE REFORMED CONFESSIONS. 175

that all who are lost are lost by their own guilt in rejecting the gospel sincerely offered to them—and this is Arminianism. Good Calvinists preach like Methodists, as if everything depended on man; good Methodists pray like Calvinists, as if everything depended on God. St. Paul himself represents the fact that *God* works in us both the will and the deed, as the reason why *we* should work out our salvation with fear and trembling. This may be logically inconsistent, but finite logic is not the ultimate standard of infinite truth. God's logic is wider and deeper than man's logic.

Election by free grace and perseverance of saints (viewed as a duty as well as a divine gift) will no doubt always remain distinctive features of Calvinistic theology, as they are clearly and strongly taught in the Bible, but the decree of reprobation (except as a judicial act for the actual guilt of unbelief) is now rarely taught and never preached. If Presbyterians preach on the mystery of predestination at all, which is very seldom, they never forget, if they are wise, to mention human freedom and responsibility, and to trace man's ruin to his own unbelief. No Reformed Synod (at least on the Continent) could now pass the rigorous canons of Dort against Arminianism, which, after a temporary defeat, has silently leavened the National Church of Holland, and which, through the great Methodist revival, has become one of the most powerful converting agencies in Great Britain and America. The five knotty points of Calvinism have lost their point, and have been smoothed off by God's own working in the history of the Church.

(*b*) *Infant Salvation.*—It has now become almost an article of faith in the Reformed Churches, that all infants dying in infancy are saved by the atonement.[1] This is a liberal but entirely

---

[1] As far as America is concerned, Dr. Hodge positively affirms that "he never saw a Calvinistic theologian who held the doctrine of infant damnation in any sense." See his *System. Theology*, vol. iii., p. 605, and my work on *Creeds*, vol. i., p. 795. [To these references should be added a remarkable paper on *Infant Salvation* by Dr. George L. Prentiss, of the Union Theol. Seminary, New York, in the "Presbyterian Review" for 1883, pp. 548 sqq.]

legitimate development of the Calvinistic doctrine of election, which allows an indefinite extension of God's saving grace beyond the ordinary and visible means of grace. All systems which hold to the absolute necessity of water-baptism for salvation, lead logically to the horrible conclusion that all unbaptized infants dying in infancy, as well as all the heathen, that is, by far the greatest part of the human race past and present, are lost forever. It is a poor relief if Augustin, who taught this unchristian dogma, makes a distinction between negative damnation or absence of bliss, and positive damnation or actual torment, or if an old Calvinist of New England assigns to infants "the *easiest* room in hell." Hell is hell, and was made only for impenitent sinners who refuse to be saved. Zwingli was the first, but the only one among the Reformers (except his friend and successor, Bullinger), who had the courage to oppose this dismal view, and to teach the probable salvation of all infants, and of an indefinite number of adult heathen. The second Scotch Confession "abhors and detests," among the doctrines of the Roman Antichrist, "his cruel judgment against infants departing without the sacrament." The Westminster Confession teaches that "elect infants dying in infancy, and all other elect persons who are incapable of being outwardly called by the ministry of the word, are regenerated and saved by Christ through the Spirit, who worketh when, and where, and how he pleaseth." It is true, that some Calvinists and Westminster divines, make or imply a logical distinction between elect and reprobate infants; but the Calvinistic system does not define the limits of election, and hence allows the charitable assumption that all infants dying in infancy are among the elect, and that their removal from a world of temptation before committing any actual transgression and contracting personal guilt, is a proof of God's saving mercy to them. There can be no salvation without Christ, but salvation does not necessarily require an historical knowledge of the gospel any more than damnation requires an historical knowledge of Adam's fall. Our Saviour took special delight in children, blessed them and said: "Of such is the kingdom of heaven." It is *not* the will of our heavenly Father that "one of these little ones should perish."[1] The natural inference is, that none of them will perish; for nothing can come to pass without God's will.

5. RELIGIOUS LIBERTY.—The Calvinistic (as well as the Lutheran) Confessions presuppose a Christian State and a uniformity of belief among the people, and assign to the Civil Magistrate the duty not only to support the Church and its ministry, but also to punish heresy as an offence against society. The principle and practice of persecution for religious convictions prevailed almost universally since the days of Constantine and the union of Church and State, although the persecuted party always complained of the application on the ground of its own innocency. In the age of the Reformation the Anabaptists and Socinians were the only Christians who advocated toleration from principle. The burning of Servetus for heresy and blasphemy is the one dark stain on the fair fame of the great and good Calvin, but it was justified even by the gentle Melanchthon. Anabaptists were drowned and burnt by the score in Protestant as well as Roman Catholic countries. The Church history of England from Henry VIII. down to William III. is an unbroken tragedy of persecution of Romanists against Protestants, Protestants against Romanists, Anglicans against Puritans, and Puritans against Anglicans. Even the virgin soil of New England was stained by the martyr blood of Quakers, under the theocratic rule of Congregationalism, whose champions in the Westminster Assembly had advocated, though only in a limited degree, the sacred rights of conscience. All Protestant sects, with the exception of a few which never had a chance to rule, are guilty of intolerance and persecution, though in a far less degree than the Roman Church, from which they inherited the principle, and which adheres to it to this day, as is proved by the Papal Syllabus of 1864.

[1] Comp. Matt. 18: 2, 3, 10, 14; 19: 14, 15.

178 CONSENSUS OF THE REFORMED CONFESSIONS.

The Act of Toleration in 1689, though far from the full conception of the rights of conscience, closed the dark chapter of religious persecution in England, at least under its more violent form, and inaugurated the era of religious liberty among Protestants. The Baptists and Quakers made the doctrine of religious liberty an article of their creed. By a combination of various causes it has become almost a universal belief among Protestants, at least in Great Britain and in North America, that God alone is Lord of the conscience, that faith is a free act which cannot be enforced, that all coercion in religious matters is evil, and evil only, and contrary to the teaching and example of Christ and his apostles. Spiritual errors must be spiritually judged by ecclesiastical censures, admonition, suspension, and excommunication. The Civil Magistrate has no control over heresies and schisms, and is bound to protect the liberty of conscience and of public worship as one of the fundamental and inalienable rights of all its citizens, so far as this liberty does not interfere with public morals and the peace of society.

On this subject the Anglo-Saxon Protestants are ahead of the Continental Protestants. In the United States the Episcopal Church has changed the Thirty-nine Articles, and the Presbyterian Church the Westminster Standards, so as to adapt them to this modern conviction; while in England and Scotland the objectionable clauses have become a dead letter, or are expressly disowned, or liberally explained. The battles of Christendom must hereafter be fought out on the basis of freedom and equality before the law, and without those carnal weapons which are forbidden by the spirit and letter of the New Testament.

THE REFORMED CONSENSUS AND THE PRESBYTERIAN ALLIANCE.

This is, I trust, a fair historical statement of the Consensus of the Reformed Confessions, and the present state of Evangelical theology in relation to it.

We now approach the difficult and delicate practical question of the relation of this Alliance to the Consensus. The constitution adopted in the preliminary meeting at London (21st July, 1875), lays down, as the doctrinal basis of the Alliance, "the Consensus of the Reformed Confessions." But it does not define this consensus, nor is there any recognized formula of the kind. The subject, therefore, will have to be settled sooner or later, and this is the proper time to discuss it, although we may not be prepared to take any definite action. I shall confine myself to a few suggestions which I offer with modesty and some diffidence to the consideration of wiser heads.

To avoid misunderstanding, and perhaps unnecessary apprehension, I must remark at the outset, that the question before us is not the question of a revision of the Westminster Confession, or of any other confession. This must be left with the particular Church or Churches which own that confession. The General Presbyterian Council, moreover, has no jurisdiction or legislative authority. It may indeed define its relation to the historical confessions, or set forth a new one, but it would have no binding force upon any Churches except by their own act of adopting it.

We may state our relation to the Consensus in two ways—the one negative, and the other positive.

1. The doctrinal consensus need not be formulated at all, but may be left an open question, which every delegate must decide for himself. The Council may trust the personal character of the individual members, as a living guarantee for the doctrinal purity and soundness of the body. The Christian faith is older than the Apostles' Creed, and the evangelical faith is older than the Protestant Confessions. Sooner or later questions as to the precise nature and extent of the Consensus will probably spring up; but it is not necessary to anticipate future difficulties.

2. The doctrinal consensus can be formulated by the Presbyterian Council, after long and mature deliberation. This again may be done in three ways—

(a) By a list of doctrines, or an index of the chief heads of doctrine on which agreement is desired and required as a condition of membership, without defining the doctrines themselves. There can be no doubt that the Reformed Confessions teach the same views on the divine inspiration and authority of the Scriptures, the unity and tripersonality of the Godhead, the divine-human constitution of Christ's person, the atonement by his blood, election and salvation by free grace, justification by faith, the Church and the sacraments. Such a list would be similar to the Nine Articles of the Evangelical Alliance. The prevailing theology might show itself in the order and the wording of the articles. But it would be merely a skeleton of a confession.

(b) A historical statement, or brief summary of the common doctrines of the old confessions, without additions or changes. Such a summary has been actually prepared for this Council by my friend, Dr. Krafft, professor of Church History in the University of Bonn, who is thoroughly familiar with the confessions, and in sympathy with their spirit. His paper would form a good basis for an official document of the Council, if it should deem proper to adopt this course.

(c) A new œcumenical Reformed Confession. By this I mean the Consensus of the old Reformed Confessions freely reproduced and adapted to the present state of the Church; in other words, the creed of the Reformation translated into the theology of the nineteenth century, with perhaps a protest against modern Vatican Romanism and Rationalism. This would be a work for our age, such as Cranmer invited the Reformers to prepare for their age, and would thus fulfill the joint wish of these great and good men.

A new confession would be a testimony of the living faith of the Church, and a bond of union among the different branches of the Reformed family, as the Apostles' Creed is among all Christians, or as the common English version of the Scriptures is among English-speaking Protestants. It would not necessarily interfere with the provincial authority of the numerous confessions over which this Council has no control, and with which it ought not to meddle. It would have to be prepared by a body of able, wise, and godly divines, representing all the Churches of the Presbyterian Alliance, for *quod tangit omnes debet tractari ab omnibus.* Its authority would of course depend upon the general consent of the Churches.

The preparation of such a confession would afford an excellent opportunity to simplify and popularize the Reformed system of doctrine, to utter a protest against the peculiar errors and dangers of our age, and to exhibit the fraternal attitude of this Alliance to the other evangelical Churches which have sprung up since the Reformation and have been blessed by God. It ought to be truly evangelical and catholic in spirit. A confession which would intensify Presbyterianism and loosen the ties which unite us to the other branches of Christ's kingdom, I would regard as a calamity. We want a wall to keep off the wolves, but not a fence to divide the sheep; we want a declaration of union, not a platform of disunion.

The right to frame a new confession or to revise the old ones is beyond dispute. The desirableness of a common doctrinal bond of union among the Reformed Churches is likewise apparent. But the expediency of such a work at the present time is, to say the least, very doubtful. The pear may be ripening, but it is not ripe yet. If we were ready for it, I would say, let us take this course, but we are not prepared for it at this time, and perhaps not for a number of years. Let me state the reasons.

In the first place, creeds and confessions of faith which have vitality and power, usually spring from great doctrinal controversies and deep religious commotions. They cannot be made to order, like political platforms. No amount of theological learning and literary ability is sufficient. They require a religious fervor and enthusiasm that is ready for any sacrifice, even the death of martyrdom. They are solemn acts of faith, and the product of a higher inspiration.

In the second place, our theology is in a transition state, and has not yet reached such clear and definite results as could be embodied in a form of sound words. It would be impossible to unite all the Reformed Churches under an elaborate theological confession such as were those of the sixteenth and seventeenth centuries. The new Form of Concord might become a Form of Discord. The Anglo-American Churches would require a maximum of orthodoxy, the Continental Churches would be content with a minimum of orthodoxy. The recent Continental confessions framed by the Free Church of the Canton de Vaud, 1847 (thirty printed lines), the Free Church of Geneva, 1848 (seventeen articles, one hundred lines), the General Synod of the Reformed Church of France, 1872 (fifteen lines), of the Evangelical Church Association of Switzerland, 1871 (twenty-two lines), of the Free Church of Italy, 1872 (eight articles, thirty-eight lines), of the Free Church of Neuchatel in 1874 (a dozen lines), are very brief, and leave room for a great variety of views.[1] So are the Nine Articles of the Evangelical Alliance.

It seems to me, therefore, that the most we can do in the present Council is to intrust this whole subject to the hands of an able and comprehensive Committee, with instructions to gather all the necessary information about creeds and subscription to creeds within the bounds of this Alliance, and to report thereon to the next triennial meeting.

[1] We give as a specimen the Confession of the "Evangelical Church of Neuchatel, independent of the State," which is as follows:—" Faithful to the holy truth which the apostles preached, and which the reformers brought again to light, the Evangelical Church of Neuchatel acknowledges as the source and only rule of its faith the Holy Scriptures of the Old and New Testaments. It proclaims with all the Christian Church the great facts of salvation, condensed in the Creed called the Apostles' Creed. It believes in God the Father, who has saved us by the life, death, and resurrection of Jesus Christ, His only Son, our only Lord; and who has regenerated us by the Holy Spirit. And it confesses this faith in celebrating, according to the institution of the Lord, the sacraments of Baptism and the Lord's Supper." The new French Confession, which is similar to this, see in my work on *Creeds*, vol. i., p. 500; the Geneva Confession, in vol. iii., p. 781; the Free Italian Confession, in vol. iii., p. 789

One word in conclusion. A creed is a response of man to the questions of God; but God's Word is better than the best human creed. A creed is a confession of faith, but faith is better than the confession of it, and without faith the best confession is but "as sounding brass, or a clanging cymbal." Much as we esteem doctrinal unity, there is a higher unity, the unity of spiritual life, the unity of faith, the unity of love which binds us to Christ, and to all who love him, of whatever denomination or creed. Let us, with Peter and Thomas, confess Christ first and Christ last, and let our confession be an act of worship, an act of personal and collective self-consecration to him who saved us from sin and death, and leads us to immortality and glory. Let us not forget what the most logical and the most theological of all inspired apostles says, that now we see through a mirror darkly, but then we shall see face to face; that now we know in part, but then we shall know in full, even as we are known.

"And now abideth faith, hope, love, these three; but the greatest of these is love."

[NOTE.—The subject of this paper was discussed in the Council by Prof. Godet, of Neuchatel, Prof. Mitchell and Principal Tulloch, of St. Andrew's; Principal Brown, of Aberdeen; Prof. Candlish and Dr. Marshall Lang, of Glasgow; Dr. Begg and Mr. Taylor Innes, of Edinburgh, and Dr. Ormiston, of New York. See *Report of Proceedings of the First Presb. Council convened at Edinburgh, July,* 1877 (Edinb. 1877, pp. 27–51). Whereupon a Committee on Creeds and Confessions was appointed to prepare an historical report on the existing creeds and confessions and formulas of subscription of the churches composing the Ref. Alliance (*ibid.* p. 51 and 277). This Committee reported through its chairman to the Second Council held in Philadelphia, Sept. 1880 and the report is printed in the *Proceedings* published in Philadelphia (pp. 259–262; 965–1123). The same Council appointed a large committee to prepare a report on "the desirableness of defining the Consensus of the Reformed Confessions," for action by the third Reformed Council held in Belfast, June and July, 1884. This Council declared it unnecessary and undesirable at the present time to formulate the consensus, but practically defined it in a *liberal* sense by admitting the semi-Arminian Cumberland Presbyterians.]

SLAVERY AND THE BIBLE.

THE ORIGIN OF SLAVERY.

The Bible begins with the highest and noblest view of man by representing him as the bearer of the image of God, and placing him at the head of the whole creation. The divine image implies the idea of personality, that is reason and will, or intelligence and freedom. By these inestimable gifts man is far elevated above the brute, reflects the glory of his Maker, and is capable of communion with Him, and of endless felicity.

With this primitive conception and condition of man, slavery or involuntary servitude is incompatible. It has no place in paradise. God created man male and female, and thus instituted marriage and the family relation before the fall, but not slavery. He gave him "dominion over the fish of the sea, and over the fowl of the air, and over the cattle, and over all the earth, and over every creeping thing that creepeth upon the earth,"[1] but not over his fellow-man. The only slave could have been Eve, but she was equally the bearer of the divine image and the loving and beloved partner of Adam. In the language of a distinguished commentator, "the woman was made of a rib out of the side of man; not made out of his head, to top him—not out of his feet, to be trampled upon by him—but out of his side, to be equal with him, from under his arm, to be protected by him, and from near his heart, to be beloved."

But man fell from his original state by the abuse of his freedom of an act of disobedience, and was driven from paradise.

[1] Gen 1: 26, 28; Ps. 8: 6–8.

Sin is the first and worst kind of slavery, and the fruitful source of every other intellectual, moral, and physical degradation. In this sense every sinner is a slave to his own appetites and passions, and can only attain to true freedom by the Christian salvation. Hence the Saviour says: "Every one that committeth sin is the slave of sin .... If the Son shall make you free, ye shall be free indeed."

Slavery then takes its rise in sin, and more particularly in war and the law of brute force. Lust of power, avarice and cruelty were the original motives, kidnapping, conquest in war, and purchase by money were the original methods, of depriving men of their personal freedom and degrading them to mere instruments for the selfish ends of others.

But when the institution was once generally introduced, most slaves were born such and were innocently inherited like any other kind of property. Slaveholding became an undisputed right of every freeman and was maintained and propagated as an essential part of the family among all the ancient nations. In many cases also freemen voluntarily sold themselves into slavery from extreme poverty, or lost their freedom in consequence of crime.

THE CURSE OF NOAH.

Slavery, like despotism, war, and all kinds of oppression, existed no doubt long before the deluge, which was sent upon the earth because it was "filled with violence" (Gen. 6: 11). But it is not expressly mentioned till after the flood, in the remarkable prophecy of Noah, which was uttered more than four thousand years ago and reaches in its fulfilment even to our time. Bishop Newton, in his "Dissertations on the Prophecies," calls it "the history of the world in epitome." It is recorded in Genesis, 9: 25–27, and in its metrical form according to the Hebrew reads as follows:

25. "Cursed be Canaan:
　　A servant of servants[1] shall he be unto his brethren.

[1] עֶ֫בֶד עֲבָדִים, *ebhed abhadim*, i. e., the meanest or lowest of servants; a Hebrew

26. Blessed be Jehovah, the God of Shem;
And Canaan shall be a servant unto them.[1]
27. God shall enlarge Japheth.
And he [Japheth] shall dwell in the tents of Shem;
And Canaan shall be a servant unto them."[2]

Noah, a preacher of righteousness before the flood, speaks here as a far-seeing inspired prophet to the new world after the flood. He pronounces a curse thrice repeated upon one of his grandsons, and a blessing upon two of his sons, yet with regard not so much to their individual as their representative character, and looking to the future posterity of the three patriarchs of the human family. Ham, the father of Canaan, represents the idolatrous and servile races; Shem, the Israelites who worshipped Jehovah, the only true and living God; Japheth, those gentiles, who by their contact with Shem were brought to a knowledge of the true religion. The curse was occasioned by a gross indecency and profane irreverence to the aged Noah. It was inflicted upon Canaan, the youngest of the four sons of Ham, either because he was, according to an ancient Jewish tradition, the real offender, and Ham merely the reporter of the fact, or more probably because he made sport of his grandfather's shame

---

form of intensifying the idea, as in the expressions *king of kings, holy of holies, song of songs.*

[1] *Unto them* [not *unto him*], *i. e.*, unto Shem and his posterity. See the next note.

[2] עֶבֶד לָמוֹ *ebhed lamo, a servant to them* (*lamo*, poetical for *lahem*), *i. e.*, either to Japheth and his posterity (as Hengstenberg takes it), or to both Shem and Japheth, in their representative character; comp. *unto his brethren*, ver. 25. In any case it includes the posterity. The English version, Luther and many others translate in ver. 26 and 27, "*his* (Shem's) servant," and Ewald (*Hebrew Grammar*, p. 459), asserts that *amo* may sometimes denote the singular, referring to Ps. 11: 7; Job 22: 2; Deut. 32: 2; and Isa. 44: 15. Kautzsch (in the 22nd ed. of Gesenius, 1878, p. 235) admits this against Gesenius and Rödiger, who maintained the exclusive plural or collective meaning; but in this passage at all events it has the collective meaning (as also in Deut. 33: 2; Ps. 73: 10 (in reference to the people), etc.

when seen and revealed by Ham to his brothers, and was the principal heir of the irreverence and impiety of his father. But Ham was also punished in his son who was most like him, as he had sinned against his father.[1] The whole posterity of Canaan was included in the curse because of their vices and wickedness (Levit. 18: 24–25), which God foresaw, yet after all with a merciful design as to their ultimate destiny.

The malediction of Noah was first fulfilled, on a large national scale, about eight hundred years after its delivery, when the Israelites, the favorite descendants of Shem, subdued the Canaanites, under the leadership of Joshua and under divine direction, and made some of their tribes " bondmen and hewers of wood and drawers of water for the house of God " (Joshua 9 : 23–27). It was further fulfilled, when Solomon subdued the scattered remnants of those tribes (1 Kings 9: 20–21; 2 Chron. 8 : 7–9). Thus Canaan came under the rod of Shem. But he was also to be a servant to Japheth (" unto his *brethren*," ver. 25, "unto *them*," ver. 27). Under this view the prediction was realized in the successive dominion of the Persians, Greeks and Romans, all descendants of Japheth, over the Phenicians and Carthaginians, who belonged to the posterity of Canaan. The blessing of Noah was likewise strikingly fulfilled in the subsequent course of history reaching down to the introduction of Christianity. Shem was the bearer of the true religion before Christ. Japheth dwelled in the tents of Shem, literally, by conquering his territory under the Greeks and Romans, and spiritually, by the conversion of his vast posterity to the Christian religion which proceeded from the bosom of Shem. It is true here in the highest sense that the conquered gave laws to the conquerors.

But in point of fact both the curse and the blessing of Noah extend still further and justify a wider historical application.

[1] Some manuscripts of the Septuagint or Greek translation of the Hebrew Scriptures read " *Ham* " for *Canaan,* and the Arabic version " *the father of Canaan,*" in the three verses of this prophecy.

The curse of involuntary servitude, which in the text is confined to the youngest son of Canaan because of his close contact with the Israelites, has affected nearly the whole of the posterity of Ham, or those unfortunate African races which for many centuries have groaned and are still groaning under the despotic rule of the Romans, the Saracens, the Turks, and even those Christian nations who engaged in the iniquity of the African slave trade. Whether we connect it with this ancient prophecy or not, it is simply a fact which no one can deny, that the negro to this day is a servant of servants. Japheth, on the other hand, the progenitor of half the human race, who possesses a part of Asia and the whole of Europe, is still extending his posterity and territory in the westward course of empire, and holds (or till quite recently held) Ham in bondage far away from his original home.

Slavery then is represented from the start as a punishment and a curse and is continued as such from generation to generation for these four thousand years, falling with special severity upon the African race, and involving the innocent with the guilty. A dark veil still hangs over this dispensation of Providence, which will be lifted only by the future pages of history. God alone, in his infinite wisdom and mercy, can and will settle the negro question by turning even a curse into a blessing and by overruling the wrath of man for his own glory. All his punishments have a disciplinary object and a remedial character. The prophecy of Noah, it is true, has no comfort for poor Canaan, and no blessing for Ham. But David already looked forward to the time when " Ethiopia shall stretch out her hands unto God " (Ps. 68 : 31). The new dispensation gives us more light and hope and solves the mysteries of the old. The gospel of Christ who praised the faith of a daughter of Canaan (Matt. 15 : 28), and who died for all races, classes and conditions of man, authorizes us to look forward to the ultimate salvation of the entire posterity of Ham through the agency of Japheth and the severe discipline of slavery. As Japheth dwelled in the

SLAVERY AND THE BIBLE.   189

eastern tents of Shem and was converted to his faith, so we may say that Ham dwells in the western tents of Japheth and was trained in America for his final deliverence from the ancient curse of bondage by the slow but sure operation of Christianity both upon him and his master, and for a noble mission to the entire mysterious continent of Africa.

PATRIARCHAL SLAVERY.

We next meet slavery as an established domestic institution among the patriarchs of the Jewish nation, as will appear from the following passages :

Gen. 12: 16: "And Abram had sheep, and oxen, and he-asses, and men-servants, and maid-servants, and she-asses, and camels."

Gen. 14: 14: "And when Abram heard that his brother was taken captive, he armed his trained servants, born in his own house, three hundred and eighteen."

Gen. 17: 23: "And Abraham took Ishmael his son, and all that were born in his house [slaves by birth], and all that were bought with his money [slaves by purchase], every male among the men of Abraham's house; and circumcised the flesh of their fore-skin in the self-same day, as God had said unto him."

Gen. 20: 14: "And Abimelech took sheep, and oxen, and men-servants, and women-servants, and gave them unto Abraham, and restored him Sarah his wife."

Gen. 21: 10: " Wherefore she (Sarah) said unto Abraham, cast out this bond-woman (Hagar) and her son: for the son of this bond-woman shall not be heir with my son, even with Isaac." Comp. Gal. 4: 22-26.

Gen. 24: 35: "And the Lord hath blessed my master (Abraham) greatly: and he is become great: and he hath given him flocks, and herds, and silver, and gold, and men-servants and maid-servants, and camels, and asses."

Gen. 26: 14: "He (Isaac) had possession of flocks, and possession of herds, and great store of servants: and the Philistines envied him."

Gen. 30: 43: "And the man (Jacob) increased exceedingly, and had much cattle, and maid-servants, and men-servants, and camels, and asses."

Gen. 32: 5: "And I (Jacob) have oxen, and asses, flocks, and men-servants and women-servants."

Gen. 37: 28: "Then there passed by Midianites, merchant-men; and they drew and lifted up Joseph out of the pit, and sold Joseph to the Ishmaelites for twenty pieces of silver: and they brought Joseph into Egypt."

Compare Job 1: 3: "His substance also was seven thousand sheep, and three thousand camels, and five hundred yoke of oxen, and five hundred she-asses, and a very great household" [literally: very many servants. German: *grosse Dienerschaft*].

The Hebrew term employed here and throughout the Old Testament generally for servants,[1] is not necessarily degrading, like our *slave;* on the contrary *ebhed* means originally *laborer, worker*, and work was no disgrace among a people whose kings and prophets were called from the flock and the plough; yea, it is used in innumerable passages in the most honorable sense and applied to messengers of kings, to angels, to Moses, the prophets and the highest officers of the theocracy, in their relation to God. But in its usual literal sense it is universally understood to mean *bond* servants in distinction from *hired* or voluntary servants, who were comparatively rare among ancient nations and are but seldom mentioned in the Old Testament.[2] The slaves here spoken of were either born in the house (called *jelide baüth*) or in large numbers by the patriarchs and the patriarchal Job without any sense of guilt or impropriety on their side, and without a mark of disapprobation on the side of God. Their usual enumeration and collocation with sheep, oxen, asses and camels, although less degrading than Aristotle's definition of a slave purchased by money (*miknath cheseph*, Gen. 17 : 23) and owned, as a

[1] עֶבֶד, *ebhed* (from the verb עָבַד, *abhad*, first *to labor;* then *to serve* (either man or God), plural עֲבָדִים, *abhadim*, for male servants; and שִׁפְחָה, *shipheha*, plural שְׁפָחוֹת, *shephachoth*, or אָמָה, *amah*, and אֲמָהוֹת, *amahoth*, for female servants. The latter terms express the close connection with the family.

[2] The Hebrew term for *hired* servant is שָׂכִיר, Ex. 12 : 45 compared with 44; 22 : 14; Levit. 19 : 13; Deut. 24 : 14; Job. 7 : 2. Josephus (*Antiquities*, IV. 8, 38) explains the Jewish law as to hired servants thus: "Let it be always remembered, that we are not to defraud a poor man of his wages, as being sensible that God has allotted wages to him instead of land and other possessions; nay, this payment is not at all to be delayed, but to be made that very day, since God is not willing to deprive the laborer of the immediate use of what he has labored for."

SLAVERY AND THE BIBLE. 191

"living tool," or "animated possession,"[1] is very offensive to our modern ear and Christian taste, and shows the difference between the Old Testament and the New, where they are never mentioned in such connection. In one passage the servants are even put between the he-asses and the she-asses, in another between the cattle and the camels, and in a third between the gold and the camels.

But we have no right to infer from this fact that the patriarchs regarded and treated their servants no better than their favorite animals. Their whole character and religion justify the opposite conclusion. They bought, but, as far as the record goes, they never sold any of their slaves. The sale of Joseph by his brothers into Egyptian servitude, although proposed as an act of comparative mercy by Judah instead of the intended murder (Gen. 37: 27), and overruled by Providence for the good of Joseph and the whole patriarchal family, is an isolated exception and falls properly under the condemnation of kidnapping, which the law of Moses punished with death (Exod. 21: 16). There is no trace of slave traffic in the Old Testament. The patriarchal servitude was free from the low mercenary aspect, the spirit of caste and the harsh treatment, which characterized the same institution among heathen nations. It was of a purely domestic character and tempered by kindness, benevolence and a sense of moral and religious equality before God. This appears from the high confidence which Abraham reposed in Eliezer, and all those slaves whom he entrusted with arms, and still more from the significant fact that he circumcised them and thus made them partakers of the blessings and privileges of the covenant of Jehovah by divine direction.[2]

SLAVERY UNDER THE MOSAIC LAW.

Between the patriarchal and the Mosaic period the Jews were themselves reduced to hard involuntary servitude in Egypt.

[1] Ὄργανον ζῶον. or κτῆμα ἐμψυχον.
[2] Gen. 15: 2; 24: 2 sqq.; 14: 14; 32: 6; 33: 1; 17: 23, 27.

The introduction to the ten commandments reminds them of their merciful deliverance "out of the land of Egypt, out of the house of bondage," that they might be grateful for so great a mercy and show their gratitude by cheerful obedience to his will, and merciful conduct towards their servants (comp. Deut. 5: 15; 15: 15).

Moses, or God through him, neither established nor abolished slavery; he authorized and regulated it as an ancient domestic and social institution, which could not be dispensed with at that time, but he also so modified and humanized the same as to raise it far above the character of slavery among the Gentiles, even the highly cultivated Greeks and Romans.

The moral law which is embodied in the decalogue, and is binding for all times, mentions "men-servants and maid-servants" twice, but evidently and most wisely in such general terms and connections as to be equally applicable to free servants and bond servants. The fourth commandment protects the religious rights of the servants by securing to them the blessings of the Sabbath day; the tenth commandment guards the rights of the master against the passion and cupidity of his neighbor.

The civil law makes first an important distinction between the Hebrew and the Gentile servants. It regarded freedom as the normal and proper condition of the Israelite, and prohibited his reduction to servitude except in two cases, either for theft, when unable to make full restitution (Ex. 22: 3), or in extreme poverty, when he might sell himself (Levit. 25: 39). Cruel creditors sometimes forced insolvent debtors into servitude (2 Kings 4: 50; Isa. 50: 1; Nehem. 5: 5; comp. Matth. 18: 25), but this was an abuse which is nowhere authorized. The Hebrew servant moreover was not to be treated like an ordinary bondman, and regained his freedom, without price, and with an outfit (Deut. 15: 14), after six years of service, unless he expressly preferred from attachment to his master or wife and children to remain in bondage. The remembrance of Israel's bondage of Egypt and the merciful deliverance by the hand of the Lord, should inspire every Israelite with kindness to his bondmen. The jubilee, or every fiftieth year, when the whole theocracy was renewed, gave liberty to all slaves of Hebrew descent without distinction, whether they had served six years or not, and made them landed proprietors by restoring to them the possessions of their fathers. Consequently the law, in permitting the Hebrew to be sold, merely suspended his freedom for a limited period, guarded him during the same against bad treatment, and provided for his ultimate emancipation. This is clear from the principal passage bearing on the subject.

"If thou buy an Hebrew servant, six years he shall serve: and in the seventh he shall go out free for nothing. If he came in by himself, he shall go out by himself; if he were married, then his wife shall go out with him. If his master have given him a wife, and she have born him sons or daughters, the wife and her children shall be her master's, and he shall go out by himself. And if the servant shall plainly say, I love my master, my wife, and my children; I will not go out free; then his master shall bring him to the door, or unto the door post; and his master shall bore his ear through with an awl; and he shall serve him for ever." [1] Exod. 21: 2-6.

"And if thy brother that dwelleth by thee be waxen poor, and be sold unto thee; thou shalt not compel him to serve as a bond-servant: but as an hired servant, and as a sojourner, he shall be with thee, and shall serve thee unto the year of jubilee: and then shall he depart from thee, both he and his children with him, and shall return unto his own family, and unto the possession of his fathers shall he return. For they are my servants which I brought forth out of the land of Egypt: they shall not be sold as bondmen. Thou shalt not rule over him with rigor: but shalt fear thy God." Levit. 25: 39-43. Comp. Deut. 15: 12-18.

"This is the word that came unto Jeremiah from the Lord, after that the king Zedekiah had made a covenant with all the people which were at Jerusalem, to proclaim liberty unto them; that every man should let his man-servant, and every man his maid-servant, being an Hebrew or a Hebrewess, go free; that none should serve himself of them, to wit, of a Jew his brother." Jerem. 34: 8, 9.

---

[1] *i. e.*, become permanent and inheritable property like the slaves of heathen origin (Lev. 25: 46); or, as the Jewish doctors take it, till the year of jubilee. Such limitations seem to be justified by Lev. 25: 41, 10.

Concerning the heathen bondmen who constituted the great majority of slaves among the Hebrews, the law was more severe, and attached them permanently to their master and his posterity.

"Both thy bondmen and thy bondmaids, which thou shalt have, shall be of the heathen that are round about you; of them shall ye buy bondmen and bondmaids. Moreover of the children of the strangers that do sojourn among you, of them shall ye buy, and of their families that are with you, which they begat in your land: and they shall be your possession. And ye shall take them as an inheritance for your children after you to inherit them for a possession; they shall be your bondmen for ever: but over your brethren, the children of Israel, ye shall not rule one over another with rigor." Levit. 25: 44-46.

But the Mosaic dispensation no where degraded even the heathen slave to mere property, or a thing, as the Roman law did. It regarded and treated him as a moral and religious being, admitted him to the blessings of the covenant by circumcision (Gen. 17: 12, 13, 23, 27; Exod. 12: 44), secured him the rest of the Sabbath and the festival days and other religious privileges, and protected him against the passion and cruelty of the master and restored him to freedom in case he was violently injured in eye or tooth, that is, according to the spirit of the law, in any member whatever. Finally it numbered kidnapping, or the forcible reduction of a freeman, especially an Israelite, to servitude in time of peace, among the blackest crimes, and punished it with death. Take the following passages which refer to all slaves:

"If a man smite his servant, or his maid with a rod, and he die under his hand, he shall be surely punished. Notwithstanding if he continue a day or two, he shall not be punished; for he is his money." Exod. 21: 20, 21.

"If a man smite the eye of his servant, or the eye of his maid, that it perish, he shall let him go free for his eye's sake. And if he smite out his servant's tooth, he shall let him go free for his tooth's sake." Exod. 21: 26, 27.

"The seventh day is the Sabbath of the Lord thy God: in it thou shalt not do any work, thou, nor thy son, nor thy daughter, thy man-servant, nor thy maid-servant," etc. Exod. 20: 10.

.... "that thy man-servant and thy maid-servant may rest as well as thou. And remember that thou wast a servant in the land of Egypt," etc. Deut. 5: 14, 15. Comp. Deut. 16: 11, 12, 14 with reference to the annual festivals.

"And he that stealeth a man, and selleth him, or if he be found in his hand, he shall surely be put to death." Exod. 21: 16.

"If a man be found stealing any of his brethren of the children of Israel, and maketh merchandize of him, or selleth him, then that thief shall die; and thou shalt put evil away from among you." Deut. 24: 7.

Such guarantees contrast very favorably with the Roman slave code which knew of no civil and religious rights of the slave, reduced him to the level of mere property and gave the master authority to torture him for evidence and to put him to death. Hence we never read of slave insurrections among the Jews, as among the Greeks and Romans. The difference in treatment was the natural result of a different theory. For the Old Testament teaches the unity of the human race, which is favorable to general equality before the law, while heathen slavery rested on the opposite doctrine of the essential inferiority of all barbarians to the Greeks and Romans and their constitutional unfitness for the rights and privileges of freemen.

If we consider the low and degraded condition of the idolatrous heathen tribes, with whom the Jews in their early history came into contact, we have a right to think that slavery was an actual benefit to them and a training school from barbarian idolatry and licentiousness to the knowledge and worship of the true God. This would explain the more easily a passage in Deut. 23: 15, 16:

"Thou shalt not deliver unto his master the servant which is escaped from his master unto thee: he shall dwell with thee, even among you, in that place which he shall choose in one of thy gates, where it liketh him best: thou shalt not oppress him."

This can, of course, not be understood as applying to all slaves indiscriminately, without involving the law in self-contradiction; for the servants of the Jews were protected by law, like any other property (Exod. 20: 17), they had to be restored, if lost (Deut. 22: 4; comp. 1 King 2: 39, 40), and passed as an inheritance from parents to children (Lev. 25: 46). The passage refers, as all good commentators hold, to *foreign* slaves only, who escaped from the surrounding *heathen* nations to the boundaries of the theocracy, and who, if returned, would have been punished with cruel tortures or certain death. Extradition, in such cases, would have been an act of inhumanity repugnant to the spirit of the Jewish religion. Such unfortunate fugitives found an asylum in Israel, as they did even in heathen temples, and since Constantine in every Christian church. In the same way political and religious refugees find a hospitable asylum in England and the United States and are not required by international obligation to be returned to their native land.

From all that has been said then thus far, we may conclude that, according to the Old Testament, the institution of involuntary and perpetual servitude dates from after the fall, and first appears as a punishment and curse; that it was known and practised by the patriarchs; recognized and protected by the Mosaic legislation, but also softened and guarded against various abuses; and that every returning jubilee made an end to Jewish servitude. It does not appear, indeed, that slaves of heathen descent were included in the blessing of jubilee. Their exclusion would have to be explained on the ground of the particularism of the old economy, which was intended merely as a national training school for the universal religion of the gospel. But on the other hand, the fact that all slaves in Jewish families seem to have been circumcised (Gen. 17: 12, 13, 23, 27), at least if they wished (comp. Exod. 12: 44), and were thus incorporated into the Jewish church, seems to justify a more general application of the blessing of jubilee, to all slaves, or at least to all who were circumcised, whether of Jewish descent or not. The language in Levit. 25: 10 makes no exception: "And ye shall hallow the fiftieth year, and proclaim liberty throughout the land *unto all the inhabitants thereof:* it shall be a jubilee unto you; and ye shall return *every man* unto his possession, and ye shall return *every man* unto his family." At all events the jubilee was a type of that "acceptable year of the Lord" (Isa. 61: 1; Luke 4: 19) which gave spiritual deliverance to all, and will be finally realized in the restoration of all men to their original dignity, freedom and equality, through the Christian salvation from every form of bondage.

GREEK AND ROMAN SLAVERY.

Before we proceed to explain the relation of the New Testament to slavery, it may be well to cast a glance at the extent and character of this institution in those highly civilized heathen nations, among which Christianity was first established.

The ancient republics of Greece and Rome had no idea of general and inalienable rights of men. They consisted in the rule of a small minority of freemen over a mass of foreigners and slaves. The Greeks and Romans looked with aristocratic contempt upon all other nations as barbarians and unfit for freedom. Their philosophers and law-givers regarded slavery as a natural, normal and perpetual condition of society, and assumed a constitutional or essential difference between the free-born and the slaves. Aristotle calls a *doulos* or slave "an animated tool, just as a tool is a soulless slave." Occasionally slaves distinguished themselves by great talent or some special merit, and were then used as teachers, or were emancipated, or they bought their liberty. But these were exceptions, which confirmed the rule. The great mass remained in a degraded and wretched condition, whether they belonged to the State as the Helots in Sparta, or to individuals. An active slave trade was carried on, particularly in the Euxine, the eastern provinces, the coast of Africa, Britain, and in the city of Rome where human beings from every tongue and clime were continually offered for sale, generally as nature made them and with a scroll around their neck, on which their good and bad qualities were specified.

The Romans made no distinction between race and color in this respect. All captives of war, whether Scythians, Phrygians, Nubians, Jews, Gauls, Spaniards, Britons, Germans, also insolvent debtors and criminals were generally sold into slavery. The distinguished Latin poets Terentius and probably Plautus, the former an African, the latter an Italian by birth, were originally slaves, but acquired their freedom by their talents and industry; and Horace, who moved in the highest circles of the Roman aristocracy, descended from a freedman. The Jewish synagogue at Rome consisted mostly of freedmen. During the Jewish war, Josephus tells us, ninety-seven thousand Jews were made captives and either sold to individuals as cheap as horses, or condemned as slaves of the State to hard work in the Egyptian mines or put to death.

Slavery extended over every province and embraced, according to Gibbon's low estimate, sixty millions, or at least one half of the entire population of the empire under the reign of Claudius; but according to more recent calculations the slaves outnumbered the citizens three to one. For in Attica, the classical spot of Greece, there were, three hundred years before Christ, four hundred thousand slaves (who were counted per head, like cattle) to only twenty-one thousand free citizens (exclusive, however, of women and minors) and ten thousand foreign residents. In Sparta the disproportion seems to have been still greater, and to keep down their numbers the Helots were sometimes cruelly and treacherously massacred by thousands. Many wealthy Romans possessed from ten to twenty thousand slaves for mere ostentation. Roman ladies of rank and fashion kept as many as two hundred for their toilet alone. The slaves did all kind of work in the house, the shop, and the kitchen. The Latin language has a great many names for the various classes into which they were divided according to their occupation.[1]

In the eyes of the Roman law till the time of the Antonines the slaves were in the fullest sense of the term the property of the master and reduced to the level of the brute. A distin-

---

[1] Those, for instance, who attended to the table alone were subdivided into *pistores, coqui, fartores, obsonatores, structores, scissores, pocillatores;* those who were employed for the wardrobe and toilet, into *vestiarii, textores, tonsores, ornatrices, ciniflones, unctores, balneatores,* etc., etc.

guished writer on civil law thus describes their condition: " The slaves were in a much worse state than any cattle whatsoever. They had no head in the State, no name, no title, no register; they were not capable of being injured; they had no heirs and therefore could make no will; they were not entitled to the rights of matrimony, and therefore had no relief in case of adultery; nor were they proper objects of cognation and affinity, but a quasi-cognation only; they could be sold, transferred, or pawned, as goods or personal estate, for goods they were, and as such they were esteemed; they might be tortured for evidence, punished at the discretion of their lord, and even put to death by his authority; together with many other civil incapacities which I have no room to enumerate." Cato the elder expelled his old and sick slaves out of house and home. Hadrian, one of the most humane of the emperors, wilfully destroyed the eyes of one of his slaves with a pencil. Roman ladies punished their waiters with sharp iron instruments for the most trifling offences, while attending half dressed to their toilet. Such legal degradation and cruel treatment had the worst effect upon the character of the slaves. They are described by the ancient writers as mean, cowardly, abject, false, voracious, intemperate, voluptuous, also hard and cruel, when placed over others. A proverb prevailed in the Roman empire: " As many slaves, as many enemies." Hence the constant danger of servile insurrections which more than once brought the republic to the brink of ruin and seemed to justify the severest measures in self-defense.

It is true, self-interest, natural kindness, and education had their due effect even among the heathen and prompted many masters to take proper care of their slaves. Seneca, Epictetus, and Plutarch gave excellent advice which tended to mitigate the evil wherever it was carried out. Legislation also began to improve in the second century under the Antonines, and the influence of the Stoic philosophy, and transferred the power over the life of the slave from the master to the magistrate. But at that time the humanizing influence of Christianity already made itself felt even upon its enemies and impregnated the atmosphere of public opinion.

Roman slavery then was far worse than Jewish servitude. It regarded and treated the slaves as chattels and things, while the latter still respected them as persons, provided for their moral and religious wants, and cheered them with the hope of deliverance in the year of jubilee.

THE NEW TESTAMENT AND SLAVERY.

Such was the system of slavery when Christ appeared, to deliver the world from the bondage of sin and death and to work out a salvation for all races, classes and conditions of men.

The manner in which Christianity dealt with an institution so universally prevalent in its worst forms and so intimately interwoven with the whole private and public life in the Roman empire, is a strong proof of its practical wisdom and divine origin. It accomplished what no other religion has even attempted before or since. Without interfering with slavery as a political and œconomical question, without encouraging any revolution or rebellion, without denouncing the character or denying the legal rights of the slave-holder, or creating discontent among the slaves, without disturbing the peace of a single family, without any appeals to the passions and prejudices of men on the evils and abuses of slavery, without requiring or even suggesting immediate emancipation, in one word, without changing the outward and legal relation between the two parties, but solemnly enforcing the rights and duties arising from it to both; Christ and the apostles, nevertheless, from within by purely spiritual and peaceful means, by teaching the common origin and common redemption, the true dignity, equality and destiny of men, by inculcating the principles of universal justice and love, and by raising the most degraded and unfortunate classes of society to virtue and piety, produced a radical moral reformation of the system and prepared the only effectual way for its gradual extinction. The Christian Church followed this example and dealt with the system of slavery in the same spirit wherever it found it as an established fact. Any other method would have either effected nothing at all, or done more harm than good. An attempt at sudden emancipation with such abundant materials for servile wars in the old Roman empire, would have thrown the world into hopeless confusion and brought dissolution and ruin upon the empire and the cause of Christianity itself.

The relation of the gospel to slavery wherever it still exists, remains the same to-day as it was in the age of the apostles. The New Testament was written for all ages and conditions of society. It rises above sectional and partisan views. It no where establishes or abolishes the institution of slavery, as little as monarchy or any other form of government; it never meddles with its political and financial aspects, which belong to the secular rulers. But it tolerates and ameliorates it wherever it exists as an established fact; it treats it under its moral bearings, and enjoins the duties and responsibilities of masters and servants; it corrects its abuses, cures the root of the evil, and provides the only rational and practical remedy for its ultimate extinction. Yet, in profound and far-seeing wisdom, it does all this in such a manner that its teachings and admonitions retain their full force and applicability, though every trace of involuntary' servitude should disappear from the earth, as no doubt it will.

Hence the unlearned reader of the New Testament seldom observes its allusions to slavery, and may read the Gospels and Epistles without dreaming of the fact, that at the time of their composition more than one-half of the human race was kept in literal bondage. Our popular versions have properly and wisely avoided the words *slave-holder* and *slave*—like the framers of the American Constitution—and have mostly substituted the words *master* and *servant*, which are equally applicable to a free state of society, or the general distinctions of superior and inferior, ruler and subject, which will continue to the end of time. The usual term for *servant*, as its etymology from the Latin suggests, was originally employed in the menial sense, but has acquired a nobler meaning under the influence of Christianity upon all domestic and social relations.

The Greek language has a number of terms for the various kinds of servants, six or seven of which occur in the New Testament.[1] We will explain three as having a bearing upon the present discussion.

1) *misthios* and *misthotos* mean a *hired* servant or *hireling*, and are so translated in the five passages of the New Testament where they occur. They may be slaves and hired out by their masters, or they may not.

2) *doulos* is more frequently used than all other terms put together. We find it, if we made no mistake in counting, one hundred and twenty-three times, namely seventy-three times in the Gospels, three times in the Acts, thirty-three times in the Epistles, and fourteen times in the Apocalypse.[2] It is uniformly translated *servant* in our English Bible, except in seven instances in the Epistles and in Revelation, where it is rendered either *bond* or *bondman*.[3] *Doulos* (originally an adjective, *bound*, from

---

[1] θεράπων, *therapon*, translated *servant* (*minister* would be better, to distinguish it from *doulos*), occurs but once, and then of Moses, in an honorable sense, Heb. 3 : 5; ὑπηρέτης, *hyperetes*, generally translated *officer*, sometimes *servant*, or *minister*, occurs several times in the Gospels and Acts, and once in the Epistles (1 Cor. 4 : 1); διάκονος, *diakonos*, which the Common Version mostly renders *minister*, sometimes *servant*, and when used in its official sense, *deacon*; μίσθιος and μισθωτός, *misthios, misthotos* (corresponding to the Hebrew שָׂכִיר), a *hired* servant; δοῦλος, *doulos* (see above); οἰκέτης, *oiketes*, a *domestic doulos* or *household servant*, and so translated in Acts 10 : 7; παῖς, *pais*, often translated *servant*, sometimes *child*, the least ignominious term for slave, and rather a title of endearment like the Latin *puer* and the English *boy*.

[2] Besides the masculine δοῦλος the feminine δούλη occurs three times, twice of the Virgin Mary, the *handmaid* of the Lord (Luke 1 : 38, 48, and in a more general application Acts 2 : 18); the neuter δοῦλον twice (Rom. 6 : 19: Yield your members *servants* to righteousness); the noun δουλεία five times and is uniformly rendered *bondage*; the verb δουλεύω twenty-five times, generally rendered *to serve*, sometimes *to be in bondage*; and the transitive verb δουλόω, *to bring into bondage, to enslave*, eight times.

[3] Namely 1 Cor. 12 : 13; Gal. 3 : 28; Eph. 6 : 8; Col. 3 : 11; Rev. 6 : 15; 13 : 16; 19 : 13. The Revised Version has *bondman* in nine passages.

the verb *deo*, *to bind*), like the Latin *servus*, means properly a *bond* servant, or a *slave*, especially one by birth, and is opposed to *eleutheros, free-born*, or *freed, made free*.[1] Yet, like the Hebrew *ebhed*, of which it is the Greek equivalent in the New Testament, it is not necessarily degrading, but simply a term of government and may signify a subject from the highest to the lowest ranks. Ammonius, an ancient writer on Greek synonyms, of the fourth century, gives the word this general sense,[2] and the Greeks called the Persians *douloi*, as subjects of an absolute monarch. The Bible frequently uses the word of the highest and noblest kind of service, the voluntary service of God, which is perfect freedom, as St. Augustin says: *Deo servire vera libertas est.* Moses, the prophets, the apostles and all true Christians are called *douloi* or servants of God and Christ, as being entirely and for life, yet voluntarily and cheerfully devoted to his service.[3] St. Paul glories in this title,[4] and so does St. Peter, St. James, St. Jude, and St. John.[5] It would be quite improper in any of these passages to substitute *slave* for *servant*.

[1] Trench, in his little work on the *Synonyms of the New Testament*, N. York ed. 1857, p. 53, defines δοῦλος as "one in a permanent relation of servitude to another, and that altogether apart from any ministration to that other at the present moment rendered; but the θεράπων is the performer of present services, without respect to the fact, whether as a freeman or as a slave he renders them; and thus, there goes constantly with the word the sense of one whose services are tenderer, nobler, freer than those of the δοῦλος." Compare also J. Theod. Vömel, *Synonymisches Wörterbuch*, Frankf. 1819, p. 78, 79 and p. 218, 219.

[2] Δοῦλοι, he says, as quoted by Vömel, εἰσὶ καὶ οἱ ἡδονῶν, καὶ πάντες οἱ ὑποτεταγμένοι ὑπὸ τὸν βασιλέα (all who are subjected to the king)

[3] Compare Luke 12: 37: "Blessed are those servants whom the Lord when he cometh shall find watching;" Acts 16: 17: "These men are the servants of the most high God, which show unto us the way of salvation;" 1 Pet. 2: 16: "as the servants of God;" Rev. 1: 1: "to show unto his servants;" 10: 7: "declared to his servants the prophets;" 15: 3: "the song of Moses the servant of God;" 19: 5: "Praise our God, all ye his servants."

[4] Rom. 1: 1: "Paul a servant (*doulos*) of Jesus Christ;" Gal. 1: 10; Phil. 1: 1; Tit. 1: 1.

[5] 2 Pet. 1: 1; Jas. 1: 1; Jude, ver. 1; Rev. 1: 1.

3) *andrapodon*[1] means always a *slave*, especially one *enslaved in war*. This term is degrading in its etymology and neuter gender, and is used in the vile and abject sense, when the slaves are statistically enumerated or otherwise represented as mere property, or chattles, or things. Now it is a remarkable fact, that the New Testament, which so frequently uses the term *doulos* and about half a dozen words more or less resembling it in meaning, never employs the term *andrapodon*, except once in the derivative compound, *andrapodistes*, a *man-stealer*, or *slave-trader*, and then in the worst possible company with murderers, whore-mongers, liars, perjurers, and other gross sinners.[2] As the term is of very frequent occurrence among the classics and must have been perfectly familiar to the apostles, the omission is significant and must imply the condemnation of the idea involved in it. It suggests to us two different conceptions of slavery, the one represented by the word *doulos*, the other by the word *andrapodon;* the one prevailing among the Jews, the other among the heathen; the one which still regards and treats the slave as a person, the other which degrades him to mere property; the one recognized or tolerated by the apostles, the other disowned by them as irreconcilable with the spirit of the gospel.

Slavery indeed always implies the double relation of lordship or government, and of possession or property. The former makes the slave-holder simply a ruler and patron of his subject, and although liable to abuse, like every other kind of power in the

---

[1] ἀνδράποδον either from ἀνήρ and πούς, the foot of the conqueror placed on the neck of the conquered, to indicate complete subjugation, or from ἀνήρ and ἀποδόσθαι, to sell a man.

[2] 1 Tim. 1: 10. The English Version and most commentators translate this word *menstealer*, or *kidnapper*, who enslaves free persons and sells them,—a crime punished with death under the Old Testament, Exod. 21: 16; Deut. 24: 7. But some dictionaries assign to ἀνδραποδιστής also the more general meaning of *slave-trader*, just as κερματιστής is not a *money-stealer*, but a *money-changer* (John 2: 14). The apostle would, no doubt, have embraced all persons engaged in the horrors of the African slave-trade under the same category and condemnation.

hands of sinful and erring man, may be unselfish, humane and beneficial; just as an absolute monarchy may be a good form of government in the hands of a good monarch who rules in the fear of God and with a single eye to the happiness of his subjects while incapable of self-government. The latter makes the slaveholder the proprietor or owner of the slave and gives him the legal—though not the moral—right to turn the *doulos* into an *andrapodon*, the person into a mere thing or "animated tool," and to dispose of him as of any other article of merchandise for his own profit. The predominance of the one or the other of these ideas determines the character of the institution and tends either to the elevation or the degradation of the slave. In the Jewish servitude the governmental idea strongly prevailed over the mercenary; in the Roman, the mercenary over the governmental. The New Testament retains and recognizes the governmental idea as an existing fact, and nowhere denounces it as sinful in itself, but it divests it of its harshness and guards it against abuse, by reminding the master of his moral responsibility and inspiring him with kindness and charity to his slave as a brother in Christ and fellow-heir of the same kingdom of glory in heaven. But the mercenary idea is entirely ignored in the New Testament, or indirectly condemned with every other form of selfishness. Hence we find not a word about traffic in men, about buying and selling human beings; the very idea is utterly repugnant to the spirit of the gospel. The slave, without distinction of race and color, is uniformly spoken of as a personal being clothed with the same moral rights and duties, redeemed by the same blood of Christ, sanctified by the same Spirit, and called to the same immortality and glory as his master. Wherever the governmental idea holds the mercenary so completely in check and yields to the influence of Christian morality, it may be a wholesome training school for inferior races, until they are capable to govern themselves.

Christianity attaches comparatively little importance to slavery and freedom in the civil and political sense. Its mission lies far deeper. It is a new moral creation, which commences with the inmost life of humanity, although it looks to the resurrection of the body and the glorious liberty of the children of God as its final consummation. It is intensely spiritual in its nature and takes its position far above the temporal relations of this world, which is continually changing and passing away. Wholly occupied with the eternal interests and welfare of man, it sinks all the social distinctions of earth and time in the common sinfulness and guilt before God and the common salvation through Christ. Rising above the limits of nationality and race, it proclaims a universal religion and opens a fountain of pardon and peace, where the Jew and the Gentile, the Greek and the barbarian, the freeman and the slave, on the single condition of renouncing sin and turning to God, may receive the same spiritual and eternal blessings and unite in a common brotherhood of faith and love. It is so pliable and applicable, so free and independent in its own elevated sphere, that it can accommodate itself to every condition and can be practised in every calling of life. It requires no man to give up his occupation after conversion, unless it be sinful in its nature; but remaining in it, he should faithfully serve God and honor his profession. If a slave can legitimately gain his freedom, so much the better, for freedom is the normal condition of man; but if he cannot, he need not be discouraged, for by faith in Christ he is a freeman in the highest and best sense of the term, a brother and fellow-heir, with his believing master, of eternal glory in heaven. Civil bondage may be a great evil, but not near as great as the moral bondage of sin; civil freedom may be a great good, but only temporal at best, and not to be compared with the spiritual freedom which elevates the humblest Christian slave far above his heathen master. All earthly distinctions and blessings vanish into utter insignificance when compared with the eternal realities of the kingdom of heaven.

This is clearly the view which St. Paul takes in the following passages:

"There is neither Jew nor Greek, there is neither bond (*doulos*) nor free (*eleutheros*), there is neither male nor female: for ye are all one in Christ Jesus." Gal. 3 : 28.

"Where there is neither Greek nor Jew, circumcision nor uncircumcision, barbarian, Scythian, bond, *nor* free: but Christ *is* all, and in all." Col. 3 : 11.

"For in one Spirit were we all baptized into one body, whether *we be* Jews or Gentiles, whether *we be* bond or free; and were all made to drink of one Spirit." 1 Cor. 12 : 13.

"Let every man abide in the same calling wherein he was called. Art thou called being a servant (*doulos*, bond-servant)? care not for it; but if thou mayest be made free, use *it* rather [namely *freedom*].[1] For he that is called in the Lord, being a servant, is the Lord's freeman : likewise also he that is called, being free, is Christ's servant. Ye were bought with a price: be not ye the bond-servants of men. Brethren, let every man, wherein he is called, therein abide with God." 1 Cor. 7 : 20-24.

From the elevated stand-point above the changing and passing distinctions of time and sense, the apostles approach the master and the servant alike with the same call to repent and believe, with the same offer of the gospel salvation, requiring the same change of their heart, though not of their outward condition, admitting both to the Christian Church, inviting them to the same table of the Lord, and urging them as church members to a faithful discharge of the general Christian duties and of those special duties which grow out of their legal and social relation to each other. Take the following exhortations:

[1] It is a singular fact that Chrysostom, and the ancient commentators supply δουλεία, *slavery*, to the verb and make the apostle say : even if, or although thou mayest be free, remain rather a slave in order to show the more by contrast thy spiritual freedom. The same view is taken by De Wette, Meyer, Kling, and apparently by Stanley, who urge the drift of the context. But Calvin, Beza, Grotius, Whitby, Doddridge, Olshausen, Neander, Hodge, and most modern interpreters supply ἐλευθερία *freedom*,—an exposition already mentioned although not approved by Chrysostom, and clearly preferable on account of the verb *use*. the particles *but* and *rather* (ἀλλά—μᾶλλον) and of ver. 23 ("be not ye the bond-servants of men"), as well as for internal reasons. For it can not be doubted for a moment that Paul, himself a Roman citizen, regarded freedom as the normal and far preferable state, wherever it could be legitimately and honorably attained.

Eph. 6: 5–9: "Servants (*douloi*), be obedient to them that are *your* masters (lords, *tois kyriois*) according to the flesh, with fear and trembling, in singleness of your heart, as unto Christ; not with eyeservice, as men-pleasers, but as the servants of Christ, doing the will of God from the heart; with good will doing service, as to the Lord, and not to men: knowing that whatsoever good thing any man doeth, the same he shall receive again from the Lord, whether *he be* bond or free. And ye masters (*kyrioi*), do the same things unto them, and forbear threatening: knowing that both their Master and yours is in heaven; and there is no respect of persons with him."

Col. 3: 22–25: "Servants (*douloi*) obey in all things *your* masters according to the flesh; not with eyeservice as men-pleasers; but in singleness of heart, fearing God; and whatsoever ye do, do *it* heartily, as to the Lord, and not unto men; knowing that from the Lord ye shall receive the reward of the inheritance: for ye serve the Lord Christ. But he that doeth wrong, shall receive again for the wrong which he hath done: and there is no respect of persons."

Col. 4: 1: "Masters, render unto *your* servants that which is just and equal; knowing that ye also have a Master in heaven."

1 Tim. 6: 1–2: "Let as many servants as are under the yoke [*i. e.* bond-servants] count their own masters worthy of all honor, that the name of God and his doctrine be not blasphemed. And they that have believing masters, let them not despise *them,* because they are brethren; but rather do *them* service, because they are faithful and beloved, partakers of the benefit. These things teach and exhort."

Tit. 2: 9, 10: "*Exhort* servants to be obedient to their own masters *and* to please *them* well in all *things* [which legitimately belong to them in their capacity as masters]; not gainsaying; not purloining, but shewing all good fidelity; that they may adorn the doctrine of God our Saviour in all things."

1 Peter 2: 18–20: "Servants [*oiketai*, domestic slaves, or household servants], *be* subject to *your* masters (*tois despotais*) with all fear; not only to the good and gentle, but also to the froward. For this is thankworthy, if a man for conscience toward God endure grief, suffering wrongfully. For what glory *is it*, if, when ye be buffeted for your faults, ye shall take it patiently? but if, when ye do well, and suffer *for it,* ye take it patiently, this *is* acceptable with God."

The sense of all these passages is plain and can not be mistaken, except under the influence of the strongest prejudice.

First, as to the servants, they are nowhere exhorted or advised to run away from their masters, however hard their condition may have been, and no doubt was at the time, especially in heathen families, nor to revolt and disobey, but on the contrary to obey their masters, whether heathen or Jewish or Christian, whether hard and cruel, or gentle and kind, in all things belonging to their proper authority and not conflicting with the authority of God and the law of conscience, and to obey cheerfully, in the fear of God and from a sense of duty, and thus to adorn and commend their holy profession; remembering always in their outward bondage that they enjoy spiritual freedom in Christ which no man could take from them, and that in the prospect of everlasting glory in heaven they might well forego the comparatively small advantage of civil freedom in this present transient life.

Secondly, the masters are nowhere required or exhorted to emancipate their slaves. This matter, like all direct control over private possessions and secular business, the apostles regarded as lying beyond their proper authority; for Christ himself, with his unfailing wisdom, refused to be a divider of property, and simply warned the contending parties against covetousness (Luke 12 : 14). Hence they left it to the free choice of the slaveholders and their own sense of duty, which depends upon the effects of the measure or the probable benefit arising from it to both parties, especially the slave himself. Christ never alludes to the subject of emancipation in his personal teaching; but if the servant of the gentile centurion was a slave, as in all probability he was,[1] we would have a strong proof from his own mouth for the compatibility of slaveholding with a high order of Christian piety; for he said of the centurion: "I have not found so great faith, no, not in Israel"

---

[1] In Luke 7 : 2 he is called δοῦλος, *doulos,* and in Matth. 8 : 6 παῖς, *pais,* which is the least ignominious term for slave. It is evident both from Matth. 8 : 9 and Luke 7 : 8, that the centurion had many soldiers and servants under his authority. He was probably a proselyte of the gate, or a half convert to Judaism, but certainly uncircumcised, and hence was held up to the Jews as an example of faith.

(Matt. 8 : 10 ; Luke 7 : 9). The apostles expressly denounce men-stealing or — if we choose to give *andrapodistes* this wider sense—slave-trading (1 Tim. 1 : 10); but they never enumerate slaveholding in any of their catalogues of sins and crimes, however complete and minute;[1] they nowhere make non-slaveholding a term of church membership; on the contrary, St. Paul speaks of certain masters of "servants under the yoke," *i. e.*, slaveholders, who are " faithful and beloved, partakers of the benefit," (1 Tim. 6 : 1, 2); and addresses Philemon, who was a slaveholder at the time, as " a brother, dearly beloved and fellow-laborer," that is, either an officer of the congregation at Colossæ, or an active lay-member (Philem. vers. 1, 7). On the other hand the apostles still less recommend the masters to sell their slaves and to make money out of them, and by doing so perhaps to sunder the sacred ties between husband and wife, parents and children. But they uniformly exhort them to give to their slaves all that is just and equitable; to treat them with humanity, kindness and charity, even as they would like to be treated according to the well known maxim of Christ; to forbear even threatening, not to mention those cruel punishments which the Roman law authorized and which were so common at the time; and in this whole relation to remember that they, too, have a Master in heaven, that the Christian slaves are freedmen of Christ and their brethren by faith, and that God is no respecter of persons. All this, undoubtedly, looks towards manumission as a logical result of moral duty. Hence Christian slave-holders in many cases set their slaves free, and such acts were highly commended in the Church from the beginning.

PAUL AND PHILEMON.

The most striking example of the moral reformation which the spirit of Christianity carried into the institution of slavery,

[1] Such catalogues we have in Rom. 1 : 29, 31; Gal. 5 : 19, 21; compare Matth. 15 : 19; Mark 7 : 21, 22; 1 Cor. 5 : 11; 6 : 9, 10; Eph. 5 : 5; Col. 3 : 8, 9; 1 Tim. 1 : 9, 10; 2 Tim. 3 : 2, 3, 4.

without interfering with its legal rights, is furnished by St. Paul's Epistle to Philemon. The apostle had converted the runaway slave Onesimus at Rome, and although he might have made good use of him, he sent him back to his rightful master Philemon, yet "no longer as a servant or slave (*doulos*) but more than a servant, a brother beloved, especially to me, but how much more unto thee, both in the flesh [*i. e.*, in his temporal or earthly relations as a servant, compare Eph. 6: 5] and in the Lord" [*i. e.*, in his spiritual relation as a Christian brother]; adding the request to receive him as he would the apostle himself (vers. 16, 17).[1]

Here we have the whole doctrine and practice of Christianity on this subject as in a nut-shell. Paul exhibits in this most touching letter the highest type of the Christian gentleman and philanthropist. He acknowledges the legal and social relation as it existed between Philemon and Onesimus, and combines the strictest regard for the rights of the one with the deepest interest in the welfare of the other. He addresses the slaveholder as a "brother, dearly beloved and fellow-laborer," and restores to him his servant, but as a Christian brother, pleading for him as for his own child, offering reparation if he had done wrong, demanding a remission of all penalty, soliciting the sympathy and affection of the master for the penitent fugitive, and promising to receive these favors as bestowed upon himself. This is the love of an inspired apostle, himself a prisoner at the time, for a poor runaway slave! And yet it is only a spark of that love which induced the eternal Son of God to shed his own blood for a sinful world.

Paul's letter to Philemon, in its spiritual and logical bearing, contained a pretty clear, though most delicate, hint at emancipa-

[1] That Onesimus was a slave, is manifest both from the general tenor of the Epistle, and the implication in οὐκ ἔτι ὡς δοῦλον, *no more as a slave*, v. 16, and is universally conceded by all ancient and modern commentators of any note. It was left for an American writer to make the discovery that Onesimus was an *apprentice* because "it is quite as common for apprentices to run away, as it is for slaves!"

tion. We do not know whether Philemon actually set Onesimus free. If he did, he only acted in the spirit of the apostle's advice; and tradition says that Onesimus not only received his freedom, but became a bishop in a Christian church.

CONCLUSION.

Christianity cured the root of the evil, and created a new state of society on the basis of a common brotherhood in Christ. It made emancipation possible, desirable, and beneficial, and always favored it in individual cases. The legal extinction of the institution of slavery is the slow process of centuries, and is not yet completed; but the progress of freedom is steady and irresistible, and will not rest until tyranny and slavery are swept out of existence.

DIE CHRISTLICHE SONNTAGSFEIER.

Eine Rede gehalten vor einer deutschen Massen-Versammlung zur Förderung der Sonntagsfeier, im Cooper Institut zu New-York, am Sonntag Abend, den 16. Oktober, 1859.[1]

"Herr Präsident!
Verehrte Versammlung!
Meine Erscheinung unter Ihnen bedarf keiner Rechtfertigung. Als ich vor ein paar Wochen von deutschen und englischen Freunden in New-York eingeladen wurde, vor einer deutschen Versammlung zur Förderung der christlichen Sonntagsfeier eine Rede zu halten, konnte ich über die Annahme dieses unerwarteten Rufes keinen Augenblick zweifelhaft sein. Es handelt sich hier um eine heilige Angelegenheit, um eine brennende Lebensfrage, welche seit einiger Zeit fast alle grösseren Städte Amerika's, vor allem aber New-York und Philadelphia, aufgeregt hat und mit den theuersten Interessen der öffentlichen Sittlichkeit und Religion, mit der wahren Wohlfahrt unseres Adoptiv-Vaterlandes und mit der Ehre des deutschen Namens aufs innigste verknüpft ist. Zur Wahrung

[1 This address is given in the language in which it was delivered. The meeting was memorable in the history of the American Sabbath, when a systematic effort was made, especially by the lager-beer and liquor-interest, to abolish all Sunday laws in New York. It was attended by Germans of all churches and classes of society. Mr. Gustav Schwab, son of the poet and one of the leading merchants of New York, presided. Nearly all the German pastors of the city and vicinity, and several English ministers as Drs. Adams, Spring, Prime, Mühlenberg, Hitchcock, Prentiss, were on the platform. Addresses were made by Rev. Mr. Garlichs, Guldin, Dr. Adams, and others, which are printed in Doc. No. 9 of the "New York Sabbath Committee."]

und Förderung dieser Güter einen Beitrag zu liefern, halte ich für meine Pflicht, für ein Vorrecht und eine Ehre. Freilich, wenn es sich blos um den Namen des Sabbaths oder Sonntags—wir brauchen diese Ausdrücke hier nach der Landessitte als gleichbedeutend—oder auch um die Differenz zwischen der anglo-puritanischen und der deutsch-evangelischen Sonntags-Theorie und Praxis handelte, so wäre ich zu Hause geblieben. Aber es handelt sich hier um Sein oder Nichtsein, um die Erhaltung eines Segenstages oder die Einführung eines Fluchtages. Der Sonntag—das bitte ich hier gleich von vorn herein zu bedenken—ist in diesem amerikanischen Freistaatenbunde, wo der Bestand der christlichen Kirche nicht auf Staatszwang, sondern auf dem freien Volkswillen, auf der Macht der öffentlichen Meinung und Sitte ruht, ein Collectiv-Name für alle Einrichtungen der christlichen Kirche und Funktionen des öffentlichen Gottesdienstes, eine Garantie für die positive Ausübung der uns durch die Landesgesetze gewährten Glaubens- und Cultusfreiheit, ein mächtiges Bollwerk um das Heiligthum der Familien und der Gotteshäuser, und ein wöchentlicher schlagender Beweis vor der ganzen Welt, dass das amerikanische Volk, trotz der Trennung von Kirche und Staat, ein *gottesfürchtiges* und *christliches* Volk ist und bleiben will.

Die Veranlassung zu dieser Versammlung ist Ihnen Allen bekannt und braucht nicht erst auseinandergesetzt zu werden. Sie ist nicht eine willkürliche und unberufene Veranstaltung einiger New-Yorker Sonntagsfreunde. Sie ist ein Bedürfniss, eine Pflicht, eine Nothwendigkeit. Die deutschen Sabbathschänder, *angeführt von einigen charakterlosen amerikanischen Politikern*, welche unsere Landsleute gerne, wie die Irländer, als Werkzeuge für ihre selbstsüchtigen Zwecke missbrauchen möchten, aber zum Glück nicht können, haben ihrem bitteren Hass gegen die Sonntagsgesetze und gute Sitte des Landes und gegen das Christenthum selbst mitten unter Tabaksqualm und trunken von Lagerbier-Begeisterung, bis zur Verletzung der allgemein-menschlichen Gesetze der Würde und des Anstandes, freien Lauf gelassen, und dadurch ihrer eignen schlechten Sache, nach dem einstimmigen Zeugniss der englischen Presse, so sehr geschadet, dass wir schon desshalb aller weiteren polemischen Rücksicht überhoben sind. Wir sind überhaupt nicht zusammengekommen, um unsere Gegner zu bekämpfen, sondern um einfach unserer eigenen Ueberzeugung einen öffentlichen Ausdruck zu geben und unsern amerikanischen Landsleuten einen factischen Beweis zu liefern, dass es zwei ganz verschiedene Klassen von Deutschen gibt, welche in dieser socialen Lebensfrage wie Feuer und Wasser, wie Licht und Finsterniss, wie Christus und Belial sich gegenüberstehen.

Und zwar glaube ich zuversichtlich behaupten zu dürfen, dass wir als Vertheidiger des göttlich eingesetzten Ruhetages nicht nur die grosse Majorität der anglo-amerikanischen Bevölkerung, von Maine bis Florida, von New-York bis San Francisco, sondern *bei weitem den besseren Theil der eingebornen und eingewanderten Deutschen* selbst auf unserer Seite haben. Zum Beweise dafür kann ich mich getrost berufen auf die mir sehr wohl bekannte deutsche Landbevölkerung, die zu den ruhigsten, fleissigsten und nützlichsten Bürgern Amerika's gehört, sowie auf die vielen hunderte von kirchlichen Gemeinden, lutherischer, reformirter, evangelischer und anderer Confession, die über fast alle Staaten dieser Union zerstreut sind und sich mit jedem Jahre vermehren. Aber es genügt, auf die gegenwärtige Versammlung deutscher Sonntagsfreunde hinzuweisen, deren imposante Grösse und würdige Haltung unsere Erwartungen weit übertrifft und unser Herz mit Dank und Freude erfüllt.

Beinahe zwei tausend und noch dazu meist eingewanderte Deutsche, wie man schon aus dem fast einstimmigen und erhebenden Gesang unserer herrlichen deutschen Choräle schliessen muss! Wahrlich, das ist die grösste deutsche, *ja sogar die zahlreichste englische* Versammlung zu Gunsten der Sonntagsfeier, die ich bis dahin in Amerika oder Europa gesehen habe. Allein wir haben, ausser der Majorität, auch die Autorität, die in solchen sittlichen Fragen besser ist; wir haben die Bibel; wir haben die Landesgesetze und die mehr als zweihundertjährige, durch die gesegnetsten Folgen bewährte Landessitte; wir haben die heilige Sache der öffentlichen Ordnung, der öffentlichen Sittlichkeit, der nationalen Wohlfahrt, kurz, wir haben göttliches und menschliches Recht auf unserer Seite. Mit solchen Bundesgenossen dürfen wir wohl den Kampf wagen und des endlichen Erfolges gewiss sein, eingedenk der alten Losung: "Mit diesem Zeichen wirst du siegen!"

Ich rede zu Ihnen nicht als Puritaner, obgleich ich gerne bekenne, vor dem Puritanismus, als einer der grossartigsten Erscheinungen der Welt- und Kirchengeschichte, einen tiefen Respect zu haben, sondern als deutscher Theologe; nicht als Vertheidiger eines ängstlichen jüdischen Sabbathismus, sondern einer freien christlichen Sonntagsfeier. Ich rede aber auch zu Ihnen nicht als ein Abkömmling von Monarchieen, sondern als ein geborner Republikaner—denn ich bin von Haus aus ein Schweizer—und als Freund der amerikanischen Glaubens- und Cultusfreiheit.

Also vom deutschen und republikanischen Standpunkte aus ergreife ich heute das Wort zu Gunsten der *physischen*, der *sittlichen* und der *religiösen Nothwendigkeit des Sonntags*, als eines Tages der *Ruhe*, der *Zucht* und des *Segens* für den Einzelnen, die Familie und den Staat.

I. Der Sabbath oder Ruhetag ist seinem Wesen und seiner Idee nach älter, als die mosaische Gesetzgebung und als das Judenthum. Er geht, wie die Einsetzung der Ehe und das Institut der Familie, zurück bis auf den Anfang des menschlichen Geschlechtes, bis in das Paradies der Unschuld: er ruht auf der ursprünglichen Schöpfung und auf der Natur des Menschen, als eines sinnlich-vernünftigen Erdenwesens. Darum weist auch das vierte Gebot auf diesen Ursprung zurück mit den Worten, welche das Gebot begründen: "Denn in sechs Tagen hat Gott der Herr Himmel und Erde gemacht und das Meer und Alles, was darinnen ist, und ruhete am siebenten Tage.

Darum segnete der Herr den Sabbathtag und heiligte ihn." Das ist natürlich nicht so zu verstehen, als ob Gott von da an aufgehört habe zu schaffen und zu wirken; es ist nicht die Ruhe des Nichtshuns, sondern die Ruhe der Vollendung, des Segnens und seligen Genusses gemeint. Gott hat, das ist der Sinn dieser populären Ausdrucksweise, am Schlusse seiner ersten Offenbarung nach aussen hin seine ewige und selige Ruhe, durch gnädige Herablassung und Accommodation, dem Menschen vorbildlich zur Anschauung gebracht und ihn dadurch angewiesen, dass auch er seine Arbeit an jedem siebten Tage durch Ruhe in Gott abschliessen und innerlich vollenden und heiligen soll. Hier haben wir also die göttliche Sanction und die göttliche Begründung eines wöchentlichen Ruhe- und Segenstages, nicht blos für Juden, sondern für *alle* Menschen. Auch in dem neuen Testamente, in der tiefsinnigen Stelle Hebr. 4:3—4, wird die Sabbathruhe auf die Schöpfung zurückgeführt und als uranfängliche Ordnung Gottes bezeichnet. Das Sabbathgebot entspricht einem allgemeinen Naturgesetze, das niemand ungestraft verletzen kann. Das menschliche Leben ist nach seiner leiblichen, geistigen und sittlichen Seite auf einen steten und regelmässigen Wechsel zwischen Arbeit und Ruhe, zwischen äusserem Wachsthum und innerer Sammlung, zwischen Ausbreitung und Vertiefung angelegt. Jede Arbeit schliesst sich in einem Ruheakte ab, und jede Ruhe ist wieder ein Ansatz zu neuer Thätigkeit. Diesem Gesetze ist selbst die Pflanze und das Thier unterworfen, und diesem Gesetze ist der Lauf der äusseren Natur, der Sonne, des Mondes und der Sterne dienstbar gemacht. Daher der Wechsel von Tag und Nacht, und die Eintheilung der irdischen Zeit in Wochen, Monden und Jahreszeiten. Was nun die Nacht ist im Verhältniss zum Tage, der Herbst und Winter im Verhältniss zum Frühling und Sommer, das ist der Sabbath, d. h. ein wöchentlicher Ruhetag, im Verhältniss zu den sechs Werktagen. Ob es der siebte oder der erste Tag der Woche sei, das ist für de allgemeine Frage hier ganz gleichgültig. Er ist die Ruhe der

Woche, wie der Schlaf die Ruhe des Tages. Leib und Seele bedürfen zu ihrem Wohlsein nicht nur der täglichen, sondern auch der periodischen wöchentlichen Ruhe von der Arbeit, der Erholung von der Anstrengung, der Kräftigung aller Gliedmassen und Fähigkeiten zu immer neuer Arbeit, und in demselben Masse, in welchem die regelmässige Befriedigung dieses Bedürfnisses versagt wird, wird auch die Gesundheit, der Wohlstand und die Arbeitsfähigkeit untergraben. Bekanntlich findet sich die Wocheneintheilung mit einer mehr oder weniger klaren Feier des siebten Tages nicht nur bei den Hebräern, sondern bei allen geschichtlichen Völkern des Alterthums, den semitischen und indo-germanischen, bei den Arabern, Aegyptern, Griechen, Römern, Chinesen und selbst den Negern der afrikanischen Goldküste, die ihren wöchentlichen Fetischtag haben, zum deutlichen Beweise, dass diese Eintheilung nicht blos temporäre und nationale, sondern allgemein menschliche Bedeutung hat und auf einem wesentlichen Naturbedürfnisse beruht. Die Siebenzahl, welche Philo "das Lebensprinzip aller Dinge" nennt, hat eine tiefe Bedeutung, nicht nur auf religiösem Gebiete als die Bundeszahl oder die Zahl der Zusammenfassung Gottes und der Welt, sondern auch in kosmischen und planetarischen Verhältnissen, und macht sich in der normalen und krankhaften Entwicklung des menschlichen Lebens überall geltend.

Der Sabbath ist also, wie Christus sagt (Mark 2:27.), für den Menschen, nicht der Mensch für den Sabbath gemacht. Er ist seiner ursprünglichen Absicht nach, wie alle Gesetze und Einrichtungen Gottes, kein Zwang, kein Joch, sondern eine wahre Wohlthat, eine Gabe und ein Recht, das Gott den Menschen, und zwar allen Menschen, besonders auch den armen und hart arbeitenden Klassen, den Dienstboten, den Fremdlingen, und selbst den unvernünftigen Thieren gegeben hat. Diese wohlthätige Absicht tritt im vierten Gebot ganz deutlich hervor. "Sechs Tage," so heisst es, "sollst du arbeiten und alle deine Werke thun, aber am siebenten Tage ist der Sabbath des Herrn, deines Gottes; da sollst du keine Arbeit thun, noch dein Sohn, noch deine Tochter, noch deine Magd, noch dein Vieh, noch dein Fremdling, der in deinen Thoren ist." Das Verbot der Arbeit,—von welchem jedoch, nach allgemeiner Zustimmung, Werke der Nothwendigkeit und der Liebe ausgenommen sind, aus dem einfachen Grunde, weil die Nothwendigkeit kein Gesetz kennt, und weil die Liebe des Gesetzes höchste Erfüllung ist,—ich sage, das Verbot der Arbeit ist nur die negative Seite und unvermeidliche Bedingung des positiven Anrechtes auf Ruhe für Leib und Seele, zur Erhaltung und Gesundheit beider.

Diese natürliche Nothwendigkeit und Wohlthätigkeit eines wöchentlichen Ruhetages für Leib und Seele wird durch die Erfahrung und durch die gewichtigsten ärztlichen Zeugnisse bestätigt. Unter den letzteren will ich aus vielen bloss einige anführen. Im Jahre 1832 liess das britische Haus der Gemeinen die Sonntagsfrage mit Rücksicht auf die arbeitenden Klassen durch eine Commission von dreissig Parlamentsmitgliedern untersuchen, zu denen Sir Andrew Agnew, Sir Robert Peel, Sir Robert Inglis, Sir Thomas Baring, Lord Ashley und andere ausgezeichnete Staatsmänner gehörten. Diese Commission consultirte eine grosse Anzahl Zeugen aus verschiedenen Ständen und Beschäftigungen, unter Andern auch den berühmten und erfahrenen Arzt Dr. John Richard Farre von London, der als Resultat seiner beinahe vierzigjährigen Praxis und Beobachtung folgendes Zeugniss aus stellte:

"Als ein Ruhetag halte ich den Sabbath für einen Ersatztag für die unzureichende Wiederherstellungskraft des Körpers unter *fortwährender* Arbeit und Aufregung. Ein Arzt nimmt immer Rücksicht auf die Erhaltung der Wiederherstellungskraft; denn wenn diese verloren ist, so hat seine Heilkunst ein Ende. Ein Arzt ist bedacht auf die Erhaltung der Gleichmässigkeit des Blutumlaufes (the balance of circulation) als nothwendig zur Wiederherstellungskraft des Leibes. Die gewöhnliche Anstrengung des Menschen schwächt den Umlauf an jedem Tage seines Lebens; und das erste allgemeine Naturgesetz, durch welches Gott seine Zerstörung verhindert, ist der Wechsel von Tag und Nacht, damit Ruhe auf Arbeit folge. Aber obwohl die Nacht scheinbar den Blutumlauf ausgleicht, so stellt sie doch das Gleichgewicht für die Erreichung eines langen Lebens nicht hinlänglich her. Desshalb ist durch die Güte der Vorsehung ein Tag unter sieben als Ersatztag dazugegeben, damit durch dessen Ruhe das animalische System vollendet werde. Diese Frage lässt sich leicht faktisch entscheiden durch den Versuch mit einem Lasthier. Man nehme z. B. das Pferd, und man wird bald finden, dass ein Ruhetag seine Kraft für die übrigen sechs Tage vermehrt und zu seiner vollen Gesundheit nothwendig ist. Der Mensch wird durch die höhere Kraft seines Geistes aufrecht gehalten, so dass sich der nachtheilige Einfluss *fortwährender* täglicher Arbeit und Anstrengung nicht so schnell und unmittelbar kund giebt als beim unvernünftigen Thiere, aber im Verlaufe bricht er rascher zusammen und verkürzt sich die Länge seines Lebens und die physische Kraft des Alters. Ich betrachte desshalb die Einsetzung des Sabbaths als eine gütige Einrichtung der Vorsehung zur Erhaltung des menschlichen Lebens, und die Beobachtung desselben als eine natürliche Pflicht, sofern nämlich zugestanden wird, dass die Lebenserhaltung eine Pflicht und die unzeitige Lebenszerstörung eine Art von Selbstmord ist. Ich sage diess blos als ein Arzt und ohne alle Rücksicht auf die theologische Seite der Frage.

Aber wenn man ferner die Wirkungen des wahren Christenthums betrachtet, nämliche Friede des Gemüths, Vertrauen auf Gott und Wohlwollen zu den Menschen, so wird man in dem höheren Gebrauch des Sabbaths, als eines heiligen Ruhetages, eine zufätzliche Quelle der Lebenserneuerung für den Geist und durch diesen auch für den Leib finden. . . . . . . Untersuchungen in der Physiologie zeigen durch die Analogie des Wirkens der Vorsehung in der Natur, dass das göttliche Gebot keine willkürliche Anordnung, sondern für das Wohl des Menschen nothwendig ist. Diess ist der Grund, auf welchen ich die Sache stelle, im Unterschied von Vorschrift und Gesetzgebung. Ich betrachte die Sonntagsruhe als nothwendig für den Menschen, und darum sind die Feinde des Sabbaths auch Feinde des Menschen. Alle starken Anstrengungen des Leibes oder Geistes, sowie alle Arten von Ausschweifung und Belustigung, welche den Blutumlauf forciren, der an diesem Tage ruhen sollte, sind ein nachtheiliger Missbrauch des Sabbaths, während die Abspannung von den gewöhnlichen Lebensforgen, der Genuss der Ruhe im Schoosze der Familie, verbunden mit den religiösen Uebungen und Pflichten, welche dieser Tag auferlegt, von welchen, gehörig verstanden, keine einzige das Leben abkürzt, den angemessenen und wohlthätigen Gebrauch des Sabbaths ausmachen." . . . . . .

Bei einer regelmässigen Versammlung der "New-Haven Medical Association," welche aus fünfundzwanzig Aerzten mit Einschluss der Professoren des medizinischen Collegiums besteht, wurden folgende drei Fragen ausführlich besprochen und *einstimmig bejahend* beantwortet: 1. Ist die Ansicht des Dr. Farre in seinem vor der Committee des britischen Hauses der

DIE CHRISTLICHE SONNTAGSFEIER. 221

Gemeinen abgelegten Zeugnisse richtig? 2. Sind Menschen, die bloss sechs Tage arbeiten, der Regel nach gesünder und leben sie länger, als solche, welche unter gleichen Verhältnissen sieben Tage arbeiten? 3. Verrichten sie mehr und besere Arbeit?—Dr. John C. Warren von Boston, Professor am medizinischen Collegium der Universität von Cambridge, gab ebenfalls seine volle Zustimmung in diesen Worten:

"Ich stimme der Ansicht des Dr. Farre, den ich persönlich als einen Arzt vom höchsten Range kenne, vollkommen bei. Die Nützlichkeit des Sabbaths als eines Ruhetages, vom weltlichen Standpunkte aus betrachtet, ruht auf einem der allgemeinsten Naturgesetze, dem Gesetze des *periodischen Wechsels* (periodicity). So weit meine Beobachtung reicht, zeichnen sich die Menschen, welche am Sabbath weltliche Sorgen und Arbeiten zu vermeiden pflegen, auch am meisten durch vollkommene Erfüllung ihrer Pflichten während der Woche aus. Der Einfluss eines Wechsels der Gedanken am Sabbath auf das Gemüth solcher Person gleicht dem Einfluss des Wechsels der Nahrung auf den Körper. Jener scheint den Geisteskräften, wie dieser den Leibeskräften, neue Frische und Energie zu geben. *Ich bin fest überzeugt, dass solche Personen im Stande sind, mehr und bessere Arbeit in sechs Tagen zu verrichten, als wenn sie alle sieben Tage arbeiteten.* Das Einathmen der reinen und erhebenden Atmosphäre eines religiösen Sabbaths erfrischt und kräftigt den Geist. Es bildet eine Epoche in unserm Leben, von der wir neue Anregung erhalten, und ist daher die beste Vorbereitung für die Arbeiten der folgenden Woche."

Eine Committee der Gesetzgebenden Versammlung von Pennsylvanien führt in einem Berichte über den Kanalbau vom Jahre 1839 die Behauptung der Sonntagsfreunde an, "dass sowohl Menschen als Vieh mehr Arbeit verrichten können, wenn sie einen Tag in sieben ruhen, als wenn sie alle sieben arbeiten," und fügt hinzu, "dass ihre eigene Erfahrung, als Geschäftsmänner, Landwirthe und Gesetzgeber, mit dieser Behauptung übereinstimme." Das Experiment ist häufig in England und Amerika mit Menschen, Pferden und Ochsen gemacht worden und hat dasselbe Resultat geliefert, und die Weisheit und Güte der göttlichen Anordnung eines wöchentlichen Ruhetages bestätigt. Ein auffallendes Beispiel zeigte sich noch vor kurzer Zeit in Californien, wo eine amerikanische Gesellschaft von Goldgräbern im Eifer für plötzlichen Reichthum den Sonntag verletzte, aber bald durch allerlei Krankheit und Seuche die Erfahrung machte, dass sie statt des Goldes vielmehr ihr eigenes Grab grub, und daher zur Feier des Ruhetages zurückkehrte, deren wohlthätige Folgen für Leib und Seele sich auch in kurzer Zeit einstellten. Zu diesen englischen und amerikanischen Zeugnissen will ich noch ein deutsches hinzufügen von einem berühmten Manne, der zwar keine theologische und religiöse Autorität ist, aber in den höchsten Kreisen weltlicher Bildung den besten Klang, und daher für unsere Gegner um so grösseres Gewicht hat.

"Ich theile ganz Ihre Meinung," sagt *Wilhelm von Humboldt* in den Briefen an sein Freundin (1850, Bd. 1. S. 282 f.), "dass die Einrichtung bestimmter Ruhetage, selbst wenn sie gar nicht mit religiöser Feier zusammenhinge, eine für Jeden, der ein menschenfreundliches, auf alle Klassen der Gesellschaft gerichtetes Gemüth hat, höchst erfreuliche und wirklich erquickende Idee ist. Es giebt nichts so Selbstisches und Herzloses, als wenn Vornehme und Reiche mit Missfallen, oder wenigstens mit einem gewissen verschmähenden Ekel auf Sonn- und Feiertage zurückblicken. Selbst die Wahl des siebenten Tages ist gewiss die weiseste, welche hätte gefunden werden können. So willkührlich es scheint, die Arbeit um einen Tag zu verkürzen oder zu verlängern, so bin ich überzeugt, dass die sechs Tage gerade das wahre, den Menschen in ihren physischen Kräften und in ihrem Beharren in einförmiger Beschäftigung angemessene Maass ist. Es liegt noch etwas Humanes auch darin, das die zur Arbeit behülflichen Thiere diese Ruhe mit geniessen."

Allein nun sagen unsere Gegner: das geben wir gerne zu, wir wollen ja auch einen wöchentlichen Tag der Ruhe, der Erholung und der Freude. Allerdings! Aber eine Ruhe, welche die grösste Unruhe und Aufregung ist, eine Erholung, welche Ermattung und Aufreibung bewirkt, und eine Freude, die mit bitterem Leide endet! Hört einmal die Sprache dieser Leute: "Der Arbeiter will einen Tag der Erholung, und zwar nicht aus dem Gesalbader eines Schwarzrockes oder aus einem brünstigen Gebetbüchlein, woran sich bloss alte Weiber und Dummköpfe erbauen können; die enge Werkstatt verlangt den Gegensatz der freien Natur, der Zwang der Arbeit drängt zur Ungebundenheit. Wir haben Sommergärten und Sommertheater, aber noch lange nicht genug; Dampfboote und Eisenbahnen müssen Sonntags erst Tausende hinaus tragen in's Freie: Musik und Tanz unter grünen Bäumen müssen ertönen, wohin man sich wendet, überall Lust und Leben und Freude." Jedermann versteht den Sinn dieser Sprache; jedermann weiss, welcher wüste und rohe Materialismus, welche Bestialität sich darunter birgt. Jedermann weiss, wie es bei diesen weltlichen Vergnügungsarten, sei es unter grünen Bäumen, sei es in den Sauf- und Spielhöllen der Stadt, am Sonntag gewöhnlich hergeht. Die Folgen derselben sind leider nur zu oft in dem physischen und moralischen Katzenjammer, in Armuth und Verbrechen, in unsäglichem Familienelend und im endlichen Ruin von Leib und Seele zu lesen. Man nehme bloss die New-Yorker Criminal-Statistik der letzten paar Jahre und die Geschichte der siebentausend siebenhundert nicht licensirten Kneipen dieser Stadt zur Hand, und man hat daran den schlagendsten und traurigsten Commentar zu dieser Sabbathschändung, der alle weiteren Beweise ersetzt. Weg mit diesen wüsten, ausgelassenen Vergnügungen, welche die Gesundheit untergraben, den Geist abstumpfen und verthieren, die Sitten zerstören und den guten deutschen Namen dem Spott und der Verachtung preis geben! Wahrlich, es giebt schönere, reinere und edlere Sonntagsfreuden, welche dem Leib und der Seele wahrhafte Erholung gewähren, sie zu neuer Arbeit stärken und eines vernünftigen sittlichen Wesens und gerade auch eines ächten deutschen Mannes allein würdig sind, Freuden an Gottes Wunderwerken in der Natur und Geschichte, Freuden im stillen Kreise der Familie, Freuden an Werken der Barmherzigkeit und Menschenliebe, Freuden an der Herzens- und Geistesbildung, Freuden der Religion und des Umgangs der Seele mit dem ewigen Urquell alles Lebens und aller Freude. Für solche Freuden, für solche Ruhe und Erholung ist der Sonntag von Gott selbst bestimmt, und von jeder wohlgeordneten christlichen Regierung aufrecht gehalten.

Denn der Sonntag hat neben seiner physischen Nothwendigkeit als Ruhetag auch eine höhere *sittliche* Nothwendigkeit und

Bedeutung, und bloss in demselben Grade, in welchem er seinem sittlichen Zwecke dient, kann er auch seinen physischen Zweck erreichen und dem Leibe des Menschen zur wahren Erholung dienen.

II. Der Sonntag ist einer der Grundpfeiler des wohlgeordneten Familienlebens, sowie der öffentlichen Ordnung und Sittlichkeit in jedem Gemeinwesen. Darum steht das Sabbathgesetz nicht bloss unter den Ceremonialgeboten, sondern in dem *Sittengesetz*, als eines der zehn Gebote, welche seitdem die sittliche Basis nicht nur des jüdischen, sondern aller christlichen Staaten gebildet haben, und bis an's Ende der Zeit bilden werden. Diese Stellung ist von der grössten Bedeutung für die allgemeine *sittliche* Nothwendigkeit und Wichtigkeit eines wöchentlichen Ruhetages und ein gewaltiges Argument zu Gunsten der anglo-amerikanischen Sonntags-Theorie und Praxis im Gegensatz gegen die laxen Ansichten vieler Theologen des Continents. Warum hat Gott, der allweise und allwissende Gott, in dem Mustergesetzbuch, das die Gesetzgebung des Solon und Lykurgus und aller Weisen des Alterthums überlebt hat und heute noch so wahr, so einleuchtend, so unentbehrlich ist als je, die Sabbathsfeier mitten in die allgemeinen und ewig gültigen Sittengesetze hineingeschoben, und die Sabbathsschändung ebenso ernstlich verboten als den Götzendienst, das Fluchen und Schwören, den Ungehorsam gegen die Eltern, den Mord, den Ehebruch, den Diebstahl und die Verläumdung des Nächsten? Gewiss lässt sich diess nur durch die Annahme eines engen Zusammenhangs des Sabbaths mit der öffentlichen Sittlichkeit, mit dem Wohl und Wehe einer Nation erklären.

Eben darum lässt sich auch von vornenherein gar nicht denken, dass Christus, der nach seiner eigenen Erklärung nicht gekommen ist das Gesetz aufzulösen, sondern zu erfüllen, das vierte Gebot seinem *Wesen* nach aufgehoben oder auch nur abgeschwächt haben sollte. Allerdings wurde der Sabbath vom siebten auf den ersten Tag der Woche verlegt, weil Christus am ersten Wochentage auferstanden ist und dadurch die höhere geistige Schöpfung und die Erlösung der Welt vollendet hat. Das ist aber bloss eine Veränderung der äusseren zeitlichen Form, nicht des Wesens. Der alte jüdische Sabbath ist mit Christo begraben worden, und am ersten Wochentage siegreich und verklärt als christlicher Sonntag, als Gedenktag der sittlichen Schöpfung, als Freudentag der vollendeten Erlösung wieder auferstanden. Allerdings treten Christus und die Apostel in mehreren Stellen des Neuen Testaments dem abergläubischen, sklavischen, werkgerechten pharisäischen Sabbathismus, wie überhaupt allem tödtenden Buchstabendienst und aller scheinheiligen Heuchelei, entschieden entgegen, aber, wohlverstanden! nicht zu Gunsten der Profanation des *Sonntags*, sondern umgekehrt im Gegensatz gegen die Profanation der *Wochentage* und im Interesse der Heiligung *aller* Tage. Das ist ein himmelweiter Unterschied. Die Sabbathfeinde wollen alle Zeit und alle Arbeit im Dienste der Welt und Selbstsucht profaniren; Christus und Paulus wollen alle Zeit und alle Arbeit dem Dienste und der Ehre Gottes geheiligt sehen. Das ist der ideale Standpunkt, der dem Christen allerdings stets als Ziel des Strebens und der Sehnsucht vor Augen schweben soll, und der auch dereinst im Jenseits, in dem ewigen Sabbath des Volkes Gottes verwirklicht werden wird. Von demselben idealen Standpunkte verbietet der Herr den Eid, der allerdings in einem Zustande vollkommener Wahrhaftigkeit wegfallen wird, ja unter wahren Christen schon hier unnöthig ist, in einer gemischten Welt voll Lüge und Trug aber nicht wohl entbehrt werden kann. Ebenso sind wir in dieser unvollkommenen Welt noch immer auf einen Wechsel zwischen Arbeit und Ruhe, zwischen Werktagen und Sonntag angewiesen, und gerade der Sonntag und seine würdige Feier ist die beste und unentbehrliche Vorbereitung zur Herbeiführung jenes idealen Zustandes, wo jeder Tag Sonntag, und jedes Werk Gottesdienst und seliger Genuss sein wird.

Daher finden wir denn auch die Feier des Sonntags, als "des Tages des Herrn," schon in der apostolischen und nachapostolischen Kirche und seitdem ununterbrochen mit grösserer oder geringerer Strenge oder Laxheit in allen christlichen Ländern und Jahrhunderten bis auf unsere Tage. Und sobald das Christenthum nach dreihundertjährigem Kampf für seine Existenz vom römischen Staate anerkannt war, erliessen Constantin der Grosse und seine Nachfolger sofort Gesetze für die *bürgerliche* Feier, oder vielmehr Gesetze gegen die bürgerliche Entweihung und zur Wahrung der religiösen Feier des christlichen Sonntags. Solche negative und protective Gesetze von grösserer oder geringerer Strenge giebt es in allen christlich civilisirten Ländern, und zwar merkwürdiger Weise vorzugsweise gerade in denjenigen, wo am meisten bürgerliche und religiöse Freiheit herrscht, wie in der Schweiz, in Holland, England und Schottland.

Vor allem aber zeichnet sich das amerikanische Volk, das freieste und lebenskräftigste Volk unseres Zeitalters, durch strenge Sonntagsfeier aus. Dieser Zug ist wahrlich keine seiner Schwächen und Mängel, sondern umgekehrt ein Zeichen seiner sittlichen Stärke und Selbstbeherrschungskraft, ein Beweis seiner Fähigkeit zum Genusse vernünftiger Freiheit, und mit ein Erklärungsgrund seines beispiellosen Gedeihens und seiner weltgeschichtlichen Grösse. Diese Sonntagsfeier ist hier ein ursprüngliches Gewächs und ein gemeinsamer Besitz, an welchem alle christlichen Benennungen Theil haben. Es ist bekannt, dass die puritanischen Pilgerväter, die Gründer von Neu-England, gleich den ersten Sonntag nach ihrer Landung in Plymouth Rock, im Jahre 1620, im kalten December, trotz aller Hindernisse der ersten Ansiedlung, ohne Obdach und in rauher Wildniss, auf die strengste und würdigste Weise feierten. Diese puritanische Sitte ist tief in den amerikanischen Nationalcharakter eingedrungen und allgemeine Volkssitte geworden. Sie hat zwar mit dem Wachsthum einer heterogenen Bevölkerung viel von ihrer ursprünglichen, zum Theil allerdings rauhen und übertriebenen Strenge verloren, besonders in den grossen Seestädten, wo die Sonntags-Gesetze neuerdings vielfach durch die Nachsicht einer schwachen und charakterlosen Administration zum todten Buchstaben herabgesunken sind, kann aber nie ausgerottet werden. Das amerikanische Volk wird sich den wöchentlichen Ruhetag nie rauben oder in einen Tag der weltlichen Zerstreuung und Lustbarkeit verkehren lassen. Die Sonntagsgesetze von New-York stehen nicht vereinzelt da; alle andern Staaten unserer Republik, mit Ausnahme von einem oder zwei, wo das französische oder spanische Element vorherrscht, haben ähnliche, zum Theil viel strengere Gesetze.

Nun tritt uns aber hier gleich die populäre und oft wiederholte Einwendung entgegen, dass der Staat nichts mit der Kirche zu thun habe, und dass die Sonntagsgesetze der amerikanischen Glaubens- und Cultusfreiheit widersprechen, also constitutionswidrig seien, folglich aufgehoben werden sollten.

Diese Einwendung ruht zunächst auf einem völligen Missverständniss der Natur und Absicht der amerikanischen Sonntagsgesetze. Sie sind nämlich gar nicht coerciv oder zwingend, sondern bloss protectiv oder beschützend; sie sind nicht sowohl positiv, als negativ; sie gebieten nicht die Sonntagsheiligung, sondern verbieten bloss die öffentliche Sonntagsentheiligung; sie zwingen Niemanden in die Kirche zu gehen, sondern beschützen bloss die Kirchengänger in ihren durch die Glaubens Freiheit des Landes ihnen gewährten und verbürgten Rechten. Diess gilt selbst vom Alttestamentlichen Sabbathgebot; es sagt nicht: am Sabbath sollst du die Stiftshütte oder den Tempel besuchen und deine Opfer bringen, sondern: Du sollst am Sabbath keine Alltagswerke verrichten, weder du, noch dein Sohn, noch deine Tochter, noch dein Knecht, noch deine Magd. Der Staat verhält sich zur Kirche ungefähr wie der Leib zur Seele, oder wie das Gesetz zum Evangelium. Er hat mit der inneren Gesinnung, mit der subjectiven Sittlichkeit und Privatfrömmigkeit, sofern sie nicht mit den Rechten Anderer in Conflict geräth, nichts zu thun, und darf die Gewissensrechte nicht einschränken; wohl aber ist es seine Pflicht, die öffentliche Sittlichkeit und die freie Ausübung der Religion zu wahren und zu schützen. Er darf nicht gebieten: Du sollst deinen Nächsten lieben und ihm Gutes thun; wohl aber muss er verbieten, dem Nächsten zu schaden, und muss daher die Verläumdung, den Diebstahl und den Mord bestrafen. Ebenso darf er, wie schon erwähnt, auch nicht die Sonntagsfeier und den Gottesdienst gebieten; wohl aber darf und muss er, so lange er auf den Namen eines christlichen Anspruch macht, die Sonntagsentweihung und die Störung des Gottesdienstes verbieten und nöthigenfalls bestrafen, und seinen Bürgern die Feier des Sonntags und die Ausübung ihrer Cultusfreiheit möglich machen. Das ist alles, und nichts mehr und nichts weniger, was wir vom Staate und seiner Gesetzgebung verlangen.

Nun wendet man aber weiter ein, der amerikanische Staat sei ja gar kein christlicher, so wenig als ein jüdischer, oder mohammedanischer, oder heidnischer; er verhalte sich gegen alle Religion ganz gleichgültig und müsse die Religionslosigkeit und den Atheismus ebenso frei gewähren lassen, als irgend eine Form der Religion.

Allerdings sind Kirche und Staat nicht nur in unserer General-Regierung, sondern auch in allen einzelnen Staaten und Territorien, mit Ausnahme des ganz abnormen und bloss temporären Mormonenterritoriums, getrennt. Allein diese Trennung ruht nicht auf Geringschätzung der Religion und Kirche, sondern auf tiefer Achtung vor beiden. Unsere Religions- und Cultusfreiheit ist nicht eine negative Freiheit, oder Emancipation *von* der Religion, sondern eine positive Freiheit *zur* Religion, die als zu hoch und heilig für die politische Gesetzgebung angesehen, und daher dem freien Gewissen des Einzelnen in seinem Verhältniss zu Gott und den kirchlichen Körperschaften überlassen wird. Der Amerikaner betrachtet die Religions- und Cultusfreiheit eben so wie die Rede- und Pressfreiheit, welche in dem bekannten Artikel der Föderal-Constitution zusammen genannt werden, als eines der unveräusserlichen Grundrechte eines amerikanischen Bürgers und verlangt von der Regierung, dass sie jeden Unterthanen in diesem Rechte, wie

DIE CHRISTLICHE SONNTAGSFEIER. 229

in seiner Person und seinem Eigenthum beschützen soll. Da nun die grosse Masse der Volkes sich zum Christenthum in seinen verschiedenen Formen bekennt und den Sabbath zur Ausübung des Christenthums für unentbehrlich hält, so muss die Regierung schon nach dem republikanischem Grundsatze der Majoritätenherrschaft ihnen den Vollgenuss ihrer Christenrechte und die Ausübung ihrer Christenpflichten, also unter anderm auch die Feier des göttlich eingesetzten Ruhetags, möglich machen, und sie darin beschützen.

Die Trennung des Staates von der Kirche ist nichts weniger als eine Trennung der *Nation* vom *Christenthum;* vielmehr ist die amerikanische Nation entschiedener christlich, als irgend eine Nation der alten Welt, wo die beiden Mächte verschmolzen sind. Das Christenthum ist ein Theil unseres von England ererbten gemeinen Rechts (Common Law), ist mit all unsern Anschauungen und Sitten verwoben, beherrscht unsere häuslichen Einrichtungen und ganze Civilisation und ist die einzig mögliche Religion für Amerika. Gerade weil es hier nicht von der Staatsgewalt aufgezwungen, sondern von ihr bloss beschützt wird, ist es nur um so mächtiger und einflussreicher. Woher denn die vielen tausend Kirchen und Geistlichen; woher die Bibel-, Missions- und Traktatgesellschaften mit ihren enormen Einnahmen; woher die zahllosen christlich-religiösen und philanthropischen Anstalten, Vereine und Liebeswerke, ohne den geringsten Beitrag aus der Staatskasse, alle gegründet, gehoben und getragen durch den freien Willen des Volkes? Sind sie nicht eben so viele Beweise und Ehrendenkmäler der Christlichkeit der amerikanischen Nation?

Ja, das Christenthum ist nicht nur die Religion des Landes, sondern auch die einzig feste Grundlage der amerikanischen Republik, ohne welches diese nicht sechs Jahre bestehen könnte. Das ist die Ansicht der bedeutendsten und weisesten amerikanischen Staatsmänner. "Während eine gerechte Regierung," sagt Washington, der unsterbliche Vater dieser Republik, der selbst ein gottesfürchtiger und bibelgläubiger Mann war, "alle

Bürger in ihren religiösen Rechten beschützt so ist andererseits wahre Religion der sicherste Schutz der Regierung." Und zwar verstand er unter Religion nichts, anderes als das Christenthum. "Das amerikanische Volk," bemerkt sein Freund und Biograph, John Marshall, der erste Oberrichter des obersten Gerichtshofs der Vereinigten Staaten, "ist ein durchaus christliches Volk; und bei uns sind Christenthum und Religion Eins und dasselbe. Es wäre in der That sonderbar, wenn die Institutionen eines solchen Volkes nicht überall das Christenthum voraussetzten." Der Oberrichter Joseph Story, sein College und der berühmteste Ausleger unserer Constitution, sagt von dem oben berührten Artikel über die Religionsfreiheit: "Die eigentliche Absicht dieses Zusatzes[1] war nicht, den Muhamedanismus, oder das Judenthum, oder den Unglauben zu beschützen, noch viel weniger zu befördern und das Christenthum zu benachtheiligen; sondern bloss, alle politische Rivalität zwischen den verschiedenen christlichen Benennungen auszuschliessen und die Gründung einer Staatskirche mit einer ausschliesslich von der Nationalregierung begünstigten Hierarchie zu verhindern." "Denn," fährt er fort, "zur Zeit der Annahme der Constitution und der Zusätze war es wahrscheinlich die herrschende, wo nicht allgemeine Ansicht in Amerika, dass das Christenthum vom Staate begünstigt und geschützt werden solle, so weit diess mit den Privatrechten des Gewissens und mit der Freiheit des religösen Cultus vereinbar ist. Ein Versuch, alle Religionen gleich zu stellen, und es zur Staatspolitik zu machen, gegen alle gleich indifferent zu sein, würde allgemeine Missbilligung, wo nicht allgemeine Entrüstung (universal disapprobation, if not universal indignation) hervorgerufen haben." Derselbe Judge Story erklärt: "Frömmigkeit, Religion und Sittlichkeit sind aufs Innigste mit der Wohlfahrt eines Staates verwoben und

---

[1] Im ersten Artikel der Zusätze: "Congress shall make no law respecting an establishment of religion, or prohibiting the free exercise thereof; or abridging the freedom of speech, or of the press; or the right of the people peaceably to assemble, and to petition the government for a redress of grievances."

für die Administration der bürgerlichen Gerechtigkeit unentbehrlich (indispensable)." Nach Daniel Webster, der sich den Ehrennamen des "Auslegers der Constitution" erworben hat, spricht alles dafür, dass das Christenthum und nur das Christenthum die anerkannte Religion der Vereingten Staaten ist.

Und nun wollen die rothen Republikaner, welche ungerufen zu uns kamen oder zu kommen genöthigt waren und die Gastfreundschaft dieses Landes undankbar missbrauchen, uns belehren, dass unsere Gesetze und Freiheit religionslos seien und das Christenthum mit dem Atheismus auf Eine Stufe stellen! Wahrlich diese Herren haben eine grundfalsche Vorstellung vom amerikanischen National-Charakter und müssen noch das A B C der wahren Freiheit lernen. Die rothrepublikanische und die amerikanische Freiheit haben nichts mit einander gemein als den Namen. Jene Freiheit ist rein negativ und besteht bloss im Hasse gegen Fürsten und Pfaffen, gegen alle beschränkenden Gesetze und Sitten; sie ist in Wahrheit Zügellosigkeit des Fleisches und eben darum die elendeste Sklaverei der Leidenschaft; sie muss im Staate nothwendig zur Anarchie und dann, auf dem Wege der unausbleiblichen Reaction, zum militärischen Despotismus führen. Schlagende Beweise dafür liefern die erste französische Revolution und die pseudo-republikanischen Missgeburten des Jahres 1848, welchen wir die Einwanderung so vieler verunglückten und verjagten Freiheits- oder Zügellosigkeitshelden verdanken.

Der Amerikaner dagegen kann sich individuelle und nationale Freiheit nur denken auf Grundlage der unantastbaren Autorität des Gesetzes und unter der Bedingung des self-government, d. h. der sittlichen Herrschaft des Bürgers und des Volkes über sich selbst. Denn das Wörtlein "selbst" oder "self" ist in diesem berühmten Losungsworte anglo-amerikanischer Freiheit nicht als Nominativ und Subjekt zu fassen, wie in dem russischen Worte "Selbst-Herrscher," self-ruler, welches die ausschliessliche Herrschaft Eines Willens, des Czaren, über das ganze Volk, also das Princip des absoluten Despotismus ausdrückt, sondern es ist das Objekt und zeigt an, dass jeder sich selbst ein Gesetz und über alle seine Leidenschaften Herr sein müsse, ehe er zur Freiheit reif ist. In ähnlichem Sinne sagt der grösste deutsche Dichter ebenso wahr als schön:

> "In der Beschränkung nur zeigt sich der Meister,
> Und das Gesetz nur kann dir Freiheit geben."

Ja, nach amerikanischer und überhaupt nach der richtigen Ansicht ist nur der ein wahrhaft freier Mann, der sich selbst Gesetz ist und jedem bestehenden Gesetze um des Gewissens willen sich freudig unterwirft. Und der letzte Grund dieser vernünftig sittlichen Freiheit oder Selbstbestimmung ist die *Gottesfurcht*. Nur wer den Herrn aller Herren fürchtet, braucht sich vor keinem irdischen König und Kaiser zu fürchten; nur wer sich von Gott abhängig fühlt, ist unabhängig von Menschen; der Dienst Gottes ist die wahre Freiheit. Das war die Freiheit der alten Puritaner und ersten Ansiedler des Landes, der Holländer, der Hugenotten, der Quäker, der deutschen Lutheraner und Reformirten und Aller, die um ihres Glaubens willen die Bequemlichkeiten des Vaterlandes mit der rauhen Wildniss vertauschten und Alles opferten, um Gott nach ihrem eigenen Gewissen anbeten zu können. Die Gottesfurcht hat sie frei und stark und zu Vätern eines unermesslichen Geschlechts und der grossartigsten Republik der Weltgeschichte gemacht. Das ist noch jetzt die Freiheit jedes ächten Amerikaners; das die Freiheit, die uns durch die Landesgesetze und Landessitte verbürgt ist, während der Missbrauch der Freiheit und die Zuchtlosigkeit hier, wie in jedem andern Lande, der gerechten Strafe unterliegt.

[Hier wandte sich der Redner in englischer Sprache an die anwesenden Anglo-Amerikaner mit mehreren Fragen zur Bestätigung des Gesagten, welche einstimmig mit Ja beantwortet wurden.]

Die Geschichte, dieses didaktische Heldengedicht Gottes, diese grosse Lehrerin der Weisheit und Erfahrung, hat längst und vielfach den positiven und negativen Beweis geliefert, dass nur eine solche Freiheit, die auf sittlicher Basis ruht, mit Ehrfurcht vor Gesetz und Ordnung Hand in Hand geht und von der

Gottesfurcht und Tugend des Volkes genährt und getragen wird, bestehen und ein Volk glücklich machen kann, während jener revolutionäre, sittenlose und religionslose Liberalismus alle Grundlagen der Gesellschaft zerstört und mit Schmach und Schande endet.

Wahre Freiheit steht also nicht im Widerspruch mit Ehrfurcht vor Gottes heiligem Worte und Gesetze, also auch nicht mit Ehrfurcht vor seinem heiligen Tage, sondern wird umgekehrt dadurch nur gestützt und gefördert. "Without support from religion," sagt ein ausgezeichneter amerikanischer Schriftsteller, "all human freedom moulders and topples into irretrievable ruin." Daher dürfen wir uns auch nicht wundern über die bedeutungsvolle, schon oben berührte Thatsache, dass gerade die freisten Völker der Welt, die Schweizer, die Holländer, vor allem aber die Engländer, Schotten und Amerikaner die strengsten Beobachter des Sonntags, als eines stillen, gottgeweihten Ruhetages sind, und ihre Freiheit gerade in demselben Masse bewahren und geniessen, als sie in der Furcht und Liebe zu Gottes heiligem Worte und Gesetze verharren.

Der wohlthätige sittliche Einfluss einer würdigen Sonntagsfeier auf das Familienleben, die öffentliche Ordnung und nationale Wohlfahrt kann leicht durch den Contrast zwischen dem kontinental-europäischen, besonders parisischen, und dem anglo-amerikanischen Sonntag und seinen unmittelbaren Wirkungen anschaulich gemacht werden. Ich frage hier jeden der anwesenden Amerikaner, die den europäischen Kontinent zum Theil mehrmals besucht haben, ob sie nicht bei aller Bewunderung vor dem vielen Herrlichen, Schönen und Guten in der alten Welt, doch gerade durch die leider so häufige Sabbathsschändung und ihre traurigen Folgen schmerzlich berührt wurden und in diesem Punkte wenigstens mit doppelter Achtung und Liebe zu ihrem amerikanischen Sabbath zurückgekehrt sind?

[Hier forderte der Redner Herrn Dr. R. Hitchcock, Professor am Theol. Seminar der Presbyterianischen Kirche in New-York, und einen gründlichen Kenner und Bewunderer der deutschen Literatur, achtungsvoll auf, der Versammlung das Resultat feiner Beobachtung in dieser Hinsicht während eines zweijährigen Aufenthaltes in Europa Anno 1848 und 1849 mitzutheilen. Darauf trat Herr Dr. H. hervor und sprach züerst in einigen deutschen Worten und dann in englischer Sprache, von dem Unterschied zwischen dem römisch-katholischen holiday und dem evangelisch-christlichen holy day, dann von der unermesslichen Wirkung der Reformation Luthers und Calvins, die als eine Eichel auf den jungfräulichen Boden Amerikas verpflanzt, ungehemmt von fremdartigen Traditionen und Einrichtungen, zu einem riesigen Eichbaum herangewachsen sei, von dem nothwendigen Zusammenhang aller wahren Freiheit mit Achtung vor göttlicher Autorität, und äusserte seine hohe Freude über das begonnene Zusammenwirken der deutschen Mitbürger zur Aufrechthaltung der amerikanischen Sabbathsfeier.]

III. Bisher habe ich mich auf die physische und sittliche Bedeutung des Sonntags beschränkt. Nun noch einige Worte über die *religiöse* und *kirchliche* Bedeutung desselben, als eines Segenstages für die Seele in ihrem Verhältniss zu Gott und zur Ewigkeit. Diese Seite der Frage, obwohl für den Christen von der höchsten Wichtigkeit, hängt eigentlich bloss mittelbar mit dem Zwecke, der uns hieher geführt, zusammen. Es handelt sich nämlich für uns bei dieser Gelegenheit zunächst bloss um die Erhaltung und Förderung des *bürgerlichen* Ruhetages, und dafür *allein* sprechen wir den Schutz des Staates an, dessen Jurisdiction hier ein Ende hat. Allein der bürgerliche Sonntag ist die nothwendige Basis für den *kirchlich-religiösen* Sonntag, und die physische und moralische Bedeutung und Feier desselben vollendet sich erst in der gottesdienstlichen Feier.

Diese gottesdienstliche Feier des Sonntags, sowie die Religion überhaupt, ist Sache der Freiheit. Sie kann ihrem Wesen nach, zumal in einem Lande, wo Kirche und Staat getrennt sind, niemanden aufgezwungen werden. Eine gezwungene Anbetung ist gar keine Anbetung. Es fällt keinem vernünftigen amerikanischen Bürger, selbst von dem strengsten puritanischen Rigorismus, auch nur von ferne ein, unsere sabbathfeindlichen Landsleute durch Staatsgesetze zum Kirchengehen zu nöthigen, so sehr er auch als Menschenfreund und Christ wünschen muss, das sie den vollen Segen des Sonntags geniessen möchten, statt denselben im Wirthshaus und Theater zu vergeuden oder in

Fluch zu verkehren. Alles, was wir von ihnen auf gesetzlichem Wege verlangen, ist, dass sie nicht durch öffentliche Sabbathsschändung unsere öffentliche Sabbathsfeier, die ein wesentlicher Bestandtheil der Ausübung unserer christlichen Religions- und Cultusfreiheit ist, stören oder gar unmöglich machen, und dadurch die öffentliche Sittlichkeit und nationale Wohlfahrt, wie ihr eignes individuelles Glück, gefährden und untergraben.

Auf der andern Seite aber hängen Religion und Sittlichkeit im Staate, wie im Einzelleben, sehr eng mit einander zusammen, und es ist die wohlbegründete Ansicht der grössten amerikanischen Staatsmänner,—um von den Theologen und Geistlichen gar nicht zu reden,—dass die Sittlichkeit ohne Religion unmöglich auf die Dauer bestehen kann. Ich erinnere sie hier, ausser dem bereits angeführten, bloss an folgende beherzigenswerthe Worte in der Abschiedsrede Washingtons, des grössten und besten Amerikaners. "Alle Einrichtungen und Gebräuche," sagt er, "welche zu politischer Wohlfahrt führen, bedürfen der Frömmigkeit und Sittlichkeit als unentbehrlicher Stützen. Vergebens würde derjenige Opfer der Vaterlandsliebe verlangen, welcher daran arbeitet, diese Hauptpfeiler des Menschenwohls, diese, festesten Grundlagen der Menschen- und Bürgerpflichten zu untergraben. Der blosse Staatsmann sollte sie, gleichwie der fromme Gläubige achten und pflegen. Ein grosses Buch könnte alle ihre Verbindungen mit dem Wohlergehen des Einzelnen, wie des ganzen Staates nicht erschöpfen.

In unserem freien Lande bedarf der Staat zu seiner Sicherheit ebenso sehr, ja noch mehr des sittlichen Einflusses der Kirche, als die Kirche des gesetzlichen Schutzes des Staates, obwohl beide mit vollem Rechte von einander geschieden und in ihrer Verwaltung unabhängig und selbstständig sind. Beide gehören gleich nothwendig zum Gesammtleben des amerikanischen Volkes, ebenso wie Leib und Seele zum Wesen des Menschen. Wir fürchten keinen Widerspruch von einem vernünftigen Zuhörer, wenn wir den Grundsatz aussprechen: *Keine Freiheit ohne Tugend, keine Tugend ohne Frömmigkeit.* Mit demselben Rechte können wir aber auch sagen: *Kein physischer Sabbath ohne bürgerlichen und sittlichen Sabbath, kein sittlicher Sabbath ohne kirchlich-religiösen Sabbath.*

Denn die Religion—das lehrt die Geschichte aller Völker—ist das geheimnissvolle Band, das den endlichen Geist mit dem unendlichen Geiste, das vernünftige Geschöpf mit dem Schöpfer, den erlösungsbedürftigen Menschen mit dem ewigen Urquell alles Lebens und Heils verbindet. Sie ist zugleich das stärkste Band der Gesellschaft, dauernder als Freundschaft und zeitliches Interesse. Die Religion ist das tiefste, allgemeinste und heiligste Bedürfniss, die Würde und Zierde, die Krone und Perle des menschlichen Daseins; sie ist der mächtigste Damm gegen Sünde, Laster und Verzweiflung; sie ist die Mutter des Glaubens, der Liebe und der Hoffnung; sie begeistert zu grossen Gedanken, edlen Gefühlen, nützlichen Thaten; sie lehrt Mässigung im Glücke und Geduld im Leiden; sie giebt Frieden im Leben und Trost im Tode; sie verknüpft das Diesseits mit einem besseren Jenseits, und verklärt den flüchtigen Jammer der Erde in den ewigen Jubel des Himmels.

Das Alles gilt aber im vollen Sinn bloss vom Christenthum, der allein wahren, der allgemein menschlichen, der vollkommnen Religion, welche die Weisheit Griechenlands, die Politik Roms, die Barberei der Celten, Germanen und Slaven ohne Schwertstreich besiegt hat und gewiss auch den modernen Unglauben wie seine Vorgänger überwinden wird, welche jetzt weiter verbreitet und tiefer begründet ist als je zuvor, welche die ganze civilisirte Menschheit beherrscht, das Ruder der Weltgeschichte führt und in ihrem friedlichen Siegeslaufe fortschreiten wird, bis alle anderen Religionen ihr zu Füssen fallen und sich zum Lobe des Dreieinigen Gottes, des Schöpfers, Erlösers und Vollenders der Menschheit, vereinigen.

Hat es aber je ein Christenthum in der Welt gegeben ohne gemeinsamen Gottesdienst? Und ist gemeinsamer Gottesdienst nach den Gesetzen des irdischmenschlichen Lebens möglich ohne einen heiligen gottgeordneten Ruhetag? Alle christlichen

DIE CHRISTLICHE SONNTAGSFEIER.   237

Confessionen und Sekten, gleichviel ob sie den Ursprung des Sabbaths auf das offene Grab des Erlösers, oder auf den Berg Sinai, oder in den Garten Eden zurückführen, gleichviel ob sie einer streng puritanischen oder einer freien evangelischen Ansicht über die Art und Weise seiner Feier huldigen, haben auf diese Fragen nur eine und dieselbe Antwort.

Ja, der wöchentliche Ruhetag ist die nothwendige Bedingung der regelmässigen Predigt des Evangeliums, des öffentlichen Gebets und Gesanges, der feierlichen Verwaltung der Sakramente, kurz aller Funktionen der christlichen Kirche und ihres unermesslichen, reinigenden, erhaltenden, erhebenden und heiligenden Einflusses auf das Volksleben. Der Ruhetag ist eine Wagenburg um das Christenthum herum; ein wöchentlich wiederkehrender Glockenruf zur Busse, zum Glauben, zur Versöhnung, zur Heiligung und Vollendung; ein Meerfels, an dem sich die wüsten Wogen des Mammonismus und Secularismus, des Unglaubens und der Unsittlichkeit immer wieder brechen; ein Hereinscheinen der Himmelssonne in die Erdennacht; ein Wegweiser aus der Zeit in die Ewigkeit.

Und zwar ist dieser Ruhetag oder der Tag des Herrn,—wie er im neuen Testamente im Unterschied von dem jüdischen Sabbath und dem heidnischen Sonnentage heisst,—für den gläubigen Christen keineswegs ein hartes Gesetz und schweres Joch, sondern seiner ursprünglichen Bestimmung gemäss ein sanftes Evangelium und süsses Vorrecht, eine köstliche Himmelsgabe und Gnadengeschenk. Er erinnert uns ja an alle Wohlthaten Gottes in der vollendeten Schöpfung und Erlösung, im Reiche der Natur und der Gnade. Er ist ja der Tag der Auferstehung, an welchem der Herr Tod, Teufel und Hölle besiegt hat, seinen Jüngern als den Lebensfürsten sich offenbart und immer aufs Neue sein "Friede sei mit euch!" ihnen zuruft. Er ist ja der Tag der Ausgiessung des heiligen Geistes, der seitdem in der Kirche gewohnt hat und uns fortwährend durch Wort und Sakrament aus der Finsterniss zum wunderbaren Lichte des Evangeliums ruft. Er ist also ein heiliger Freudentag, ein Tag der geistlichen Sonne der Wahrheit und des Lebens, ein Tag des Aufgangs aus der Höhe, ein Tag der Freiheit in der Knechtschaft, ein Recht zur Ruhe mitten in der Unruhe des Erdenlebens, eine kühle Rasenbank auf der Pilgerfahrt durch die Wüste, ein Tag der Erholung und Erquickung für Leib und Seele, eine Erinnerung an das Paradies der Unschuld und ein Vorschmack des ewigen Sabbaths im Himmel, wo alle Erdenarbeit sich zur Gottesruhe und alle Zeit in die Ewigkeit verklären und vollenden wird. Das ist die ächt christliche, das ist die deutsch evangelische Anschauung vom Tage des Herrn, wie sie in dem von uns angestimmten Liede meines theuren Lehrers und Freundes, des berühmten Theologen Dr. Tholuck, so schön und lieblich ausgesprochen ist:

> "O Sabbath, den der Herr gemacht,
> Damit Er gnädig uns bedacht,
> Erquickunstag der Frommen,
> Wo in's Getümmel dieser Welt
> Ein Strahl des ew'gen Sabbaths fällt,
> Zu dem ich einst soll kommen!
> Ja, ich Will mich
> Hier schon letzen
> An den Schätzen
> Deiner Stille
> Bis zur ew'gen Sabbathfülle."

Und diesen göttlichen Segenstag sollten wir uns von den Feinden des Christenthums entreissen und in einen Fluchtag verkehren lassen? Nein, so wahr der Herr lebt, so lieb uns unser Leib und unsere unsterbliche Seele sind, gegen dieses Zerstörungswerk wollen wir uns wie Ein Mann mit aller Kraft des Zeugnisses und der That erheben! Im Namen eurer leiblichen und geistigen Gesundheit, im Namen eurer zeitlichen und ewigen Wohlfahrt, im Namen eurer Familien, eurer Weiber und Kinder, im Namen der öffentlichen Sittlichkeit und nationalen Wohlfahrt, im Namen des Staates und der Kirche, im Namen der deutschen Gottesfurcht und Frömmigkeit, im Namen der deutschen Ehre und Würde, im Namen alles dessen, was euch als Menschen, als Bürger und als Christen heilig und theuer ist, beschwöre ich euch, dass Ihr euch mit unsern amerikanischen Landsleuten und Mitchristen vereinigt zur Rettung und Bewahrung der unschätzbaren Güter dieses heiligen Tages, unter dessen schützendem und segnendem Einflusse dieses Land und dieses Volk frei und stark, eine Grossmacht der Welt und ein Wunder der Geschichte geworden ist.

Dann wird ein reicher Gewinn von dieser Abendversammlung ausgehen, dann werden wir Deutsche ein Segen für unsere neue Heimath werden und unserm alten Vaterlande Ehre machen. Ja, Deutschland selbst wird uns dafür danken, die späteste Nachwelt in Amerika den deutschen Namen mit Achtung und Liebe nennen, und der Herr des Sabbaths uns mit seiner ewigen Sabbathruhe im Himmel belohnen.

THE CHRISTIAN SABBATH.[1]

THE ANGLO-AMERICAN THEORY OF THE LORD'S DAY.

The Sabbath, or weekly day of holy rest, is, next to the family, the oldest institution which God established on earth for the benefit of man. It dates from Paradise, from the state of innocence and bliss, before the serpent of sin had stung its deadly fangs into our race. The Sabbath, therefore, as well as the family must have a general significance: it is rooted and grounded in the physical, intellectual, and moral constitution of our nature as it came from the hands of its Creator, and in the necessity of periodical rest for health and wealth of body and soul. It is to the week what the night is to the day—a season of repose and reanimation. It is, originally, not a law, but an act of benediction—a blessing and a comfort to man.

The Sabbath was solemnly reaffirmed in the Mosaic legislation as a primitive institution, with an express reference to the creation and the rest of God on the seventh day, in completing and blessing his work, and at the same time with an additional reference to the typical redemption from the bondage of Egypt.[2] It was embodied, not only in the ceremonial and civil, but also in the moral law, which is binding for all times, and rises in

[1] An Essay read before the National Sabbath Convention, Saratoga, N. Y., August 11, 1863, on invitation of The New York Sabbath Committee.

[2] Deut. 5:15. Principal Fairbairn, *Typology of Scripture*, Vol. II. p. 120 (second edition, 1858) makes the remark: "It seems as if God, in the appointment of this law, had taken special precautions against the attempts which he foresaw would be made to get free of the institution, and that on this account he laid its foundations deep in the original framework and constitution of nature."

sacred majesty and grandeur far above all human systems of ethics, as Mount Sinai rises above the desert, and the pyramids of Egypt above the surrounding plain. There the Sabbath law still stands on the first table, as an essential part of that love to God which is the soul and sum of all true religion and virtue, and can as little be spared as any other of the sacred ten—the number of harmony and completeness. Diminution here is necessarily mutilation, and a mutilation not of any human system of legislation or ethics, but of God's own perfect code of morals. Let us remember that the fourth, like every other of the ten commandments, was immediately spoken by the great Jehovah, and that under an overwhelming and unparalleled display of divine majesty; that it was even written by his own finger—written upon tables of stone—the symbol of durability; that it was preserved in the most sacred place of the tabernacle; that it was emphatically "a sign between Jehovah and his people;"[1] that it received the express sanction of Christ and his apostles, when they comprehended all the laws of God and all the duties of man under the great law of love to God and to our neighbor, and declared that the gospel, far from overthrowing the law, establishes and fulfils it. The Saviour, according to his own solemn declaration, came not to destroy the law or the prophets, but to fulfil.[2] He was neither a revolutionist nor a reactionist, but a reformer, in the highest sense of the term; he re-enacted the law of Sinai from the mount of beatitudes with the fulness of the gospel blessing, as the fundamental charter of his heavenly kingdom; he explained, deepened, and spiritualized its meaning, satisfied its demands, delivered us from its curse, infused into it a new life, and enables us, by his Holy Spirit, to keep it, in imitation of his own perfect example.

Finally, the Jewish Sabbath rose with the Saviour from the grave, as a new creation, on the morning of the resurrection, with the fulness of the gospel salvation, and descended with the Holy Spirit from His exalted throne of glory on the day of

[1] Ezek. 20:12. [2] Matt. 5:17—19. Comp. Rom. 3:31.

Pentecost; to be observed as the Christian Sabbath, as "the Lord's day," in his church to the end of time. Its temporary, ritual form was abolished, its moral substance was preserved and renewed. The Jewish Sabbath was baptized with fire and the Holy Ghost—it was Christianized and glorified. Henceforward it was emphatically the commemoration day of the resurrection, or of the new spiritual creation and the accomplished redemption, and hence a day of sacred joy and thanksgiving, "the pearl of days," the crown and glory of the week, and a foretaste and pledge of the eternal Sabbath in heaven.

> "A day of sweet refection,
> A day of sacred love;
> A day of resurrection
> From earth to heaven above."

The Sabbath, then, rests upon a threefold basis—the original *creation*, the Jewish *legislation*, and the Christian *redemption*. It answers the physical, moral, and religious necessities of man. It is supported by the joint authority of the Old and the New Testament, of the law and the gospel. It has still a twofold legal and evangelical aspect, and we must keep both in view in order to do justice to its character and aim. Like the law in general, the fourth commandment is both negative and positive, prohibitive and injunctive; it is to all men a mirror of God's holiness and our own sinfulness; to the unconverted a wholesome restraint, and a schoolmaster to lead them to Christ, and to the converted a rule of holy obedience. But the Sabbath is also a gospel institution: it was originally a gift of God's goodness to our first parents before the fall; it "was made for man,"[1] and looks to his physical and spiritual well-being; it was "a delight" to the pious of the old dispensation,[2] and now under the new dispensation it is fraught with the glorious memories and blessings of Christ's triumph over sin and death, and of the outpouring of the Holy Spirit; it is the connecting link of creation and redemption, of paradise lost and paradise regained; a remi-

[1] Mark 2: 27. [2] Isaiah 58: 23.

niscence of the paradise of innocence, and an anticipation of the paradise in heaven that can never be lost. "It is the day which the Lord hath made; we will rejoice and be glad in it."[1] Rest in God is the end of all creation[2]—not the rest of inaction, but the rest of perfection and benediction, which is one with the highest spiritual activity and joy in unbroken peace and harmony. To this rest the Sabbath points and prepares us from week to week; it is—to borrow freely some expressions from an English poem of the seventeenth century[3]—heaven once a week; the next world's gladness prepossessed in this; a day to seek eternity in time; a lamp that lights man through these dark and dreary days; the rich and full redemption of the whole week's flight; the milky way chalked out with suns; the pledge and cue of a full rest, and the outer court of glory.

This, in brief positive statement, is the *Anglo-American*, as distinct from the *European-Continental*, theory of the Sabbath, which forms the basis for its practical observance. The difference between the two is general and radical, and strikes the attention of every traveller in its practical effects. There are a few distinguished writers in England, as Milton, Whately, Arnold, Alford, Hessey, who hold substantially the Continental view; as there are, on the other hand, some divines and ministers on the Continent—and their number is increasing—who, with slight modifications, adopt the Anglo-American view, and still more who, while differing from the theory, fully approve of the corresponding practice. But these are the exception, not the rule.

The Anglo-American theory is sometimes called the *legalistic* or *sabbatharian* theory, as distinct from the *Dominican* or *evangelical*, which bases the Sabbath exclusively on the fact of the resurrection of Christ; and from the *ecclesiastical* or *traditional* theory, which bases it on the authority and custom of the church. But we protest against the term, as one-sided and liable to misunderstanding; strictly speaking, it applies only to the Jewish

[1] Ps. 118: 24. [2] Heb. 3: 11; 4: 1—11. [3] Henry Vaughan.

and the Seventh-Day Baptist theory. The genuine Anglo-American theory, as we understand and defend it, is *evangelical* as well as legal; it combines what is true in the other theories, which are wrong, not in what they positively affirm, but in what they deny and exclude. It embraces the whole truth of the Sabbath, in its physical, moral, and religious aspects; while the other theories represent merely a fragment of it, and ensure only a small portion of the benefit which emanates from the institution in its integrity and completeness. The Anglo-American theory agrees with the evangelical theory in making the resurrection of the Lord the main—though not the only—basis of the Christian Sabbath or Lord's day; and it agrees with the ecclesiastical theory in honoring the universal custom of the church of all ages—as an additional, though by no means the only or chief, support of its authority. But it differs from both by going back to the primitive creation as the first natural basis of the Sabbath, and in holding to the perpetual obligation of the fourth commandment, as the legal basis of its authority.

OBJECTIONS ANSWERED.

We will now notice the objections which are urged against the Anglo-American theory, not only from the open enemies of the Sabbath, but also from the champions of the other theories. The objections are directed mainly against the legal feature of the true theory, or the alleged perpetuity of the fourth commandment. They would indeed have force, and drive us logically to the alternative of either giving up the Sabbath, or of adopting the view of the Seventh-Day Baptists, if we based the authority of the Sabbath *exclusively* on the decalogue; but this, as already remarked, is not the view held by the leading English and American divines of the present day. We make as much account of the resurrection of the Saviour in this connection, as the strongest champions of the evangelical view can possibly do; only, while holding fast to this New Testament basis, we do not destroy the old foundation, which was laid by the same eternal and unchangeable God, who raised Christ from the dead, and thereby completed the new spiritual creation.

1. It is objected, first, that the fourth commandment alone required a positive enactment, while all the other commandments of the decalogue are co-extensive in their obligation with reason and conscience. But a law may be positive, and yet generally binding. So is the law of monogamy, which is equally primitive with the institution of the Sabbath, and yet was equally disregarded by heathens and Mohammedans, and fell even into gross neglect among the Jews, until Christ restored it in its primitive purity and force. Where is the Christian who would on this account defend polygamy, which destroys the dignity of woman, and undermines the moral foundation of the family?

The fourth commandment, however, by pointing back to the creation, gives the Sabbath at the same time a place in the order of nature. It is not so much a new commandment, as the solemn re-enactment of an institution as old as man himself. It antedates Judaism, and therefore survives it; it combines the three elements of a permanent Christian institution, being rooted in the order of nature, enacted by positive legislation, and confirmed by the gospel of Christ.

2. The second objection is derived from the change of day from the seventh to the first, under the Christian dispensation. But this change is a mere matter of form, and does not touch the substance of the commandment. The law itself does not expressly fix on the *last* day of the week; it only requires six days for labor, and *every* seventh day, not necessarily *the* seventh day (dies *septenus*, not dies *septimus*) for the rest of worship. It undoubtedly establishes the week of seven days as a divine order, and it would be altogether wrong to substitute a decade for it, as the French Revolution, during a short period of madness, tried to do but failed. The number seven (three and four) has a symbolical significance throughout the whole Bible, being the number of the covenant, or of the union of God with man, as three is the

number of the Divinity, four the number of the world or mankind, ten the number of completeness and harmony. All days, in themselves considered, are equal before God,[1] and the selection of the particular day of the week for holy purposes depends on divine facts and commandments. In the Old Testament it was determined by the creation and the typical redemption; in the new dispensation by the resurrection and full redemption of Christ. The gospel only changed the ceremonial or ritual form of the Sabbath law, but preserved and renewed its moral substance. It is also worthy of remark, that the first Sabbath of the world, although the last day in the history of God's creation, was in fact the first day in the history of man, who was made on the sixth day, as the crowning work of God.

3. A third objection is taken from the general spirit of the Christian religion, which it is said abolished the Jewish distinction of sacred and profane times and places, and regards all time as sacred to God, and every place of the universe as his dwelling. But this argument closely pressed would turn every week-day into a Sabbath, and give us seven Sabbaths for one. This, for all practical purposes, proves too much for the anti-sabbathists. It anticipates an ideal state of another and better world. There is, indeed, an eternal Sabbath in heaven, which remaineth for the people of God. But while we live on earth, we must, by the necessities of our nature, and by God's own express direction, *labor* as well as rest, and do all our work, with the exception of one day in the week, when we are permitted to rest from *our* work, in order to do the work of *God*, and to prepare ourselves for the eternal rest in heaven. Let us by all means give to God as much of the week as we can, and let us do all our secular work for the glory of God, and thus consecrate all our time on earth to his holy service; but let us not, under the vain delusion of serving him better, withhold from him even that day which he has reserved for his special service. Let us raise the week-days, as much as we can, to the sanctity of the Sabbath, instead

[1] Rom. 14:5.

of bringing down the Sabbath to the level of ordinary workdays. Our theory, far from secularizing the week-days, has a tendency to elevate them, by bringing them under the hallowed influence of the Lord's day; while the pseudo-evangelical theory has just the opposite effect in practice; it cries out, spirit, but with the masses it ends in flesh; it vindicates liberty, but it favors lawlessness, which is death to all true freedom. There is a false evangelism as well as a false legalism, and the one is just as unchristian and pernicious as the other.

As regards *intrinsic* holiness, all times and seasons, as well as all labor and rest, are alike. This we fully grant. How could we otherwise defend the change of the day from the seventh to the first, or answer the obvious astronomical objections? God undoubtedly fills all time, as he fills all space. But God is also a God of order; he has constituted man a social being, and fitted him for public as well as private worship, which, like every other act of a finite being, must be regulated by the laws of time and space. There is no more superstition in holding to sacred seasons, than there is in holding to sacred places, provided it be not done in an exclusive sense. Both are equally necessary and indispensable for the maintenance of social and public worship. We all know that the omnipresent Jehovah may be worshipped in the silent chamber, in the lonely desert, and the dark catacomb, as well as in the temple of Jerusalem and on Mount Gerizim. But shall we on that account destroy our churches and chapels, or desecrate them by turning them into "houses of merchandise?" The objection we have under consideration, falsely assumes, that the consecration of particular days to God necessarily tends to secularize the other days, when just the contrary is the case. The keeping of the Sabbath, far from interfering with the *continual* service of God, secures, preserves, promotes, and regulates it. The meaning of the Sabbath law is, not that we should give to God the seventh part of our time *only*, but *at least*. So we should pray "without ceasing," according to the apostle's direction; but this, instead of annulling, only increases the obligation of devoting *at least* a certain time of every day to purposes of private devotion. It is not by neglecting, but by strictly observing, the custom of morning and evening prayers, that we can make progress towards our final destination, when our whole life shall be resolved into worship and praise.

4. The last and strongest argument is professedly based upon what we all admit to be the highest authority beyond which there is no appeal. Christ and St. Paul, it is urged, give no countenance to the Anglo-American theory, but deny the perpetuity of the Sabbath law.[1] But if we keep in mind the general relation of the Saviour to the law, as explained especially in the Sermon on the Mount,[2] we cannot for a moment suppose that he should have shaken the authority of any of God's commandments, the least of which he declared to be more enduring than heaven and earth. The passages so often quoted are not aimed at the Sabbath which the Lord hath made, but at the later Jewish perversion of it. They in no wise oppose the proper observance of the Sabbath by works of divine worship and charity, but the negative, mechanical, self-righteous, and hypocritical sabbatharianism of the Pharisees, who idolized the letter and killed the spirit of the law, who strained out a gnat and swallowed a camel, who exacted tithe from the smallest produce of the garden, and neglected the weightier matters of the law, judgment, mercy and faith; who, like whited sepulchres, appeared beautiful without, but within were full of dead men's bones, and of all uncleanness. Wherever the Christian Sabbath is observed in the same spirit, it is an abuse of God's ordinance, and falls, of course, under the same condemnation as the Jewish Sabbatharianism of the days of Christ. Christ is indeed "Lord of the Sabbath day."[3] But in the same sense he is Lord of all the commandments, as the lawgiver is above the law. He is also Lord of life, and yet never weakened the commandment, "Thou shalt not kill," but sharp-

---

[1] Matt. 12:1-5, 10-12; Mark 2:27; Luke 13:11-16; 14:2-5; **John 5:16,** 9:14; Rom. 14:5, 6; Col. 2:16; Gal. 4:9, 10.

[2] Matt. 5:17-19.   [3] Matt. 12:8; Mark 2:28.

ened and deepened it by condemning even the hatred of the heart against our neighbor as murder before God. He uniformly set an example of the right observance of the Sabbath by devoting it to works of worship and charity. He emphatically declared the Sabbath to be made for the benefit of man.[1] He exhorted his disciples, in the extremities of the last days, to pray that their flight be not on the Sabbath day, lest they might be tempted to desecrate it.[2] And as to St. Paul, it is certain that while he opposed the *Jewish* Sabbath and the Judaizing mode of its observance, he observed the *Christian* Sabbath by acts of worship,[3] and enjoined its observance by acts of charity upon his congregations.[4] St. John, the bosom disciple of Christ, the apostle, evangelist, and seer of the New Testament, has sufficiently defined his position on the Sabbath question by conferring upon the first day of the week the high distinction of the *Lord's Day*.[5] The apostles in retaining without dispute the divinely established weekly cycle, necessarily retained also the Sabbath, which constitutes and completes the week, and which ceased no more than the weeks to run their ceaseless round. The universal religious observance of Sunday, which we find in the Christian church east and west immediately after the apostles, would be an inexplicable historical mystery without the preceding practice and sanction of the apostles. We conclude, therefore, that they regarded the Sabbath, as it was intended to be, as a *perpetual* sign between Jehovah and his people.[6]

CHARACTERISTICS AND ADVANTAGES OF THE ANGLO-AMERICAN THEORY.

The Anglo-American theory, whatever may be its theoretical merits, has undoubtedly, for all practical purposes for which the Sabbath was instituted, many and great advantages over the

[1] Mark 2:27. [2] Matt. 24:20. [3] Acts 20:7. [4] 1 Cor. 16:2. [5] Rev. 1:9.
[6] Exod. 31:17: "It is a sign between me and the children of Israel for ever." The reason assigned goes back significantly to the primitive order, "For in six days," etc. Gen. 2:2. Comp. Ezek. 20:12, 20.

Continental European theory, whether it base the Sabbath merely on ecclesiastical authority and custom, or rise higher by deriving it from Christ and the apostles.

1. The Anglo-American theory goes back to the *primitive* Sabbath of the race, given to man as man. It plants it deeply in the original constitution of man and in the order of nature. This is of the utmost importance as a basis for all the temporal benefits of the Sabbath, and for an appeal to utilitarian considerations which must be allowed to have their proper weight upon the world at large, especially on those who cannot be reached by the higher moral and religious considerations. "For goodliness is profitable unto all things, and has a promise for this life as well as for that which is to come."

Experience which speaks louder than argument, comes to the aid of our theory by furnishing abounding proof that the Sabbath rest is favorable and necessary to the body as well as the soul, to the preservation and promotion of health, wealth, and the temporal happiness and prosperity of individuals and communities.

It is an undeniable fact that the two nations which keep the Sabbath most strictly—Great Britain and the United States—are the wealthiest and the freest on earth. The philosophy of this fact is plain. Sabbath-rest is the condition of successful week-labor for man and beast, and successful labor is the parent of wealth. The proper keeping of the Sabbath, moreover, is one of the best schools of moral discipline and self-government, and self-government is the only ground on which rational and national freedom can rest and be permanently maintained.

2. The Anglo-American theory retains the *legal* basis of the Sabbath, by teaching the perpetuity of the fourth commandment. It thus secures to the Sabbath the authority of the divine lawgiver, which attaches to all other parts of the decalogue, and appeals to the conscience of man. It raises it far above the sphere of mere expediency and temporal usefulness into the sphere of moral duty and sacred obligation. It can enforce it by

an irresistible, "Thus saith the Lord." By strengthening the decalogue in one member we strengthen all the other members, and promote the general interests of morality; while the later theories, by taking out the fourth commandment as a mere temporary arrangement, destroy the completeness and harmony of the decalogue, and tend to undermine its general authority. The Anglo-American view here has an exegetical as well as a practical advantage over the others, as on it alone can the place of the Sabbath in the *moral* law be satisfactorily explained and vindicated.

3. By placing the fourth commandment on a level with the other commandments, and bringing it especially into close contact with the fifth, which enjoins obedience to parents, and with the seventh commandment, which condemns all unchastity in thought, word, and deed, the Anglo-American theory acknowledges the inseparable connection between the strict observance of the Sabbath and the moral welfare and happiness of the *family*. The Sabbath and the family are the two oldest institutions of God on earth, both date from paradise, both look towards the happiness of man, both flourish and decay together. What God has joined together no man should dare to put asunder.

4. The Anglo-American theory makes more account of the distinction between the *religious* and the *civil* Sabbath than the Continental, and lays greater stress on the necessity of the latter. It regards the civil Sabbath as essential for public morals and the self-preservation of the state. On this distinction rest our Sabbath laws in the different states. They militate as little against religious freedom and the separation of church and state, as the laws upholding monogamy. On the contrary, they are a support to our civil and political freedom. For freedom without law is licentiousness and ruin to any people. Our separation of church and state implies mutual respect and friendship, and is by no means a separation of the nation from Christianity. The religious Sabbath lies beyond the jurisdiction of the state; it cannot, and ought not to be enforced by law; for all worship and

true religion must be the free and voluntary homage of the heart. But the civil Sabbath can and ought to be maintained and protected by legislation, and a Christian community has a natural right to look to their government for the protection of their Sabbath as well as for the protection of their persons and property. All good citizens can rally around the support of the *civil* Sabbath from moral and patriotic motives, whatever may be their religious opinions. Such coöperation is not so easy on the Continent of Europe, where church and state are inextricably mixed up.

5. But while we hold fast to all these great characteristics and advantages, let us never lose sight of the fact that the Sabbath is *gospel* as well as law, and its observance a *privilege* as well as a duty. It is law to all citizens, gospel to believers. If we insist exclusively or chiefly upon the legal element, we are in danger of relapsing into Jewish sabbatharianism, and make its observance a burden instead of a joy. Its advent will then not be hailed but dreaded, especially by the youth. There is a false legalism as well as a false liberalism, and we must keep equally clear from both extremes.

HISTORY OF THE SABBATH.

The Christian Sabbath, like every other institution and article of faith, has its *history*—a history full of instruction, warning, and precept. It is intertwined with all the fortunes of Christianity. It was frequently obscured, but never abolished at any period, or in any part of the church, except during the mad days of the reign of terror in France, and even this exception only furnished the negative proof for its indispensable necessity as a safeguard for all public and private morality. It is held in common by all Christian denominations, from the oldest to the youngest, from the largest to the smallest.

THE SABBATH BEFORE THE REFORMATION.

For the first three centuries, when the church was an illegal sect, and persecuted by the state, Sunday was a purely religious institution. With Constantine the Great, the first Roman emperor who professed Christianity, it became also a civil institution, recognised and protected by the laws of the state. Civil legislation, it is true, cannot enforce the sanctification, but it can prevent, to a great extent, the public desecration of Sunday; it cannot and ought not to be coercive and injunctive, but prohibitive and protective. Constantine and his successors prohibited lawsuits and pleadings, theatrical amusements, and physical labor on Sunday, and thus enabled all their Christian subjects to observe the day without disturbance and hindrance.

The Christian Sabbath continued ever since, without interruption, as a religious and civil institution in all Christian lands. But its authority and observance was greatly undermined during the middle ages by the endless multiplication of holy days; each day of the calendar being devoted to the memory of some saint and martyr. This was, at best, a premature anticipation of an ideal state of the future world, when the life of the Christian will be one uninterrupted festival of joy and peace. But the arrangement, in its practical effect on the people, almost inevitably tended to obliterate the distinction between Sunday and the week days, between a day of rest and the days of labor, between one *holy day* of divine appointment and the many *holidays* of human invention, to promote idleness, the worship of saints, and all manner of superstition, and to obscure the merits of Christ by interposing an army of subordinate mediators and idols between him and his people. We all know to what a fearful extent this perversion and consequent desecration of the Lord's day still prevails all over the Continent of Europe, especially in Roman Catholic countries.

THE SABBATH SINCE THE REFORMATION.

We might expect that the Reformation of the sixteenth century should have remedied the evil and revived the primitive purity of the Sabbath as well as of the general system of Christianity, on the basis of the infallible word of God. Luther, Zwingle,

Calvin, and Bucer at first favored the abolition of all holidays with the exception of the Lord's day. But their general antagonism to the Judaizing legalism and ritualism of Rome, their zeal for evangelical freedom, and their imperfect understanding of the well-known words of Christ and Paul against the negative sabbatharianism of the Pharisees, prevented the reformers from attaining to the proper view of the authority and perpetuity of the fourth commandment. This is especially true of Luther, who sometimes represents the whole law of Moses as abolished, and says of the Sabbath, "Keep it holy for its use's sake both to body and soul; but if anywhere the day is made holy for the mere day's sake, if anywhere any one sets up its observance upon a Jewish foundation, then I order you to work on it, to ride on it, to dance on it, to feast on it, to do anything that shall reprove this encroachment on the Christian spirit and liberty." But Luther must never be judged from a single sentence, but be allowed to interpret himself. In other places he represents the observance of Sunday as "good and necessary," and in opposition to the antinomian views of Agricola, he defends the law of Moses as still binding upon Christians. "He who pulls down the law," he correctly remarks, "pulls down at the same time the whole framework of human polity and society. If the law be thrust out of the church, there will no longer be anything recognized as a sin in the world, since the gospel defines and punishes sin only by recurring to the law." Had the reformers foreseen the base use which has been made of their free expressions on the subject, they would have been far more cautious and careful.

There has been no radical reform of the Sabbath on the Continent of Europe since the Reformation, but rather a fearful progress of Sabbath-desecration in inseparable connection with a growing neglect of public worship. This crying evil forms one of the greatest obstacles to the spread of vital religion among the people, and can never be successfully overcome except on the basis of a stricter theory on the Sabbath, than that which generally prevails in the greater part of the old world.

THE SABBATH IN ENGLAND AND SCOTLAND.

It was different in Great Britain. The Church of Scotland was the first among the churches of the Reformation to set the example of a more sacred observance of the Lord's day than had been customary since the days of the apostles. She took from the beginning a somewhat radical position against all the annual festivals of the church, even the ancient commemoration days of the birth, passion, and resurrection of our Saviour, and the outpouring of the Holy Ghost, which are certainly innocent in themselves, and may be observed with great benefit to the people. But the loss in this respect was a gain to the weekly commemoration-day of the risen Redeemer. The *First Book of Discipline*, which was drawn up by John Knox and five other ministers, abolishes Christmas, circumcision, and Epiphany, "because they have no assurance in God's word," but enjoins the observance of Sunday in these words: "The Sabbath must be kept strictly in all towns, both forenoon and afternoon, for hearing of the word; at afternoon upon the Sabbath, the Catechism shall be taught, the children examined, and the baptism ministered. Public prayers shall be used upon the Sabbath, as well afternoon as before, when sermons cannot be had." The third General Assembly, which met in June, 1562, resolved to petition the queen for the punishing of Sabbath-breaking, and all the vices which are to be punished according to the law of God, and yet not by the law of the realm. The Assembly of June, 1565, mentions the breaking of the Sabbath day among "the horrible and detestable crimes" which ought to be punished.

Yet, after all, this was only an approach towards the right view and practice which now prevails in Great Britain. Theoretically John Knox did not differ from his admired friend and teacher, Calvin, on the subject of the Sabbath, and the Scotch Confession of Faith, which he with five others prepared in 1561, makes no express mention of the fourth commandment. The proper Anglo-American theory and practice dates from the closing years of Queen Elizabeth's reign, and took its rise in the Puritan Party of the Church of England. It was first clearly and fully set forth in a work of NICHOLAS BOWND, D.D., a graduate of Cambridge, and minister of Norton, in Suffolk, which appeared in 1595, and in an enlarged form in 1606, under the title, "*The Doctrine of the Sabbath, plainely layde forth and soundly proved*," etc.[1] This book learnedly labors to show from the Scripture, the Fathers, and the Reformers, that the observation of the Sabbath is not a bare ordinance of man, or a merely civil or ecclesiastical constitution appointed only for polity, but an immortal commandment of Almighty God, and therefore binding on man's conscience; that the Sabbath day was given to our first parents; that it was revived on Mount Sinai by God's own voice, with a special note of remembrance, fortified with more reasons than the other precepts, and particularly applied to all sorts of men by name; that the apostles by the direction of God's Spirit, changed the day from the seventh to the eighth (first), which we now keep in honor of redemption, and which ought still to be kept by all nations to the end of the world, because we can never have the like cause or direction to change it; that the Sabbath should be spent altogether in God's service, in public and private worship, in works of necessity and charity; while we should carefully abstain from all the ordinary works of our calling, and avoid whatever withdraws our heart from the exercises of religion; and that magistrates and princes ought to provide for the observation of the fourth commandment, and compel the people to at least an outward rest, as well as to the keeping of the commandments against murder, adultery, theft, and slander.

[1] For a fuller account of this work, and the controversy to which it gave rise, we refer to James Gilfillan's book; *The Sabbath viewed in the light of Reason, Revelation, and History,* 1862, republished by the American Tract Society and the New York Sabbath Committee, 1863, pp. 66, etc. Dr. Bownd wrote, besides the Doctrine of the Sabbath, three other works, viz., *The Holy Exercise of Fasting* (1604); *A Storehouse of Comfort for the Afflicted in Spirit* (1604); and *The Unbelief of Thomas, the Apostle, laid open for Believer* (1608).

The treatise of Dr. Bownd produced a great sensation. "It is almost incredible," says Thomas Fuller, the English historian, "how taking this doctrine was, partly because of its own purity, and partly from the eminent piety of such persons as maintained it, so that the Lord's day, especially in corporations, began to be precisely kept, people becoming a law to themselves, forbearing such sports as yet by statute permitted; yea, many rejoicing at their own restraint therein. On this day the stoutest fencer laid down the buckler, the most skilful archer unbent his bow, counting all shooting besides the mark; May-games and Morish-dances grew out of request, and good reason that bells should be silenced from gingling about men's legs, if their very ringing in steeples were adjudged unlawful; some of them were ashamed of their former pleasures, like children which, grown bigger, blushing themselves out of their rattles and whistles. Others forbear them for fear of their superiors, and many left them off out of a polite compliance, lest otherwise they should be accounted licentious. Yet learned men were much divided in their judgments about these sabbatharian doctrines. Some embraced them as ancient truths consonant to Scripture, long disused and neglected, now seasonably revived for the increase of piety. Others conceived them grounded on a wrong bottom, but because they tended to the manifest advance of religion, it was pity to oppose them, seeing none have just reason to complain being deceived into their own good. But a third sort flatly fell out with these positions, as galling men's necks with a Jewish yoke against the liberty of Christians: that Christ, as Lord of the Sabbath, had removed the rigor thereof, and allowed men lawful recreations; that the doctrine put an unequal lustre on the Sunday, on set purpose to eclipse all other holy days to the derogation of the church; that the strict observance was set up out of faction to be a character of difference, to brand all for libertines who did not entertain it."

The new theory of the Sabbath, like every great movement in history, had to encounter considerable opposition, and gave rise to the first sabbatharian controversy in the Christian church. But it was ably defended by Greenham, Bishop Babington, Perkins, Dod, Bishop Andrewes, Dr. Willet, and many others, and soon worked its way into the heart of the English and Scotch people. When in 1603, at the Commencement of the University of Cambridge, the thesis, *Dies Dominicus nititur Verbo Dei*, was publicly maintained, no member of the University put up an *antithesis* in opposition to it. The judicious Hooker, whose name is revered by all parties in the Church of England, says: "We are to account the sanctification of one day in seven a duty which God's immutable law doth exact forever." The Book of Common Prayer bears strong witness to the perpetuity of the fourth commandment, and its binding character upon the Christian conscience, by requiring to each of the ten commandments the response of the people, "Lord, have mercy upon us, and incline our hearts to keep this law." The Puritan theory on the Sabbath penetrated like leaven the churches of England and Scotland, and the strict observance of that day is one of the permanent effects which Puritanism left upon the Anglican church and all its dependencies. Dr. Twisse, the Moderator of the Westminster Assembly, gave it as his opinion that if the votes of the bishops of England were taken, the major part would concur with the Puritans as touching the doctrine of the Sabbath, rather than against them.

This doctrine was permanently embodied in the Westminster standards, the Confession of Faith, the Larger and Shorter Catechism, and was thus clothed with symbolical authority for all the churches which embraced these standards. The "Westminster Confession of Faith" gives this clear and strong statement of the doctrine:[1]

"As it is the law of nature, that, in general, a due proportion of time be set apart for the worship of God; so in his word, by a positive, moral, and perpetual commandment, binding all men in all ages, he hath particularly appointed one day in seven for a Sabbath, to be kept holy unto him; which,

[1] Ch. 21, sect. 7, 8.

THE CHRISTIAN SABBATH. 259

from the beginning of the world to the resurrection of Christ, was the last day of the week; and from the resurrection of Christ, was changed into the first day of the week, which in Scripture is called the Lord's Day, and is to be continued to the end of the world as the Christian Sabbath.

"This Sabbath is then kept holy unto the Lord, when men, after a due preparing of their hearts, and ordering of their common affairs beforehand, do not only observe an holy rest all the day from their own works, words, and thoughts about their worldly employments and recreations; but also are taken up the whole time in the public and private exercises of his worship, and in the duties of necessity and mercy."

This is the doctrine of the Westminster Assembly, which, next to the Synod of Dort, is unquestionably the most important ecclesiastical Synod held in the history of the Reformed Church, and adorned by such distinguished scholars and divines as Lightfoot, Gataker, Twisse, Henderson, Rutherford, Wallis, Reynolds, and Selden. On this point there was no dispute between the Independents and Presbyterians. In Scotland the Westminster standards were at once received, and have been adhered to ever since by all the various branches of Scotch Presbyterianism. The Secession Church, the Relief Church, the Reformed Presbyterian Church, the United Original Seceders, and the Free Church, agree with the Established Church of Scotland, in holding the Westminster doctrine on the Sabbath.

This doctrine, it must be admitted, goes beyond that of any other symbolical book or confession of faith previously issued in the Christian church. But it is none the less true and scriptural in all its essential features. It is one of the noblest contributions which Great Britain has made to the cause of evangelical truth and piety. Far from being a relapse, it is a real progress in the cause of Christianity and civilization. But a progress on the rock of the Bible: for all true growth in ecclesiastical history is not a growth *beyond* Christ, but a growth *in* Christ, and a deeper apprehension and fuller application of his Spirit, word, and work. We now see the doctrine of justification by faith in every epistle of St. Paul; and yet it was only by the Reformation of the sixteenth century that it was clearly brought out from the mines of the Bible. So we are better prepared to now understand and appreciate the whole Scripture doctrine of the Sabbath, than the church was before the sixteenth century. We have the great test of an experience of more than two hundred years to assist us in taking the right view.

The whole world knows the striking difference between the Continental and the British Sabbath; and every impartial Christian observer must admit the superiority and incalculable benefits of the latter, in the promotion of every public and private virtue. Even the freedom, wealth and political greatness of England and Scotland may, to a considerable extent, be traced to the strict observance of the Lord's Day. Let us quote but one testimony, and that of a Frenchman, and a zealous Roman Catholic. "Impartial men," says the celebrated Count Montalembert, "are convinced that the political education by which the lower classes of the English nation surpass other nations—that the extraordinary wealth of England, and its supreme maritime power—are clear proofs of the blessing of God bestowed upon this nation for its distinguished Sabbath observance. Those who behold the enormous commerce of England, in the harbors, the railways, the manufactories, etc., cannot see without astonishment the quiet of the Sabbath-day."

THE SABBATH IN NEW ENGLAND.

It is one of the peculiar marks of divine favor to America, that its foundations are deeply laid in religion, and that the Sabbath, as observed in Scotland and England from the beginning of the seventeenth century, was one of the most cherished institutions of the fathers and founders of our Republic. The history of New England commences with the famous politico-religious covenant of the Pilgrim Fathers, signed on board the Speedwell, on the day of its arrival in Cape Cod harbor, on the 11th of November, 1620, which laid the foundation for independent, voluntarily, democratic self-government in church and state, and was solemnly inaugurated, on the day following, by the strict observance of a Puritan Sabbath. During the following weeks of anxious and dangerous explorations for a safe harbor and settlement on terra firma, nothing could prevent the Pilgrims from spending every Sabbath in religious retirement, which invigorated them for the severe work of the week. And when, on the ever-memorable 22d of December (new style, or December 11, old style) they landed on Plymouth Rock, not even the pressing necessities of physical food and protection, nor the cry of some Indian savages, who threatened as they thought, with an assault, could induce them to break the first Sabbath in their future home. "They were still without the shelter of a roof. At the sharp winter solstice of New England, there was but

'A screen of leafless branches
Between them and the blast.'

But it was the Lord's hallowed time, and the work of building must wait." [1]

There this small congregation of pious emigrants, the unconscious bearers of the hopes and destinies of a mighty future, met far away from friends and kindred, in a new and inhospitable clime, in dreary, cold December, on a barren rock, threatened by roaming savages, under the stormy sky of heaven, and, in the exercise of the general priesthood of believers, offered the sacrifices of broken hearts, and the praises of devout lips to their God and Saviour, on his own appointed day of rest. The Pilgrims

[1] See Palfroy's *History of New England*. Boston. 1859. Vol. I., p. 173. This first Puritan Sabbath on the American continent fell on the 24th of December. On Monday the 25th, being Christmas, all were busy felling, sawing, riving or carrying timber. "No man rested all that day," which they regarded as of purely human invention. In this opposition to annual festivals in honor of Christ, and to the whole idea of a church-year, the Puritans evidently went too far. But we may readily excuse their weakness, in view of their eminent services to the Lord's Day. For Christmas they afterwards substituted the Day of Thanksgiving which continues to be the great annual thanksgiving and home-festival of New England; but Christmas, Easter, and Pentecost are reasserting their historic claims and spreading more and more in the American churches.

were first and last true to God, and therefore in the best sense true to themselves, and true to the world. They made religion the chief concern of life, and regarded the glory and enjoyment of God the great end of man, to which everything else must be subordinated. They reasoned, and reasoned correctly, that all lower goods are best secured by securing the highest. They first sought the kingdom of God and his righteousness, well assured that all other things necessary would be added unto them. They knew that the fear of the Lord is the beginning of all wisdom. Their constant sense of dependence on God made them feel independent of men. Being the faithful servants of Christ, they became true freemen, and the fathers and founders of a republic of self-governing sovereigns.

The noble example of the Pilgrim fathers was followed by all the Puritan emigrants. The strict observance of the Lord's day was a universal custom in New England from the beginning, and has continued without interruption to the present day. It was there ably defended in sermons and tracts, from time to time, by the most distinguished divines, as Jonathan Edwards, President Timothy Dwight, Dr. Humphrey, Dr. Justin Edwards, who have enriched the Sabbath literature by contributions of abiding value. It is there interwoven with the whole structure of society—it enters into the sanctuary of every family, it is identified with the earliest and most sacred recollections of every man, woman, and child. The strictness of the New England Sabbath is proverbial, and has only its equal in the Scotch Sabbath. In former days it was no doubt frequently carried to excess, and observed more in the spirit of Jewish legalism than of Christian freedom; but along with Puritan rigor and austerity went the blessings of the Sabbath. Its strict observance was an essential part of that moral discipline which made New England what it is to-day, and is abundantly justified by its fruits, which are felt throughout the whole Christian world.

It is unnecessary, even in these days of sectional prejudice, party animosity, and slander, to say one word in praise of New

THE CHRISTIAN SABBATH. 263

England. Facts and institutions always speak best for themselves. We might say with Daniel Webster, giving his famous eulogy on Massachusetts a more general application to her five sister States: "There they stand: look at them, and judge for yourselves. There is their history, the world knows it by heart: the past at least is secure." The rapid rise and progress of that rocky and barren country called New England, is one of the marvels of modern history. In the short period of two centuries and a half it has attained the height of modern civilization, which it required other countries more.than a thousand years to reach. Naturally the poorest part of the United States, it has become the intellectual garden, the busy workshop, and the thinking brain of this vast republic. In general wealth and prosperity, in energy and enterprise, in love of freedom and respect for law, in the diffusion of intelligence and education, in letters and arts, in virtue and religion, in every essential feature of national power and greatness, the people of the six New England States, and more particularly of Massachusetts, need not fear a comparison with the most favored nation on the globe.[1]

But the power and influence of New England, owing to the enterprising character of its population, extends far beyond its

---

[1] Dr. Robert J. Breckinridge, of Kentucky, in a patriotic letter to the Hon. Robert C. Winthrop, dated June, 25, 1863, thus speaks of New England: "It may be the will of God that the most dreadful changes await our country. If the very worst comes, I look that true and regulated liberty will perish last in New England. In past years I have spoken freely in disapprobation of much that has been felt as an evil influence from New England, as it appeared to me. But I never doubted—and now less than ever—that the roots of whatever produces freedom, equality, and high civilization, are more deeply set in New England than in any equal population on the face of the earth." We are sure that this noble testimony will be heartily responded to by thousands of Christians in the Middle, Western, and even the Southern States, who are able to rise above the passions of the hour, and to subordinate their sectional and denominational interests and preferences to truly national and catholic considerations. [Dr. Breckinridge, who wrote this letter in the midst of the civil war, was the Uncle of the Secretary of War of the Southern Confederacy, and formerly Vice-President of the United States in Buchanan's administration.]

own limits, and is almost omnipresent in the United States. The twenty thousand Puritans who emigrated from England within the course of twenty years, from 1620 to 1640, and received but few accessions until the modern flood of mixed European immigration set in, have grown into a race of many millions, diffused themselves more or less into every State of the Union, and take a leading part in the organization and development of every new State of the great West to the shores of the Pacific. Their principles have acted like leaven upon the whole lump of American society; their influence reaches into all the ramifications of our commerce, manufactures, politics, literature, and religion; there is hardly a Protestant church or Sabbath-school in the land, from Boston to San Francisco, which does not feel, directly or indirectly, positively or negatively, the intellectual and moral power which constantly emanates from the classical soil of Puritan Christianity.

The Southern enemies of our government, who in former years resorted to New England institutions for an education, acknowledge this fact by applying the term *Yankee* reproachfully to the whole people of the North. But it is rather a term of honor, of which no one need be ashamed. The New Englanders have their idiosyncracies and faults, like every people under the sun, and are apt to run into extremes and all sorts of *isms* in politics, philosophy and religion; but they have counterbalancing virtues of sterling value, which make them a real blessing to the race. Wherever they go, they carry with them their industry and enterprise, their love of freedom and zeal for education, and, what is better than all, their native, traditional reverence for God's holy word and holy day; and this, far from being a weakness, is one of the chief sources of their strength and prosperity, and an unspeakable benefit to the whole country. Let us never forget the debt of gratitude which we owe to New England for the observance of the Lord's Day.

THE AMERICAN SABBATH.

But the Sabbath is by no means a Puritan or New England institution simply: it is truly national American; its sacredness and influence is as wide as the continent from Maine to Georgia, and from the Atlantic to the Pacific. It enters into the bone and sinew of the American character. It is entrenched in our national habits, embodied in our creeds, and guarded by our civil legislation. It is an essential part of American Christianity and morality, and one of the strongest common bonds which unite the different Protestant denominations. The Episcopalian, whether high, or low, or broad in his views of doctrine or policy, the Presbyterian, the Dutch Reformed, the German Reformed, the Lutheran, the Methodist, the Baptist, the Quaker, unite with the Puritan Congregationalist in zeal for the honor of the Lord's day, and in abhorrence of its desecration. The venerable French scholar, Duponceau, after long familiarity with America, made the remark, "that of all we claimed as characteristic, our observance of the Sabbath is the only one truly national and American, and for this cause, if for no other, he trusted it would never lose its hold on our affections and patriotism."

This was so, we may say, from the beginning of our nation. The laws of nearly every colony and State (with the exception of Louisiana, which is owing to its French and Roman Catholic origin) recognise this national sentiment, and protect the Christian Sabbath against abuse and desecration. A kind Providence has watched over our legislation in this important matter with singular care. It was influenced by the truly Christian and patriotic conviction of that eminent judge of the Supreme Court of the United States, expressed in this significant sentence: "Where there is no Christian Sabbath, there is no Christian morality; and without this, free government cannot long be sustained." The earlier legislation of New York, for instance, both under Dutch and English rule, shows the profoundest respect for the civil Sabbath, and the strongest conviction of its public utility and necessity.[1] Legislation in a republican country like ours always reflects and embodies the ruling sentiment of the community. It is certainly so in this case. It has been asserted by one, especially competent to judge, by long and wide observation,[2] that "at least nine-tenths of the American-born population, and probably a large majority of the foreign-born, esteem the Sabbath too sacred to be spent as a frivolous holiday. With trifling exceptions, the Christian churches of every name regard the Sabbath as a day to be kept holy unto the Lord, and to be employed in acts of religious worship and charity: so that millions of our citizens are grieved, and justly grieved, as they think, by a systematic perversion of the day into a mere carnival of sensuous pleasure."

It is true that the combined influences of the various denominations of non-Puritan descent, and the flood of the more recent foreign immigration from Europe, have softened the rigor of the Puritan Sabbath, especially in our large cities. But the essential features remain unchanged in the heart of the people. I know of no serious American Christian, of any evangelical denomination, who would be willing to exchange the Anglo-American Sabbath theory and practice for that of the Continent of Europe, or of Mexico, and Central, and South America. All intelligent foreigners, too, who appreciate the interests of religion and virtue, must after a few months or years of observation, see and acknowledge the great superiority of the American observance in

[1] Here belong the Decrees and Ordinances of Peter Stuyvesant, 1647-8, the Acts of the General Assembly of the Colony of New York, passed in 1695, the laws of the State Legislature in 1813, the Municipal Ordinances, 1797-1834, etc. They are conveniently brought together in the first published document of the New York Sabbath Committee, under the title, "The Sabbath in New York," New York, 1858. [More fully in Doc. xlvii., published N. Y., 1883, under the title: *Sunday Laws of the State of New York and Judicial Decisions sustaining them.*]

[2] The Secretary of the New York Sabbath Committee, the Rev. R. S. Cook, in Doc. No. xi. p. 15.

THE CHRISTIAN SABBATH. 267

its practical bearings and effects upon the individual, the family, and the people. The foreign German population, for instance, in two large meetings, held at Cooper Institute, New York, the one in October, 1859, the other in March, 1861, have given strong and emphatic testimony to the Anglo-American Sabbath, and pledged to it their moral and material support.[1]

Our theory has stood the strongest of all tests, which the Saviour requires in the words, "By their fruits ye shall know them." Even the extreme of strict Sabbath observance is comparatively harmless, and far less dangerous than the opposite extreme of laxity. There has been much senseless talk against the Judaizing legalism of American Sabbath-keeping by men who ignore the world as it is, and misconceive the essential relation of the gospel to holiness. Daily experience tells us that the

[1] Compare Documents No. ix. and No. xvi. of the New York Sabbath Committee, which contain, in the German language, a full account of the two memorable German mass meetings in Cooper Institute. We quote the resolutions heartily and unanimously adopted by the first meeting, which was attended by over fifteen hundred Germans of all classes.

"*Resolved* That we, as Germans, do solemnly protest against the perversion of Sunday from a day of rest and devotion, into a day of noisy excitement and dissipation, which is only too frequent among some of our German countrymen, and brings dishonor on the German name; and that we request our fellow-citizens by no means to charge the fault of many upon the *whole* people and upon Germany, where for many years past noble efforts are successfully making towards the promotion of the better observance of Sunday.

"*Resolved,* That we regard the strict observance of Sunday, which was introduced into this country with the very first settlements of European immigrants, and has ever since been the common custom of the land, by no means as a defect, but on the contrary, as a great advantage and blessing to America, and we will cheerfully assist in keeping it up, and handing it down to future generations.

"*Resolved,* That in the Sabbath laws of this country, as they obtain in nearly every State of our great republican confederacy, we see nothing that conflicts with the cherished principles of civil and religious liberty; on the contrary, we regard them as one of the strongest guarantees of our free institutions; as a wholesome check upon licentiousness and dissipation, and as a preventive of the pauperism and crime which must necessarily undermine and ultimately destroy the liberty of any people."

great mass of mankind needs the restraint of law as much as ever, and most of all in a free republic like ours. The law is still a schoolmaster to lead men unto Christ, and true freedom is not freedom *from* law, but freedom *in* law. Our country must stand or fall with respect for law and order, for religion and virtue.

TRIALS AND TRIUMPHS OF THE AMERICAN SABBATH.

The American Sabbath had its days of trial and temptation, but so far it has manfully and successfully weathered the storm.

1. Its first great trial was the war of the Revolution. War, whatever be its ultimate benefits, is proverbially demoralizing in its immediate effects, by accumulating and intensifying the vices of all classes of society. It is especially regardless of the third and fourth commandments, under the convenient cover of military necessity, and the old bad maxim, *Inter arma silent leges.* But fortunately for the country, the commander-in-chief and the father of this nation, who will ever stand "first in war, first in peace, and first in the hearts of his countrymen," was a God-fearing man, and issued, August 3, 1776, a general order, which, from a lofty eminence above the passions and strifes of the day, still speaks with telling effect to the armies of the North and of the South, solemnly protesting against the kindred vices of Sabbath breaking and profanity, as follows:

"That the troops may have an opportunity of attending public worship, as well as to take some rest after the great fatigue they have gone through, the General, in future, excuses them from fatigue duty on Sundays, except at the shipyards, or on special occasions, until further orders. The General is sorry to be informed, that the foolish and wicked practice of profane cursing and swearing, a vice hitherto little known in an American army, is growing into fashion. He hopes the officers will, by example as well as influence, endeavor to check it, and that both they and the men will reflect that we can have but little hope of the blessing of Heaven on our arms, if we insult it by our impiety and folly. Added to this, it is a vice so mean and low, without any temptation, that every man of sense and character detests and despises it."[1]

[1] Sparks' *Writings of Washington,* vol. iv. p. 28.

THE CHRISTIAN SABBATH. 269

When, after the successful termination of the war and the achievement of our national independence, the federal Constitution was formed for the permanent organization of our Union, everything was carefully avoided which might tend to introduce the evils resulting from a union of the church and state in the old world—and that not from disrespect, but respect for religion, which was regarded by our fathers as too sacred to be subjected to the contaminating influence of political interests and secular control. Yet it is very significant and characteristic that in this very document the authority of the Christian Sabbath is incidentally acknowledged, by exempting it from the working days of the chief magistrate of the country in the signature of the bills of Congress;[1] and this, with the *Anno Domini* of the date, is the only express indication of the Christian origin of the magna charta of the American Union. Congress has always respected the national habit, and never meets on Sundays, nor does the nation celebrate its birth-day on the fourth of July when it happens to fall on the sacred day of rest.

2. More recently the American Sabbath had to encounter another and more fearful danger, arising from the increasing tide of foreign Sabbath desecration, with its accumulating crimes and general demoralization. It culminated in New York among the teeming thousands of foreign residents of every nation and tongue. A few years ago the anti-sabbath movement threatened to sweep away the Sabbath alike from our statute books and from our streets, and endangered not only the public morals, but even the material interests of the whole community. But just in the time of the greatest danger, in 1857, God raised up the New York Sabbath Committee, and through its quiet and unobtrusive, but faithful and persevering labors, saved the Sabbath, shut the new flood-gates of drunkenness and crime, restored order and security to the metropolis, secured the coöperation of

---

[1] Constitution of the United States of America, Art. I., Sect. 7: "If any bill shall not be returned by the President within ten days (*Sundays excepted*) after it shall have been presented to him, the same shall be a law," etc.

the better part of the foreign population, enriched our sabbath-literature by valuable tracts and sermons, and so influenced the legislature and the judiciary of the Empire State, that they not only maintained the old Sunday laws, but committed themselves more strongly than ever in favor of the maintenance of the civil Sabbath.[1] In every one of the successive suits for the violation of the Sunday theatre act, the question was decided in favor of the constitutionality of laws for the protection of the Christian Sabbath as a civil and political institution, which in the State of New York, as in all other States, exists as a day of rest, by common law, and without the legislative action to establish it, so that all that the legislature attempt to do in the Sabbath laws is to regulate its observance and to protect it from desecration. The opinions of the different courts on this controversy, especially the opinion of Judge Allen of the Supreme Court,[2] are extremely valuable as a basis for all needful legislation, and a bulwark against future attempts to overthrow or evade the laws of the land.

[1] Compare for details the *Documents of the New York Sabbath Committee*, published from 1858 to 1863 [1884], which will always fill an important place in the history of the American Sabbath. Also an excellent article on the *Perpetual Observance of the Sabbath*, partly in review of these documents, by Professor Egbert C. Smyth, in the *American Theological Review*, for April, 1862, pp. 296-327. Prof. Smyth thus sums up the results of the labors of the New York Sabbath Committee: "A score of Sunday theatres have been closed, the liquor traffic greatly restricted, Sunday news-crying abolished, much useful labor expended among the foreign population, documents in English and German prepared and distributed in great numbers, a manifest advance secured in the popular apprehension of the claims and benefits of the civil Sabbath, the legal right of every man to a weekly season of repose and worship vindicated; and, in brief, a Sunday characterized by traffic, noise, drunkenness, and vice, made to give place to 'a Sabbath marked by refreshing stillness and sobriety,' and an impulse given to similar reformatory movements in other large cities in this country, and also across the Atlantic. Such results are a sufficient proof of the wisdom and energy with which the efforts of the Committee have been conducted. They shed light also upon the true method of prosecuting reformatory measures under a free government."

[2] It is published in the series of Reports of the Supreme Court of New York, and in an authorized abridgement, as Doc. No. XVIII. of the series of the Sabbath Committee.

3. But our cherished institution had hardly been vindicated from the deadly grasp of foreign enemies, when it had to face a more dangerous domestic foe. The severest trial through which the American Sabbath, in common with our whole national Government and Union, with its principles of republican self-government, ever had to pass, or is likely to pass in future, is the civil war which has now been raging with increasing fury for more than two years. The desecration of the Sabbath, together with profanity and intemperance, soon after the outbreak of the war, increased at a most alarming rate, and threatened the people with greater danger than the rebellion itself. But fortunately there was an organization at hand which understood its duty; and rising from a metropolitan to a national importance, elicited from the highest military and civil authorities of the land a testimony in favor of the Sabbath, even more explicit and direct than ever issued from a professedly Christian government.[1]

Soon after assuming supreme command of the Army of the Potomac, Major-General George B. McClellan issued the following admirable order:

(General Orders No. 7.)

"HEAD-QUARTERS, ARMY OF THE POTOMAC, WASHINGTON, Sept. 6, 1861.

"The Major-General commanding desires and requests that in future there may be more perfect respect for the Sabbath, on the part of his command. We are fighting in a holy cause, and should endeavor to deserve the benign favor of the Creator. Unless in the case of an attack by the enemy, or some other extreme military necessity, it is commended to commanding officers, that all work shall be suspended on the Sabbath; that no unnecessary movements shall be made on that day; that the men shall, so far as possible, be permitted to rest from their labors; that they shall attend divine service after the customary Sunday morning inspection; and that officers and men shall alike use their influence to insure the utmost decorum and quiet on that day. The General commanding regards this as no idle form. One day's rest in seven is necessary

---

[1] See Document No. XIX. of the New York Sabbath Committee, "A plea for the Sabbath in War."

to men and animals,—more than this, the observance of the holy day of the God of mercy and of battles is our sacred duty.

"GEORGE B. MCCLELLAN,
Major-General Commanding.

"*Official:* A. V. COLBURN, Assistant Adjutant-General."

Still more important is the order of the President of the United States, issued in consequence of an interview with a deputation of the New York Sabbath Committee, which were accompanied by the Secretaries of War and the Navy, and Rear-Admiral Foote, and introduced by Governor Morgan, of New York.[1]

"EXECUTIVE MANSION, WASHINGTON, Nov. 15, 1862.

"The President, Commander-in-Chief of the Army and Navy, desires and enjoins the orderly observance of the Sabbath, by the officers and men in the military and naval service. The importance for man and beast, of the prescribed weekly rest, the sacred rights of Christian soldiers and sailors, a becoming deference to the best sentiment of a Christian people, and a due regard for the Divine will, demand that Sunday labor in the army and navy be reduced to the measure of strict necessity. The discipline and character of the national forces should not suffer, nor the cause they defend be imperilled, by the profanation of the day or name of the Most High. 'At this time of public distress,' adopting the words of Washington, in 1776, 'men may find enough to do in the service of God and their country, without abandoning themselves to vice and immorality.' The first general order issued by the Father of his Country, after the Declaration of Independence, indicates the spirit in which our institutions were founded and should ever be defended:

"'*The General hopes and trusts that every officer and man will endeavor to live and act as becomes a Christian soldier, defending the dearest rights and liberties of his country.*' ABRAHAM LINCOLN."

These orders, which were read by millions of people on the very day of their publication, and translated into the German, French, and other tongues, have become part of our national history, and will remain a precedent to our rulers as long as our nation shall endure.

Thus God has overruled even the fearful profanation of the Sabbath, for its defence, by those who represent and reflect his authority in our land.

[1] See the facts of the interview, in Document No. XXIII.

CONCLUSION.

But the danger is by no means overpast. Notwithstanding the noble orders from the highest civil and military authorities of the land, and the thrilling sermons of the Almighty God of battles, there is still a most shocking amount of the kindred vices of profanity and Sabbath-breaking in our army, which fills every Christian and patriotic heart with sorrow and grief, and makes it tremble for the future. Unfortunately too many of our officers, even high in command, set the worst possible example to the soldiers. Eternal vigilance is the price not only of our liberty, but also of our Sabbath. Let all the friends of the good cause lift up their hearts and stretch out their hands for the rescue of one of the most conservative and benevolent institutions of the land. An immense work is before them. Even after a successful military settlement of the present gigantic struggle, there remains the task of a political and social solution of our national difficulties, and in this work of reconstruction, Christianity and humanity, wisdom and charity, must take the lead. We have every encouragement to labor in this cause. We have on our side the laws of the land, the traditions of our fathers, the national tastes and habits, the dearest interests of our families and firesides, and the authority of God's word, which is more powerful than all armies and navies.

The Sabbath, like every institution of God intended for the benefit of man, must be either a great blessing, or a great curse, a savor of life unto life, or a savor of death unto death. This is especially the case with us. We need the Sabbath more than any other nation on earth. With us Christianity must stand on its own independent merits, and be rooted and grounded in the affections of a free people. It can never look to the secular power for direct support. Hence the surpassing value of pious national habits and customs, among which the reverent observance of the Lord's Day is one of the most important. It stands not isolated and alone, but implies our most sacred rights and privileges, and all the blessings which emanate from public worship. Our energy and restless activity as a nation, our teeming wealth and prosperity, and our very liberty, makes the weekly day of rest a special necessity for us; for it is a powerful check upon secularism and the degrading worship of the almighty dollar, and upon radicalism and licentiousness, which is death to all true freedom.

The loss of the sacred day of rest, with all its purifying and ennobling influences, would be an irreparable disaster to our country. Take away the Sabbath, and you destroy the most humane and most democratic institution which was made for man, and more particularly for the man of labor and toil, of poverty and sorrow. Take away the Sabbath, and you destroy a mighty conservative force, and dry up a fountain from which the family, the church, and the state receive constant nourishment and support. Take away the Sabbath, and you shake the moral foundations of our national power and prosperity: our churches will be forsaken, our Sunday-schools emptied, our domestic devotions will languish, the fountains of public and private virtue will dry up; a flood of profanity, licentiousness, and vice will inundate the land; labor will lose its reward, liberty be deprived of its pillar, self-government will prove a failure, and our republican institutions end in anarchy and confusion, to give way, in due time, to the most oppressive and degrading military despotism known in the annals of history. Yea, the end of the Sabbath would be for America the beginning of the unlimited reign of the infernal idol-trinity of Mammon, Bacchus, and Venus, and overwhelm us at last in ruin.

But we confidently hope and believe that, under the protecting care of the Lord of the Sabbath, and the watchfulness of his people, it will survive the shock of this terrible civil war, and the attacks of all its foreign and domestic foes. The Sabbath will mitigate the horrors of war as long as it may last, and when it shall have spent its fury and given way to an honorable and lasting peace, it will be one of the means to remedy its evils, to heal up its wounds, to build up its desolations, to cement the Union, and to regenerate the whole nation on a sound and permanent moral and religious foundation. It will continue its weekly testimony to the world at large that our freedom rests in law and order, that we are independent of human tyranny, because we feel dependent on the Sovereign Ruler of Nations, and bow in sacred reverence before the majesty and authority of the Lord of lords and the God of gods. It will continue to be one of our most cherished and sacred traditions, an essential characteristic of American Christianity, an intellectual educator, a feeder of public and private virtue, a school of discipline and self-government, a pillar of civil and religious liberty, a bond of union among all Christian denominations, and a "sign" between us and our God as long as this nation shall endure. If we honor the Lord of the Sabbath, he will honor us, sanctify and overrule our present calamities for our own good, and make us a shining light and example among the nations of the earth.

"Blessed is the nation whose God is the Lord, and the people whom he hath chosen for his own inheritance."

THE DEVELOPMENT OF RELIGIOUS FREEDOM.[1]

It is as clear as the sun, and is now universally admitted, except by the blind, that religious persecution is opposed to the teaching and example of the Founder of Christianity. He came to save the world, not to destroy it. He summed up the whole law in supreme love to God and love to our fellow-men. He declared that his kingdom is not of this world. He rebuked the hasty Peter for using the sword even in defense of his Master; and he preferred to suffer and to die rather than to call the angels of God to aid against his enemies. His apostles spread the gospel by spiritual means, and condemned all carnal weapons. For three hundred years Christianity spread, and triumphed at last by the force of truth and a holy life; the Church suffered persecution from Jews and Gentiles, but never persecuted as long as she was true to the example of her Head, who won the crown by his cross. She retained in the darkest of the Dark Ages a remembrance of this Christ-like position in the principle: *Ecclesia non sitit sanguinem.*

Persecution is of heathen origin, and passed into the Christian Church at the time of her union with the State. That union was the source of much good and of much evil. When Constantine the Great espoused the cause of Christianity, he transferred his power as high-priest of the Roman state religion to his new position as the temporal head of the Church. The Christian emperors now persecuted the heathen religion as the pagan

[1] Reprinted, by permission, from "The North American Review," April, 1884. Slightly enlarged.

emperors had persecuted the Christian religion. Not only so, but they persecuted also every departure from the established orthodox creed; they recognized but one legitimate form of Christianity, which was represented by the Catholic Church, and they treated every heresy and schism as a crime against the state. In this attitude they were aided by the theological dogma framed by the fathers, of the exclusiveness of the Catholic Church, which they confounded with the kingdom of God, out of which there is no salvation. The imperial legislation from Constantine the Great to Justinian is filled with penal laws against Arians, Donatists, Manichæans, Gnostics, Montanists, Quartodecimans, Novatians, Appollinarians, Nestorians, Eutychians, and all other sects that dissented from the dogmas and canons of the ruling state Church, and who were punished as enemies of society with deposition, fines, banishment, and even with death. The first blood of heretics was shed in the execution by the sword of some Priscillianists of Spain by order of the Emperor Maximus, in 385; but St. Ambrose of Milan, and St. Martin of Tours, loudly protested against it and broke off communion with the bishops who had approved the cruel act. The anti-heretical laws of the Byzantine emperors were incorporated in the Justinian code, and this was gradually adopted, together with the ecclesiastical or canon law, all over the continent of Europe. Rome ruled once more by law as she had so long ruled by the sword, and ruled over the children of those barbarians who had broken up her empire.

England alone, favored by her isolation and protected by the surrounding sea, resisted the introduction of the Roman civil law and the canon law; she preferred her own customs, inherited from Anglo-Saxon times, and built on them her common law (or *lex non scripta*) and her statute law (or *lex scripta*). But as to her religion, England was as thoroughly Catholic, and even Roman Catholic, as any country on the Continent. The first Archbishop of Canterbury, St. Augustine, who was sent by Pope Gregory I. to convert the Anglo-Saxons, could not tolerate the older and more independent Christianity of the Britons, which was driven to the mountains of Wales. The statute on the burning of heretics was in force even to the times of Queen Elizabeth and King James. Wiclif escaped persecution during his life, but was not spared after his death, and the Council of Constance, which burned Huss and Jerome of Prague as heretics, condemned Wiclif and his writings to the flames; whereupon his remains were solemnly ungraved, burned to ashes, and cast into the brook Swift, which (as Fuller says) "conveyed them into the Avon, Avon into Severn, Severn into the narrow seas, they into the main ocean; and thus the ashes of Wiclif are the emblem of his doctrine, which now is dispersed all the world over." Five hundred years after the completion of Wiclif's Bible translation his memory was celebrated in five continents. What a change!

The mediæval persecution reached its height in the crusades against the Waldenses and Albigenses, in France, and in the Inquisition of Spain. Both were ecclesiastico-political. The Church defined and condemned the heresy, and the State punished it by the sword, using carnal force against spiritual offenses. The Spanish Inquisition was instituted by Ferdinand and Isabella, with the express sanction of the Pope, for ridding the state of all enemies, Moors, Jews, and heretics. It is stated that during the first twenty years of its existence, from A. D. 1478 to 1498, when the terrible Inquisitor-General Torquemada resigned his office, over 8080 persons were burned alive, 6500 in effigy, and 90,004 punished in other ways. The sum total of persons condemned to death by the Spanish Inquisition during the 330 years of its existence (from 1478 to 1808) is stated to be 30,000. Roman Catholic writers, like Balmez and Hefele (the latter in his work on Cardinal Ximenes), in defense of the institution, question the figures of Llorente (who, however, was a Spanish priest and secretary of the Inquisition from 1789–1791), and claim for the Inquisition as a good result that it saved Spain from the horrors of religious wars, which would have cost far more victims, and might have ruined the country. But the peace of a grave-yard is much worse than war. France, Holland, Germany, and England have all passed through the ordeal of religious wars, and left Spain, once the proudest monarchy of Europe, far behind in everything that makes up the glory of a nation.

The Reformation of the sixteenth century was the grandest movement in history since the introduction of Christianity, and carried in it the modern principles of religious and civil liberty. But at first it was simply an emancipation from the thraldom of Popery, which, from being a school-master of the barbarous nations of Europe, had become an intolerable tyrant. The Reformers had no idea of religious freedom beyond their own creed, nor of a separation of church and state. They were intensely convinced of the scriptural truthfulness of their views, and deemed it right and proper to deny to others the right of dissent which they claimed and exercised for themselves. They appealed to the civil magistrate for the support of the new churches and the suppression of heresy. And the civil magistrates were only too anxious to secure the control of religion in this dominion. Statecraft and priestcraft are alike hostile to individual and personal rights and aim at conformity and uniformity in the public exercise of religion. The Lutheran princes in Germany and Scandinavia acted on the principle *Cujus regio ejus religio*, and made themselves supreme bishops or little popes in their territories. The republican magistrates of Zurich, Bern, Basel, Geneva, and other Swiss cantons, did the same. In England this principle was carried to the extreme of Erastianism. Henry VIII. simply cut off the Roman head from the English hierarchy and put his own crown on the bloody trunk. He called himself the "supreme head" of the Church of England, and his daughter Elizabeth, being a woman, only softened it into "supreme governor." Anabaptists and Socinians were persecuted in Protestant as well as in Roman Catholic countries. The only difference is in the extent of persecution and the degree of severity, in which Romanism has an unenviable pre-eminence, because it had more power and once ruled supreme in Europe.

Calvin consented to the burning of Servetus, by the civil authorities of Geneva, for denying the trinity and the divinity of Christ, though he had begged the magistrate in vain to mitigate the punishment by substituting the sword for the fagot. The burning was fully justified by all the surviving reformers, Farel, Beza, Bucer, Bullinger (Zwingli's successor in Zurich), and the mild and gentle Melanchthon. Beza called liberty of conscience a diabolical dogma. Castellio, once a friend, then an enemy of Calvin, and expelled from Geneva, was the only Protestant of that age who denounced the execution; and he did it for the rationalistic reason that errors on speculative doctrines, as the trinity, predestination, etc., which are impenetrably obscure, have no influence on morals, and are therefore innocent. Luther and Zwingli, who had died long before that tragedy in Geneva, in obedience to their liberal instincts, might possibly have disapproved of its severity, but not of the principle. Luther once made the excellent remark that if heretics were to be burned the hangman would be the best theologian; but Luther would not have tolerated Zwingli or Œcolampadius in Saxony, whom he refused to acknowledge as brethren at Marburg, though they agreed in fourteen out of fifteen articles of doctrine, and differed only on the mode of Christ's presence in the eucharist. The Melanchthonians (or Philippists), Krypto-Calvinists, and all professors, clergymen, and school teachers who would not subscribe to the Formula Concordiæ of 1577, lost their places in Saxony; and Chancellor Nicholas Crell, who had supported Calvinism, was, after ten years imprisonment, beheaded at Dresden as a traitor (1601). "Since that time the name of a Calvinist became more hateful in Saxony than that of a Jew or Mohammedan." In Scandinavian countries, till the middle of the nineteenth century, Lutherans only were allowed the privilege of public worship and the rights of citizenship, and apostasy to any other church was punishable with confiscation and exile. In England, the penal laws, enacted under Queen Elizabeth, were a systematic attempt to uproot every form of dissent, whether Roman Catholic or Protestant, and were carried out with cruel severity. John Knox declared that one Popish mass in Scotland was more obnoxious and dangerous than a French army of invasion. Archbishop Laud was as bigoted and intolerant as any Inquisitor in Spain. The puritan Assembly of Westminister expelled two thousand beneficed Episcopal clergymen, and Charles II. on his restoration took double vengeance on the Non-conformists in England and the Covenanters of Scotland. Cromwell was the most tolerant of the statesmen of the seventeenth century, but even he exempted "Popery and Prelacy" from his scheme of toleration. Milton, the most eloquent advocate of liberty in the English tongue, made the same exception. Baxter was comparatively liberal, yet he pronounced universal toleration to be "soul-murder," and "the way to man's damnation." Jeremy Taylor, when in exile, eloquently defended the principle of toleration in his "Liberty of Prophesying," but abandoned it when the Episcopal Church regained her power, and apologized for the publication of that book.

Nor is our own America free from the reproach of persecution. The first English settlers fled from persecution in their native land, and sought freedom of worship for themselves, but for themselves only. With the exception of the Baptist colony of Rhode Island, the Quaker colony of Pennsylvania, and the Catholic colony of Maryland (in its earliest stage), the principle of State churchism was as fully recognized and established in our colonial period as in England. Congregationalism was the established Church in Massachusetts and nearly all New England; Episcopacy in Virginia, the Carolinas, and New York. There was a time when dissenters were fined, imprisoned, exiled, and even hanged for religious opinions, to the extent of the power of the civil authorities of our free country, even in the enlightened State of Massachusetts, and such persecution was justified on the basis of the union of church and state.

Wherever this principle is acknowledged and established, persecution becomes even a duty of conscientious rulers. The worst persecutors among the Roman emperors (with the exception of Nero, who persecuted the Christians, not for religion, but on the false charge of incendiarism) were influenced by motives of patriotism and duty to the integrity of the ancestral religion, and are numbered among the best emperors—Trajan, Marcus Aurelius, Decius, Diocletian, and Julian. And so we must dismiss the idea that every Christian persecutor is necessarily a cruel and bad man. He may be very conscientious, kind and forgiving to personal enemies. The great and good St. Augustin was the first among the fathers who formulated the very principle of persecution by his famous misinterpretation of "Compel them to enter in."[1] Innocent III., who inspired the horrible crusade against the Albigenses and Waldenses, was one of the purest, as well as ablest among popes. Cardinal Ximenes, the third Inquisitor-General of Spain, is the originator of the first Polyglot Bible, a work of gigantic magnitude in those days, now one of the rarest and costliest of books. Calvin, who shares with the Geneva magistrate the guilt of burning Servetus, is not only the greatest theologian among the Reformers, but surpassed them all in zeal for purity of doctrine and holiness of life. Archbishop Laud was personally a pure and devout man, like his master Charles I. The intolerance of the old Puritans while in power, sprang from their

---

[1] Lecky says ("Hist. of Rationalism in Europe," vol. ii., p. 28): "The writer, who was destined to consolidate the whole system of persecution, to furnish the arguments of all its later defenders, and to give to it the sanction of a name that long silenced every pleading of mercy and became the glory and the watchword of every persecutor, was unquestionably Augustin, on whom, more than any other theologian,—more, perhaps, even than on Dominic and Innocent, —rests the responsibility of this fearful curse." In his earlier writings Augustin condemned persecution, but he changed his view during the Donatist controversy, and retracted his condemnation in his Retractations. Although he had himself been a Manichæan heretic, he considered heresy the greatest crime. It must be added, however, that his heart did not sympathize with his head, and that he exerted his influence to change the death-penalty into banishment.

zeal for what they regarded as the genuine religion of Christ, and their abhorrence of error. Lecky, who abhors persecution, goes so far as to say (in his able " History of Rationalism in Europe," vol. I., pp. 353, 354):

> "The burnings, the tortures, the imprisonments, the confiscations, the disabilities, the long wars, and still longer animosities, that for so many centuries marked the conflicts of great theological bodies, are chiefly due to men whose lives were spent in absolute devotion to what they believed to be true, and whose characters have passed unscathed through the most hostile and searching criticism. In their worst acts the persecutors were but the exponents and representatives of the wishes of a large section of the community, and that section was commonly the most earnest and unselfish. It has been observed, too, since the subject has been investigated with a passionless judgment, that persecution invariably accompanied the realization of a particular class of doctrines, fluctuated with their fluctuations, and may therefore be fairly presumed to represent their action upon life."

Lecky derives religious persecution from the intensity of religious conviction, and the belief that there is no salvation beyond the limits of a certain system of orthodoxy. But here we must decidedly dissent from him. That the degree of earnestness and exclusiveness of belief determines the degree of severity of persecution we admit; but we utterly deny that religious earnestness or orthodoxy, in any shape, is necessarily persecuting. Otherwise, Christ and the Apostles would have been the greatest persecutors, at least in principle, as they could not be in fact. Religious convictions were as deep and strong in the first three centuries, when orthodox Christians suffered from persecution, as in the Middle Ages, when Christians persecuted Jews, heretics, and infidels. There are now in America plenty of Congregationalists, Episcopalians, Presbyterians, Lutherans, and even Roman Catholics, who are as orthodox, as sincere, as earnest, even as exclusive in their theological opinions, as their ancestors, and who yet utterly disavow their persecuting principles and practices. They all profess the opposite principle of toleration and freedom. As to Baptists, Quakers, Methodists, and Moravians, they have never persecuted in fact, and disown the *principle* of persecution.

We maintain, then, that persecution arises from the union of church and state; while religious freedom is the inevitable result of a peaceful separation of the two. The closer the union, the severer the persecution; the looser the union, the milder the persecution. A state may become tolerant in practice from sheer indifference to religion, or from policy; but as far as it is connected with any particular creed, it has the right to persecute dissenters, and may at any time exercise it. Full freedom requires separation of the secular and spiritual powers, and the complete independence of the latter. Church and state are both of divine origin and equally necessary for the well-being of man, but in their nature and aim as distinct as soul and body, as eternity and time. The state represents the law, protects life, property, and all the rights of citizens; it promotes their temporal welfare, and enforces its authority by temporal rewards and temporal punishments. The church represents the gospel, is concerned with the spiritual and eternal welfare of man, uses moral suasion, and deals with spiritual rewards and spiritual punishments. The state is intrusted with the sword for the punishment of evil-doers. The church exercises discipline by admonition, deposition, and excommunication; and these punishments are simply remedial, and look toward repentance and restoration. Civil punishment for civil offenses; spiritual punishment for spiritual offenses.

The founder of the Christian religion settled the question of principle in a few words, the wisest ever uttered in answer to an entangling question: "Render to Cæsar the things that are Cæsar's, and render to God the things that are God's." Here is separation of church and state, not as two hostile forces, but as two legitimate institutions equally necessary for society and entitled to our loyalty and obedience. The celebrated Leopold Ranke, who, as a youthful octogenarian, is publishing a history of the world, declares in the third part (1883), where he reverently touches upon the origin of Christianity, the sentence just quoted to be "the most important and influential word of Christ," and adds, "Jesus saw in religion a sacred jewel of man which can and ought not to be darkened by any political addition or interference."

This is, we may say, the American idea of religion, and the sense of the article in our Constitution which forbids Congress to legislate on the subject of religion, or to prohibit the free exercise thereof. We make a distinction between religious toleration and religious liberty. Toleration is an expedient and a concession; liberty is a principle and a right. We tolerate what we cannot prevent, though we may hate it; we tolerate even a nuisance, if it is unavoidable. The government of the Sultan tolerates the Christian sects, though he despises the Christian "dogs," and would kill them all if he could. But religion is the most sacred possession of man; it belongs to his inmost soul; it connects him with his Maker; it inspires him to do good; it enables him to suffer wrong; it fortifies him against danger and temptation; it cheers and comforts him in affliction; it dispels the darkness of death by opening the vision of an endless life beyond. It is too sacred to be dragged into the arena of politics. Freedom of religion, like freedom of thought and of speech and of the press, is one of the inalienable rights of man, and it is the most valuable and fundamental of these rights, which the Government is bound to protect like every other right, and which it ought never to curtail or oppress. Freedom, of course, is limited by duty to our fellow-men. No one has a right to interfere with the freedom of his neighbor. The Government, in guarding and protecting the liberty of all, cannot allow any one to abridge the liberty of others, or to endanger the peace and order of the community. All Christian denominations and sects (with the exception, perhaps, of Mormonism) have proved not only consistent with, but actually favorable to, the preservation and promotion of the national peace and welfare.

The theory of the sacredness and freedom of conscience which implies freedom of public worship as a necessary consequence is as old as Christianity itself. It entered into the world and fought its way through a hostile world by the purely moral force of truth and righteousness. Tertullian, in the second century, gave vigorous utterance to this view when he boldly challenged the heathen persecutor, and told him : " It is no part of religion to force religion (*nec religionis est cogere religionem*); everybody has a natural right and power to worship God according to his conviction ; all compulsion in matters of conscience is wrong, and no form of worship has any value whatever, except as far as it is the voluntary homage of the heart." [1] Lactantius also, a contemporary of Constantine, and tutor of his son Crispus, condemned persecution in the strongest terms, which he never recalled. " Religion," he says, " is the most voluntary thing (*nihil est tam voluntarium quam religio*); when the mind and heart are not in it, it ceases to be religion." [2] Even Constantine himself at first, after his victory over Maxentius at the Milvian Bridge, which decided the downfall of idolatry and the triumph of Christianity, proclaimed the policy of toleration to all religions of the empire (A.D. 313). The decree gives both to Christians and all others the right to follow whatever religion they please ("*et Christianis et omnibus potestatem sequendi religionem quam quisque voluisset*"). But this was merely a temporary policy to pave the way for the introduction of Christianity as the state religion, and this, of necessity, involved the gradual suppression of paganism. The instinct and tradition of power in the head of the Roman empire was too strong to abandon the prerogative of a supervision of public worship. Consequently Constantine, even before he was baptized, convened the first Œcumenical Council (328), exiled Arius, and excluded heretics and schismatics from the freedom and privileges of the orthodox Catholic Church.

Nevertheless, the voice of liberty and the protest against persecution was never silent. Every persecuted sect in the church became a witness for toleration and for the sacred rights

[1] *Ad. Scapulam*, c. 2; *Apol.* c. 24.   [2] *Inst. div.*, V. 20.

of conscience. The blood of martyrs and patriots is the seed of religious and civil liberty.

We cannot trace the history of liberty through the Middle Ages and modern times, but we may indicate briefly the most salient points. The battle was fought chiefly in England. The Reformation broke down the tyranny of the papacy. The Puritan rebellion revolted against the semi-popery of Archbishop Laud and the Stuart dynasty. The restoration of the episcopacy and royalty, under Charles II., apparently destroyed all that had been gained, but by its own folly provoked the Revolution of 1688, with the Act of Toleration, under William and Mary (1689). This, for the first time, gave a breathing spell to nonconformists, and allowed them to organize separate self-supporting and self-governing churches, though with certain restrictions, as the subscription of thirty-six out of the thirty-nine Articles of the Church of England.[1]

From that time dates the division of English Christianity into several distinct and independent organizations, which had previously existed only as parties struggling for recognition. The same toleration was gradually extended to Unitarians, Roman Catholics, and Jews, who may now sit in Parliament, and occupy all but a few of the highest offices of the government. To all intents and purposes, the subjects of Queen Victoria enjoy as much religious liberty as the citizens of the United States, and there is more religion in Great Britain now than ever before. Nevertheless, England still holds to the principle of establishment, and distinguishes between the national church and the

---

[1] The Act (1 William and Mary, c. 18), designated "An act for Exempting their Majesties' Protestant subjects Dissenting from the Church of England from the Penalties of certain Laws," does not relax the provisions of the Corporation and Test Acts, and excludes Roman Catholics and Unitarians; it requires from all dissenting preachers an approval of the thirty-six doctrinal articles, but allows them on this condition to hold assemblies for religious worship with open doors, and permits the Quakers in certain cases to substitute an affirmation for an oath. It is very far, therefore, from the modern theory of religious freedom.

dissenting sects; or rather she recognizes two ecclesiastical establishments, episcopacy in England, and presbytery in Scotland, the Queen being the supreme governor of both, and taking the holy communion from an Anglican bishop when in England, and from a Presbyterian pastor when in Scotland. Episcopalians are dissenters in Scotland; Presbyterians are dissenters in England. This is a curious anomaly, which is not likely to outlast the present century. The experience in Ireland (since 1869) and the United States justifies the expectation that neither the Episcopal Church in England, nor the Presbyterian Church in Scotland, is likely to lose anything in moral and spiritual force by being disestablished and placed on the voluntary principle of self-support and self-government.

The United States made an important step beyond England to the full recognition of religious liberty, and equality of all churches and sects within the limits of public morality and order. This was evidently the providential aim of the settlement of the country by colonists from all nations and churches of Europe, seeking freedom from persecution for the sake of their religious convictions. Puritans, Quakers, and Catholics from England, Presbyterians from Scotland and Ireland, Huguenots from France, Lutherans from Salzburg, German Reformed from the Palatinate, fled from persecution or vexation to this country to worship God according to the dictates of their consciences; while Episcopalians, Dutch Reformed, and other colonists, who were not molested at home, set up their churches. Several of the colonies, especially Massachusetts and Virginia, were at first exclusive and intolerant in their policy, but they were forced to yield to circumstances, and to make concessions to the growing number of Dissenters in their jurisdiction. The battle began in Virginia with the Revolution and Declaration of Independence; and by the combined influence of Dissenters (Presbyterians, Baptists, Quakers, Methodists), of liberal Episcopalians, and the Deistic Jefferson (who fought for freedom of unbelief), the Episcopal establishment was sacrificed to the principle of equal justice

THE DEVELOPMENT OF RELIGIOUS FREEDOM. 289

to all, and the separation of church and state was carried through the Virginia Legislature in successive acts from 1776 to 1785.

The General Government was inevitably led to the same position from the beginning of its existence. It never had any connection with a church, and hence found no rights which might be violated. It arose from a combined effort of all the colonies for political independence, and the establishment of a separate nationality. Religious motives and aims did not enter into the contest at all, but members of all denominations took part in it But all advocates of independence were opposed to a hierarchical state church which might prove disastrous to civil liberty. Hence, the only way for the framers of the Federal Constitution, after the close of the war, was either to ignore religion altogether, or more wisely, to guarantee full religious liberty to all American citizens within the jurisdiction of the United States. The latter was done in justice to the people. The Constitution, adopted under Washington in 1787, provides (Act VI., section 3) that "No religious tests shall ever be required as a qualification to any office or public trust under the United States." And to make the matter more plain and emphatic, the first amendment to the Constitution, enacted by the first Congress in 1789, declares:

"Congress shall make no law respecting an establishment of religion, or prohibiting the free exercise thereof, or abridging the freedom of speech, or abridging the freedom of the press, or of the rights of the people peaceably to assemble, and to petition the Government for a redress of grievances."

This important amendment which was suggested by several State legislatures in the interest of religious liberty, has a negative and a positive feature: it prevents Congress from ever recognizing one religion or church to the exclusion of the rest, and thus effectually prevents persecution; but it secures at the same time equal liberty to all churches and sects. It puts religion on a par with other fundamental and inalienable rights of man. Congress was not influenced by the spirit of infidelity or even indifference, like the French Revolution, which began with proclaiming universal toleration and ended with the abolition of Christianity; but, on the contrary, it was animated by respect for religion as a sacred domain which belongs to the Lord of conscience and lies beyond the competency of political rulers. This difference accounts in large measure for the fact that the French Republic failed, while the American Republic succeeded. Religious liberty is the best, yea, the only safe basis of civil liberty. Church and state were not set opposite to each other as foes, but side by side, as two different spheres of the social life, in the conviction that each had best restrict its jurisdiction to its own immediate concerns, because the attempt of one to rule the other was sure to issue disastrously. The power of the state is consequently, in the United States, reduced to narrower limits than in Europe, where it controls the church also. The American status of the church differs from the hierarchical patronage of the state by the church, from the imperial and royal patronage of the church by the state, and also from the pre-Constantinian separation and persecution of the church by the heathen state. The United States present a new phase in the history of the relation of the two powers.

This separation between church and state is not to be understood as a separation of the nation from Christianity, for the state represents, in America, only the temporal interests of the people. The churches care for the religious and moral interests; and the people are religious and Christian as much as any other, and express their sentiments in different ways,—by the voluntary support of their numerous churches, by benevolent organizations of every kind, by attendance upon public worship and respect for the ministry (who are second to none in dignity and influence), by a strict observance of Sunday (which is not equaled anywhere, except in Scotland), by constant zeal for home and foreign missions, by reverence for the Bible, by a steady stream of edifying books, tracts, and periodicals, and by their public morals. Congress nominates chaplains of different confessions and opens every sitting with prayer. The President appoints chaplains for the

THE DEVELOPMENT OF RELIGIOUS FREEDOM. 291

army and navy. Fast-days have been frequently observed in particular emergencies, as in 1849, during the cholera; in 1865, on the assassination of President Lincoln; and in 1881, on the death of President Garfield. A Thanksgiving-day is yearly celebrated in November in all the States, on the proclamation of the President and the concurrent action of the governors of the different states. Indeed, religion, it may be justly claimed, has all the more hold upon the people, just because it is left to the personal conviction and free choice of every man. Religious coercion breeds hypocrisy and infidelity.

Christianity thrives best in the atmosphere of freedom, and is abundantly able to support and govern itself without any aid from the government, except the simple protection of law. This is the lesson of American Church history.

THE
DISCORD AND CONCORD OF CHRISTENDOM;[1]
OR,
DENOMINATIONAL VARIETY AND CHRISTIAN UNITY.

The Churches of Christendom. The Christian world embraces three great divisions:—the Greek or Oriental, the Latin or Roman, and the Protestant or Evangelical. As to numbers, the Roman Church is the largest, and nearly equals the other two combined; the Greek Church is the smallest. As to age, the Greek is the oldest, the Protestant is the youngest. As to territory, the Greek Church may be called the Christianity of the East; the Roman Church, the Christianity of the South; Protestantism, the Christianity of the North and West. The first is based upon the Greek nationality, but has taken hold also of the Slavonic race; the second is founded upon the old Roman nationality, and controls the Latin races of Southern Europe and South America; the third is identified with the Teutonic nations in Germany, Switzerland, Holland, Scandinavia, England and North America. The Greek Church represents ancient Christianity in repose; the Roman Church, mediæval Christianity in conflict with liberal progress; Protestantism, modern Christianity in motion.

[1] This address was freely delivered in German before the Eighth General Conference of the Evangelical Alliance, held at Copenhagen, September 2d, 1884, in presence of a representative audience of different nationalities and churches, including many distinguished ministers and scholars, and the royal courts of Denmark and Greece. It was received with unexpected enthusiasm, and elicited many oral and written expressions of cordial approval.

Protestantism again is subdivided into three main divisions, the Lutheran, the Anglican, and the Reformed. Lutheranism prevails in Germany and Scandinavia; Anglicanism, in England and the British Colonies; the Reformed communion, in Switzerland, France, Holland and Scotland. To these must be added several large and influential evangelical organizations, as the Independents, the Methodists, the Baptists, which are offshoots of the Reformation of the sixteenth century, and especially of the Church of England, since the Toleration Act of 1689. On the Continent, where they have but few adherents, they are usually called sects; in England, Dissenters; in America, denominations or churches, on equal footing with the others before the law. The tendency of Protestantism to division and multiplication of denominations is not yet exhausted.

These three great branches of Christendom are the growth of history, and embody the results of centuries of intellectual and spiritual labor. They represent as many distinct types of the one Christian religion, each with characteristic excellencies and defects.

The Greek Church. The Greek Church produced most of the ancient fathers from the apostles down to John of Damascus, and elaborated the œcumenical doctrines of the Holy Trinity and the Incarnation, with a vast body of invaluable literature, which must be studied even to this day in every school of theological learning. Hers are the Apostolical fathers, the apologists, exegetes, divines, historians, and orators of the early Church; hers a long line of martyrs and saints; in her language the Apostles and Evangelists wrote the inspired records of our religion; to her we owe nearly all the manuscripts of the Greek Testament and the Septuagint; and it was from fugitive scholars of Constantinople that Europe received and learned to read again, in the original, the Gospels and Epistles, as well as the ancient Greek classics. Though stationary and immovable, one of her scholars (Dr. Bryennios, Metropolitan of Nicomedia), has recently surprised the West by the discovery and *editio princeps* of two most important documents of primitive antiquity (the *entire* text of the Clementine Epistle to the Corinthians, and the "Teaching of the Twelve Apostles"). The Eastern Church held fast to her traditions during the dark centuries of Saracen and Turkish oppression; she controls the religious life of the vast empire of Russia, and she looks forward to a day of freedom and resurrection, which may God speed on.

The Latin Church. The Latin Church gave us the works of the great African father, Augustin, which inspired the thinking of schoolmen, mystics, and reformers, and the Latin Bible of Jerome, which, for many centuries, interpreted the Word of God to the Western nations. She saved Christianity and the Roman classics through the chaotic confusion of the migration of nations; she christianized and civilized, by her missionaries, the barbarian races which overthrew the old Roman empire; and she built up a new and better society on the ruins of the old. She converted the Anglo-Saxons, the Franks, the Germans, the Scandinavians; she built the Gothic cathedrals, founded the mediæval Universities, and educated such schoolmen as Anselm and Thomas Aquinas, and such mystics as Bernard and the author of the inimitable "Imitation of Christ." Even the Reformers of the sixteenth century are her children, baptized, confirmed and ordained in her bosom; though she cast them out as heretics with terrible curses, as the Synagogue had cast out the Apostles. She dates from that congregation to which St. Paul wrote his most important epistle; she stretches in unbroken succession through all ages and countries; she once ruled nearly the whole of Europe; and, though deprived of her former power in just punishment for its abuse, she still guides for weal or woe millions of consciences, and is full of zeal and energy for the maintenance and spread of her doctrine and discipline in all parts of the globe.

The Protestant Churches. The various Protestant Churches have the unspeakable advantage of evangelical freedom; of direct access to the fountain of God's word and of God's grace; of unobstructed personal union and communion with Christ; of the general priesthood of believers. The Reformation emancipated a large portion of Christendom from the yoke of human traditions and spiritual tyranny, made God's book the book of the people, secured the rights of nationality and private judgment in the sphere of religion, and gave a mighty impulse to every department of intellectual and moral activity. Protestantism pervades and directs the freest and strongest nations in both hemispheres; it carries the open Bible to all heathen lands; it is cultivating, with untiring zeal, every branch of sacred literature, and popularizes the results of scientific research for the benefit of the masses; it favors every legitimate progress in science, art, politics and commerce; it promotes every enterprise of Christian philanthropy; and it is identified with the cause of civil and religious liberty throughout the world.

Defects and sins of churches. This is the bright side of the three sections of Christendom. We do not mean to deny that each one has also its defects as well as its virtues. Nor need we wonder at it. There is nothing perfect under the sun. The Jewish Church, of God's own planting and training, repeatedly apostatized to idolatry; her hierarchy crucified the Messiah, and persecuted and excommunicated his disciples. There was a Judas among the twelve apostles whom Christ himself had chosen; an Ananias and a Sapphira in the first congregation at Jerusalem; and there is scarcely an epistle in the New Testament which does not rebuke grievous sins and errors in the professing members of Christ. Even the Rock-Apostle, in an hour of weakness, denied his Lord, and twenty years later he acted inconsistently at Antioch, so as to incur the public censure of his brother Paul. Conversion does not emancipate us from the frailties of human nature. There are Satanic, as well as divine, influences at work in all ages of the Church. Antichrist seeks and finds a seat in the very temple of God.

Persecution. One of the greatest sins of which the churches and sects, with few exceptions, are, or have formerly been, more or less guilty, is the sin of intolerance and exclusiveness, which, in spite of Christianity, springs from the selfishness of the human heart. They vainly imagine that they possess the monopoly of truth and piety, and look down upon other communions as heretical and schismatical sects, or even as synagogues of Satan. They have, in their polemics, exhausted the vocabulary of reproach and vituperation. They have excommunicated and persecuted each other, either by fire and sword, or by prescriptive legislation, worse than heathen Rome persecuted Christianity.

The persecution of all sorts of heretics and dissenters, and witnesses of the truth, beginning with the crucifixion of our Lord, is the darkest, we may well say, the Satanic chapter in church history, though it has been overruled by Providence for the progress of religious truth and liberty; for "the blood of martyrs is the seed of the Church." Even great and good men, including St. Augustin and John Calvin, have justified persecution as a necessary consequence of the strength of religious conviction; as a protection of truth against error; and as a duty of the Christian magistrate. But "error is harmless when truth is left free to combat it." Darkness must flee before the light of day. God is stronger than his greatest adversary. The devil is mighty, but God is almighty.

Persecution opposed to the spirit of Christianity. It is not a part of religion, says Tertullian, to enforce religion. It loses all its value if it is not free and voluntary. The whole teaching and example of Christ and the apostles are against violence in matters of conscience. Our Saviour expressly declared that his kingdom is not of this world; he rebuked the sons of Zebedee for their carnal zeal against the hostile Samaritans, and Peter for drawing the sword, though it was in defence of the Master; he "came not to destroy men's lives, but to save them;" and he submitted to the bitter cross rather than to call a legion of angels to his protection.

By persecuting, abusing and excommunicating each other, the churches do cruel injustice to their common Lord and his followers. They contract his kingdom and his power; they lower him from his kingly throne to the headship of a sect or party or school; they hate those whom he loves, and for whom he died; they curse those whom he blesses, and they violate the fundamental law of his gospel. "How the Christians love one another, and are ready to die for one another," was the wondering exclamation of the ancient heathen. "How the Christians hate and denounce and devour one another," is only too often the well-founded charge of modern infidels. All forms of bigotry are the results of ignorance or selfishness, and are an insult to Christ and his religion.

> "Was wehret ihr den Brudernamen
> Dem Jünger, der mit euch nicht geht?
> Was lästert ihr den guten Samen,
> Den eure Hand nicht ausgesät?
> Ein grosser Herr braucht manches Knechtes;
> Viel Hände kämpfen für sein Reich,
> Und im Gedränge des Gefechtes
> Ist für euch, wer nicht wider euch."

An act of humiliation. We look hopefully for a reunion of Christendom and a feast of reconciliation of churches; but it will be preceded by an act of general humiliation. All must confess: We have sinned and erred; Christ alone is pure and perfect. We take to ourselves shame and confusion of face; to him, our common Lord and Saviour, be all the glory and praise.

Fortunately, the theory and practice of persecution are doomed, and most churches now repudiate them. The principle of religious freedom (which is far more than mere toleration) is becoming more and more an essential element of Christian civilization and enlightened government. In connection with it, the problem of mutual recognition and Christian union is attracting increased attention, and is slowly but surely approaching a solution which can only be effected on the basis of freedom. It is true, there has been within the present generation a powerful revival of ecclesiasticism in the Roman Catholic and in several

Protestant denominations, but the tendency to a reunion of Christendom is also widening and deepening.

How is this union of Christendom to be brought about, or to be promoted?

Denominationalism not sectarianism. Not by a crusade against denominations. Such a crusade would be a mere waste of time and strength. The evil lies not in denominationalism and confessionalism, but in sectarianism; not in variety, but in selfish exclusiveness.

Denominationalism or confessionalism grows out of the diversity of divine gifts, and may co-exist with true catholicity and large-hearted charity. But sectarianism is an abuse and excess of denominationalism, and is nothing but extended selfishness, which may be found in any church, the largest as well as the smallest: it is evil and evil only. It is the spirit of the Pharisee who boasts of his righteousness, and thanks God that he is better than the publican.

We must, first of all, make a distinction between Christian union and ecclesiastical or organic amalgamation. The former is possible without the latter and must, at all events, precede it. Christian union is the soul, ecclesiastical organization is the body or outward form, and is empty and useless without the soul.

Diversity in unity. Diversity in unity is the law of God's physical and moral universe, and the condition of all beauty and harmony. Variety is life; uniformity is death. "There are diversities of gifts, but the same Spirit. And there are diversities of ministrations, but the same Lord. And there are diversities of workings, but the same God who worketh all things in all. But to each one is given the manifestation of the Spirit to profit withal." (1 Cor. 12: 4-7.)

There is infinite variety in nature; no two trees or leaves, no two rivers or valleys or mountains are precisely alike, but each has its own kind of beauty, and each type of variety has the power of further variation and adaptation to new conditions.

There is still greater diversity in history than in the realm of nature. Every man and woman, every family, every community, every tribe, every nationality, every race, every age, every century, every generation has its own character and individuality, its peculiar endowment and mission. No two persons are alike. Every one has a special talent, or five or ten talents, and is expected "to trade herewith" till the Lord comes to call him to account. No one can do the work of another; every one is responsible to God for his trust, whether it be high or low, large or small. And what is true of individuals is true of whole nations. What a marked difference between the ancient Jews, Greeks, and Romans, or the modern English, French, and Germans, not only in language, but also in manners, customs, laws and- institutions! None of these nationalities could be improved by being transformed into another. And if all nationalities were melted into one, the world would lose all the beauty, charm and wealth of life which spring from the variety and multiplicity of gifts. But for all that, the various nations belong to the same human family, and may and ought to respect each other, not in spite of, but on account of the characteristic varieties of type which they respectively represent.

Denominations necessary and useful. The same law of diversity in unity holds good in regard to churches. The one universal Church, founded by Christ for all ages and nations, is adapted to every grade of society and culture, from the lowest to the highest. It resembles a mighty cedar of Lebanon, which spreads its branches in every direction; or a grand temple, with many chapels and altars; or a conquering army, which is all the more effective for being divided into corps, divisions, brigades, regiments, battalions and companies, each under its own head, and all subject to the general-in-chief. Every Christian church or denomination has its special charisma and mission, and there is abundant room and abundant labor for all in this great and wicked world. The Roman Church can not do the work of the Greek, nor the Protestant that of the Roman, nor the Lutheran that of the Reformed, nor the Anglican that of the Independent or Wesleyan. We do not wish the Episcopalian to become a Presbyterian or Congregationalist; nor the Lutheran to become a Calvinist; nor the Calvinist to become an Arminian, or *vice versa*. The cause of Christ would be marred and weakened if any one of the historic churches should be extinguished, or be absorbed into another. Every denomination ought to be loyal to its own standards, and walk in the paths of its ancestry, provided only its *esprit de corps* do not degenerate into spiritual pride and sectarian bigotry.

There may be sects indeed, which after having accomplished their mission to protest against a prevailing error, or to do some specific work, ought to disband or unite with a cognate organization, and thus diminish the number of divisions. I am no champion of sects and schisms, and I regard it as a serious defect in Protestantism that it has a tendency to needless and injurious distraction. It is in this respect the very antipode of Romanism; it is onesidedly centrifugal, while the other is onesidedly centripetal; it gives too much liberty to individual dissent, while the other exercises too much authority. One extreme runs into license and anarchy; the other into despotism and slavery. It is the great task of history to adjust and harmonize the claims of authority and freedom, of unity and variety.

But we do affirm that at present none of the leading denominations of Christendom which faithfully do their Master's work, could be spared without most serious injury to the progress of the gospel at home and abroad. If we consider the appalling amount of ignorance, immorality and vice, of infidelity and indifference in Christian lands, and the fact that nearly two-thirds of the human family are still buried in idolatry, we ought to thank God that he has raised so many agencies for the defence and spread of his kingdom of truth and righteousness throughout the world, and we should heartily rejoice in the building of every new church or chapel, and in the conversion of every soul, by whatever name and agency. St. Paul opposed the party-spirit of the Christians in Corinth, and fought the bigoted Judaizers in Galatia with all his might; nevertheless in noble liberality he rejoiced again and again if only Christ was proclaimed by friend or foe "in every way, whether in pretence or in truth."

Liberty favorable to Christianity. Experience teaches that most of those countries which recognize and tolerate but one organized form of Christianity are most backward in spiritual life and energy; while those in which all forms have fair play are most active and progressive. An honorable rivalry in good works is profitable to all. The Roman Church has greatly gained inwardly by the Reformation, and shows more purity and vitality in Protestant than in exclusively papal countries or districts. The Church of England, which grants freedom to all Dissenters, was never more zealous and fruitful in good works than at the present day. And in the United States, where all denominations are equal before the law and stand on the same voluntary footing of self-support and self-government, the Christian activities keep pace with the enormous tide of immigration and the intellectual, social and commercial growth of the people; and churches, schools, colleges, seminaries, libraries, home and foreign missionary societies, and all sorts of benevolent institutions are there, by the joint zeal of the different denominations, multiplying with a rapidity that has no parallel in the annals of the past.

Organic union never realized nor promised. The Christian Church was never visibly and organically united in the strict sense of the term. The apostolic churches were of one faith and animated by one love, but maintained a relative independence without a visible head. The Greek Church never was subject to the Bishop of Rome, and never acknowledged his supremacy of jurisdiction, but only a primacy of honor. The quarrel between Photius and Nicolas only brought to a head a difference between the Patriarch and the Pope, between New Rome and Old Rome, which had been gathering strength from the second century. And the great schism has not been healed to this day.

Unity of outward organization is not absolutely necessary for the unity of the Church. This is essentially spiritual. Our Saviour promised that there will be "one *flock* and one shepherd" (as the Greek original and the Revised Version have it), but not one "*fold*" and one shepherd (as the Latin Vulgate and the Authorized Version wrongly and mischievously render the passage in John x. 16). There may be many folds, and yet one and the same flock under Christ, the great arch-shepherd of souls. Even in Heaven there will be "many mansions."

<small>Good and evil in Denominationalism.</small> Denominationalism or Confessionalism has no doubt its evils and dangers, and is apt to breed narrowness, bigotry and uncharitableness. But the worst we can say of it is that in the present state of Christendom it is a *necessary* evil, and is overruled by God for the multiplication of regenerating and converting agencies. It is not the best state of the Church, but it is far better than a dead or tyrannical and monotonous uniformity. It will ultimately pass away in its present shape and give place to a better state, when Christians shall no more be divided by human designations and distinctions, but be perfectly united in the great Head. He will not ask us, on the day of reckoning, to what denomination we belong, to what creed we subscribe, what are our preferences for this or that form of church polity or mode of worship, but simply, "Lovest thou me?"

Yet whatever is good in any portion of his kingdom, and in any age of history, will be woven as an ornament in the crown of the Redeemer. The perfection of the Church does not require an obliteration of the past. History is no child's play; it is not "the baseless fabric of a vision leaving no wreck behind," but the evolution of God's thoughts and purposes which have an eternal significance and power. No true servant of God has labored in vain. The end of history will be the rich harvest of the preceding growth in summer and spring. The temporary scaffolding will be taken down, but the building will stand; the wood, hay and stubble will be burned, but the gold, silver and costly stones will remain; the dust of earth will be shaken off, the smoke of battle will disappear, the wounds will be healed; in one word, all human imperfections, sins and errors will be done away, that the work which *God* has wrought through all

THE DISCORD AND CONCORD OF CHRISTENDOM. 303

these ecclesiastical and denominational agencies, may appear in all its purity, beauty and grandeur. The Lord will in his own good time bring cosmos out of chaos, and overrule the discord of Christendom for the deepest concord.

<small>Christian union not to be created.</small> Our present duty is to recognize, to maintain and to promote Christian unity in the midst of ecclesiastical diversity as far as truth and conscience permit. Christian unity has not to be created, but already exists as to its basis. There is now and always has been a Concord as well as a Discord. Christian unity underlies all denominational diversity and is consistent with it. We recognize the general humanity which all races and nations have in common, and so we must recognize the general Christianity which underlies all ecclesiastical distinctions. A man is a man, and a Christian is a Christian first and last, whatever he may be besides.

We all profess to believe in "the communion of saints," as an existing fact, as an ever-present reality. It necessarily flows from the living union of believers with Christ. All Christians are one in Christ, and therefore one among each other. They are members of his mystical body, they are redeemed by the same blood, baptized into the same triune name, justified by the same grace through faith, sanctified by the same Spirit, animated by the same love to God and man, and they travel or different roads to the same Father's house.

> "The saints in heaven and on earth
> But one communion make;
> They join in Christ, their living head,
> And of his grace partake."

This unity is felt just in proportion as Christians become personally acquainted and work together and pray together.

We may trace this unity in the various departments of church life.

<small>Unity in Doctrine.</small> As to doctrine, all the three great branches of Christendom accept the canonical Scriptures of the Old and New

Testaments as the inspired word of God, and the articles of the old œcumenical faith from the creation to the resurrection of the body and the life everlasting, as laid down in the Apostles' Creed. These articles are sufficient, and more than sufficient for salvation. Living faith in Jesus Christ as our Lord and Saviour is enough to make one a Christian. Peter's creed consisted only of one article: "We believe that thou art the Christ, the Son of the living God." The creed of Thomas was still shorter: "My Lord and my God." And Paul required no more from the jailor at Philippi, as a condition of baptism and salvation, than that he should "believe in the Lord Jesus Christ." If we examine and compare the most elaborate systems of Greek, Roman, and Protestant theology, say the systems of John of Damascus, Thomas Aquinas, John Calvin, and John Gerhard, we shall find that the heads in which they agree are far more numerous and far more important than those in which they differ. The only important dogma which has divided the Greeks and Romans for more than a thousand years is the question of the *Filioque*, or the double procession of the third person of the Trinity; but this belongs to metaphysical rather than practical theology, and sinks into insignificance when compared with the regenerating and sanctifying *work* of the Holy Spirit. The differences between Romanism and Protestantism, and between the various sections of Protestantism, are more numerous and weighty; but even in these controverted doctrines there are always strong points of contact and possibilities of adjustment. Take, for instance, the controversy about Scripture and tradition, or church teaching: Roman Catholics and Protestants acknowledge the importance and necessity of both, but assign them a different position, the former making tradition a *joint* rule of faith with the Scripture, the latter subordinating tradition to the Scripture as the *sole* rule. So, in the controversy on justification, both parties recognize the necessity of faith and good works, but to the one the works are a joint *condition* of justification with faith, to the other an *evidence* of faith. Paul suggests the ultimate solution in the pregnant sentence, "faith working by love." (Gal. v. 6.) The problem of eternal decrees and their relation to human freedom and responsibility has exercised and divided many of the profoundest minds in the days of Augustin, of Gottschalk, of Calvin, of Arminius, and of Wesley and Whitefield, and it remains still unsolved. But, practically, all true Christians agree that they are saved by grace alone, and that unbelievers perish by their own guilt. Arminians pray like Calvinists, as if everything depended upon God, and Calvinists preach and work like Arminians, as if everything depended on man. And Paul again suggests the solution of the difficulty in the apparent paradox: "Work out your own salvation with fear and trembling, for it is God who worketh in you both to will and to work, for his good pleasure." God's work in us is the ground and stimulus of our own work. Bitter controversies arose in the Middle Ages, and again in the period of the Reformation, about the mode of Christ's presence in the sacrament, whether it be by transubstantiation, or by consubstantiation, or whether it be spiritual and dynamic; and yet the different theories agree in the more vital points that the Lord's Supper is a divine ordinance to be observed to the end of time, that it is a commemoration of his sacrifice on the cross for the sins of the world, that Christ is spiritually present to all believers with his power and blessing, and that it is truly a feast of union and communion with him and his people.

Unity in Morals. In the moral teaching, all Christians are happily agreed that the whole duty of man consists in love to God and love to our neighbor. Higher than this law of laws no system of ethics can rise. "On these two commandments hangeth the whole law and the prophets." It is, moreover, universally admitted that our Saviour realized in his earthly life this love to God and man, or piety and virtue, in sinless perfection, and set the highest example for imitation. And who can deny that there are true followers of Jesus in every denomination and sect? And who will deny them the hand of fellowship?

Church Polity. As regards church government, the Greek Church holds to a patriarchal oligarchy, the Roman to a papal monarchy; the Protestants are divided between episcopacy, presbytery, and independency. But Christ has not prescribed any particular form of polity, leaving the Church free to adapt itself to circumstances. He uses the term "church" or "congregation" only twice in the Gospels, once in a local, and once in a general sense. He instituted only the apostolate, and says nothing about patriarch or pope, or bishop, priest and deacon.

Worship. As regards worship, the modes are widely different. In the Greek and Roman Churches the mass is the centre of public worship, and believed to be an actual, though unbloody, repetition of the atoning sacrifice on the cross for the sins of the world; while Protestants ascribe chief importance to the preaching of the word of God. Episcopalians and Lutherans prefer liturgical forms, Presbyterians and Independents prefer free prayer under the inspiration of the occasion. But do not all worship the same God the Father through the same Christ and in the same Holy Spirit? Do not all use the same Lord's Prayer, and the same Psalter of the Old Testament with the same devotion and benefit? Can not all join with the same fervor in the grand old *Te Deum*, and the *Gloria in Excelsis* of the ancient Church, or the classical hymns of the Middle Ages, or of modern times? The *Dies Iræ*, the *Stabat Mater*, the *Jesu Dulcis Memoria*, the *Salve Caput Cruentatum*, have found as many, if not more admirers and translators among Protestants than among Roman Catholics; and, on the other hand, I have seen Protestant hymns, like *Rock of Ages*, in Roman Catholic collections, though without the name of the author, lest it might spoil the effect. The history of hymnology is a history of Christian life and devotion in the festive dress of poetry, and exhibits more than any other branch of literature the communion of saints. The nearer Christians of whatsoever name approach the throne of grace, the more intense their devotion, the nearer they are to one another, though they know it not. Forty years ago I witnessed the edifying scene of a pious French Calvinist and a pious German

Lutheran, after a hot dispute about the real presence, falling on their knees in the worship of their Saviour, who so manifested his presence and welded their hearts together that they parted in tears. Quite recently, I had a similar experience of spiritual communion of an American Presbyterian with an orthodox and pious Russian priest.

Promotion of Christian Union. If, then, Christian union exists as a most real and powerful fact beneath and behind all differences and varieties of doctrine, polity and worship, why should it not be manifested and strengthened on every proper occasion? Not only as a demonstration against superstition and unbelief, not only as a means to an end, but even more for its own sake, as a thing desirable in itself. The cultivation of fraternal fellowship is essential to the nature of Christianity as a religion of love to God and man, and is a precious privilege as well as a sacred duty.

Hindrances of Christian union. The actual manifestation of Christian union is seriously hindered by differences of language, nationality and customs, but still more by various forms of sectarian exclusiveness. Every church has the right and duty to defend its own faith and practice; and everybody should belong to that denomination which he conscientiously prefers to any other, and in which he can do most good. But this is quite consistent with the recognition of the rights of others. The Orthodox Greek Church holds to the single procession, and refuses communion with any who hold to the *Filioque*. Rome is constitutionally exclusive, and recognizes no church, no ministry, no sacraments (except lay-baptism) and no saving ordinances beyond the limits of the papacy; and yet there is scarcely a right-minded and charitable Catholic who would seriously affirm that all Greeks and Protestants are lost. A certain school of Episcopalians disown every ministry outside of the apostolic succession and Episcopal ordination; and yet their hymn-books are enriched by hymns of Watts and many other dissenters. There are Lutherans who would not commune at the Lord's table with a Zwinglian or a Calvinist; and yet in Prussia, and other German states, the Lutheran and Reformed Churches are merged into one. Strict Baptists recognize no baptism except by immersion, on profession of faith; and yet they would not question for a moment the Christian character and standing of Pedobaptists. There are happy as well as unhappy inconsistencies. The piety of the heart often protests against the theology of the head, and love is better than logic.

If these and other forms of exclusiveness were removed, the Evangelical Alliance might be extended into a *Christian* Alliance, and present a spectacle which angels would delight to behold, anticipating that higher and holier Alliance in heaven,

> "Where saints of all ages in harmony meet,
> Their Saviour and brethren transported to greet."

But nothing short of a divine miracle, or a universal outpouring of the Holy Spirit of love, can remove these walls of partition. And as long as they exist, the ideal of Christian union can not be fully realized. The Lord's sacerdotal prayer, which is the Holy of holies in his life on earth, still remains unanswered, and must be offered up again and again, "that they all may be one, as thou, Father, art in me and I in thee, that they also may be one in us: that the world may believe that thou hast sent me."

<small>Christian catholicity.</small> But let us do what we can on a more humble and limited scale. We should not refuse the hand of fellowship to the lowliest disciple of Christ. There is, indeed, a negative liberalism which is indifferent to the distinction between truth and error; but there is also a positive liberalism or genuine catholicity which springs from the deep conviction of the infinite grandeur of truth and the inability of any single mind or single church to grasp it in all its fullness and variety of aspects. If we love only the members of our own church or sect, we do no more than the heathen, the Jews and the Turks. But if we take into our sympathy and affection the members of other denom-

THE DISCORD AND CONCORD OF CHRISTENDOM. 309

inations, we increase our happiness, and become more Christlike and Godlike. Love is not weakened, but strengthened and deepened by being widened. He loves best who loves most. The sun in heaven sends the same rays of light and heat upon all objects within his reach. The "quality" of love like "mercy"

> "is not strained:
> It droppeth as the gentle rain from heaven
> Upon the earth beneath. It is twice blessed:
> It blesses him that gives and him that takes."

Controversy is all right and proper in its place, and it will never cease in the Church militant on earth. It is necessary for the development of truth and the refutation of error. Every great doctrine, every new idea, every good cause, has to be tried by the fire of opposition before it is clearly understood and appreciated. The Johannean age of peace may yet be afar off. But "the truth should be spoken in love," and the warfare against sin and error be conducted by spiritual weapons, with all severity against error, with all charity for the erring brethren. Polemics must look to Irenics; war is carried on for the sake of peace. St. Paul, that fearless gospel-lion, opposed, with all his might, the tenets of false teachers, and withstood even St. Peter to his face at Antioch, when he compromised the principle of Christian liberty; yet he praised love in language of seraphic eloquence and beauty, as the queen of Christian graces; and, rising above all bigotry and party spirit, he proclaimed, in his most polemic epistle, the great principle: "In Jesus Christ neither circumcision availeth anything nor uncircumcision"— may we not add, in the same spirit, Neither immersion nor pouring, neither episcopacy nor presbytery, neither Lutheranism nor Calvinism, neither Calvinism nor Arminianism, neither Romanism nor Protestantism, nor any other ism—"availeth anything but a new creature. And as many as walk according to this rule, peace be on them, and mercy, and upon the Israel of God."

To conclude the whole matter: *Let our theology and our charity be as broad and as deep as God's truth and God's love.* Then shall we be Christians after the pattern of Christ, and best promote the work for which he came into the world, and for which he established his Church.

www.ingramcontent.com/pod-product-compliance
Lightning Source LLC
Chambersburg PA
CBHW050336230426
43663CB00010B/1875